Portraits of Persistence

JOE R. AND TERESA LOZANO LONG SERIES IN LATIN
AMERICAN AND LATINO ART AND CULTURE

Portraits of Persistence

INEQUALITY AND HOPE IN LATIN AMERICA

Edited by Javier Auyero

University of Texas Press   *Austin*

All photos are courtesy of the chapter authors unless otherwise specified.

Copyright © 2024 by the University of Texas Press
All rights reserved
Printed in the United States of America
First edition, 2024

Requests for permission to reproduce material from this work should be sent to:
Permissions
University of Texas Press
P.O. Box 7819
Austin, TX 78713-7819
utpress.utexas.edu

♾ The paper used in this book meets the minimum requirements of ANSI/NISO Z39.48-1992 (R1997) (Permanence of Paper).

Library of Congress Cataloging-in-Publication Data

Names: Auyero, Javier, editor.
Title: Portraits of persistence : inequality and hope in Latin America / edited by Javier Auyero.
Other titles: Inequality and hope in Latin America | Joe R. and Teresa Lozano Long series in Latin American and Latino art and culture.
Description: First edition. | Austin : University of Texas Press, 2024. | Series: Joe R. and Teresa Lozano Long series in Latin American and Latino art and culture | Includes bibliographical references and index.
  Identifiers: LCCN 2023029013
  ISBN 978-1-4773-2898-9 (hardback)
  ISBN 978-1-4773-2899-6 (paperback)
  ISBN 978-1-4773-2900-9 (pdf)
  ISBN 978-1-4773-2901-6 (epub)
Subjects: LCSH: Latin Americans—Biography. | Latin Americans—Social conditions. | Latin Americans—Economic conditions. | Latin America—Biography. | Latin America—Social conditions. | Latin America—Economic conditions. | Latin America—Politics and government—Social aspects.
Classification: LCC F1407 .P67 2024 | DDC 305.8092368—dc23/eng/20230822
LC record available at https://lccn.loc.gov/2023029013

doi:10.7560/328989

Contents

INTRODUCTION 1
Alison Coffey and Javier Auyero

CHAPTER 1
Soraya: La Reina del Sur in Nicaragua 21
Dennis Rodgers

CHAPTER 2
Maíra: Mothering in the Shadow of State Violence 39
Alison Coffey

CHAPTER 3
Rodrigo: "Many Secrets, Nothing to Hide"—Security Entrepreneurship in Mexico City 59
Eldad J. Levy

CHAPTER 4
Fabio and Angélica: The Resistance of Staying Put 82
Alex Diamond

CHAPTER 5
Doris Huaiquian: *Newen*, Tenacity of Spirit 104
Cinthya E. Ammerman

CHAPTER 6
Aurelia: Displacement, Toxicity, and the Struggle for Home 124
Maricarmen Hernández

CHAPTER 7
Hamid: A Life Deferred in Brazil 145
Katherine Jensen

CHAPTER 8
María: Obligated by Circumstances—From Temporary to Precariously Permanent in the United States 163
Jennifer Scott

CHAPTER 9
Ezequiel: A *Laburante* in Argentina's Relegated Neighborhoods 185
Marcos Emilio Pérez

CHAPTER 10
Nelson and Celia: Feeling Potholes and Debt in the Bones 205
Jorge Derpic

CHAPTER 11
Big Love: A Political Broker at Work 225
Javier Auyero and Sofía Servián

CHAPTER 12
Alberto: Service Work and Social Change in Argentina 243
Katherine Sobering

AFTERWORD 263
Javier Auyero

Acknowledgments 266
Contributors 267
Index 270

INTRODUCTION

Alison Coffey and Javier Auyero

This book tells twelve stories about contemporary life in Latin America. In the pages that follow, we meet a diverse group of individuals from across the continent: grassroots activists and political brokers, service industry workers and private security entrepreneurs, female drug dealers, shantytown dwellers and rural farmers, as well as migrants finding routes into and out of the region. They are courageous as well as ordinary, seemingly unspectacular people, all grappling with the challenges of daily life in a region marked by some of the deepest inequalities in the world.

Each chapter offers an intimate portrait of one or two individual lives. Carefully and respectfully constructed over long periods of time, in deep and often difficult conversations between interlocutors and authors, the stories presented here examine the subjective experiences of living and laboring in Latin America today. Bringing readers into the social worlds of many different individuals, these portraits illuminate the paths their lives have taken, the triumphs and hardships they have experienced, and the aspirations they hold for the future.

While reconstructing the trajectories of particular individuals, each story also has something important to reveal about the broader social, economic, and political processes that structure contemporary life in the region. They highlight a multitude of issues necessary for understanding Latin America today: urban violence and gender inequality, precarious labor and land dispossession, drug flows and population movement, climate change and ecological destruction, and poor people's politics and forms of collective action, among others.

Each of our contributors was tasked with not only reconstructing the life stories of their interlocutors but also conveying, with care and rigor, the national and local contexts necessary for understanding their experiences: the workings of the state and politics, the role of economic restructuring, processes of colonial and racial domination, and the cultural development of particular communities and collective identities.

While acknowledging significant regional diversity, this volume does not attempt to offer a comprehensive view of present-day Latin America of the kind offered by very good introductory texts (e.g., Green 2012; Skidmore, Smith, and Green 2013; Kirby 2014; Berryman 2016; Gutmann and Lesser 2016; Munck and Luna 2022). Rather, contributors invite readers to immerse themselves in the lives of Angélica, Fabio, Hamid, Rodrigo, Aurelia, and others, and to think with them about the many intricacies of social life in contemporary Latin America. Our hope is that these twelve stories, read alongside one another, offer unique and personal windows into the region's complex and multilayered reality.

The Origins and Makings of *Portraits*

Social sciences in and about Latin America have thoroughly described and explained objective inequalities of class, race, and gender and the mechanisms that generate them, detailing their contemporary manifestations as well as their deep historical roots (Nun 2001; Reygadas 2008; Svampa 2015; Bada and Rivera-Sánchez 2021). Yet, when it comes to understanding the varied cultural forms in which individuals, alone or in groups, experience and grapple with these multiple and intersecting inequities and the manifold ways they are legitimized or questioned, much empirical work remains to be done. With that in mind, one deceptively simple question organized our dive into these individual lives: how and why do people put up with, perpetuate, or push back against the conditions that produce their suffering? Through a granular reconstruction of individual lives, *Portraits* offers windows into many key social, economic, and political processes that structure life in the region and, more generally, invites readers to examine this lived, subjective dimension of social inequality.

The idea for this book first germinated a year before the COVID-19 pandemic sent the world into massive lockdown. In early 2019, many of the authors of this volume—graduate students who are members of the Urban Ethnography Lab at UT Austin—began a conversation about a collective project that would illuminate salient processes shaping contemporary life in the region through the intimate reconstruction of individual life stories.[1] We were soon joined by Ethnography Lab alumni and collaborators based at other institutions, in what would become a horizontal joint effort of graduate students, junior professors, and senior scholars.

The protagonists featured are everyday people whose life stories help illuminate a significant social issue in their local or national contexts, with

INTRODUCTION

relevance for understanding the region more broadly. They were recruited in the context of ethnographic fieldwork that each author was carrying out before we began to meet (some of them for doctoral dissertations, some as part of other research endeavors). In selecting the stories we would feature, we aimed to include individuals from a wide array of countries and social locations in order to highlight diverse experiences of living in contemporary Latin America. In many cases, interviews continued over Zoom, WhatsApp, or in person while we were working on this book. Thus, the stories presented in this volume were reconstructed out of months and years of intimate encounters. Each author spent a long time with the protagonists of each chapter, thus bringing to light a deep familiarity not only with the actual person but also with the social world they inhabit.

Meeting monthly via Zoom over the course of two years, our authors collaboratively workshopped drafts, developing each chapter's storyline and honing the connections between biographical details and structural analyses in their narratives. Once final drafts were ready, we met in person during a two-day workshop in Austin to discuss the manuscript in its entirety.

We are certainly not the first to focus attention on individual lives to illuminate larger social issues. A rich tradition of *testimonio* literature in Latin America has served to elevate the stories and voices of people at society's margins. In the social sciences, case studies based on one person or a few individuals have offered compelling windows into broader social, economic, and political processes (Lewis 1975; Hellman 1995; James 2001; Jesus 2003; Gay 2005, 2015; Kertzer 2008; Menchú 2010; Ginzberg 2013). The narratives in this volume share this detailed attention to the intersections of biography, structure, and history. Bringing together life history interviews with long-term ethnographic engagement, the contributors offer us finely crafted accounts that speak not only to the structures that shape contemporary life but also to the nuanced ways people experience them. How does inequality feel in the minds, hearts, and bodies of people who live it? How do everyday people make sense of the challenges they face? And how do these circumstances influence what people imagine to be possible?

Our commitment in this endeavor was not only to comprehend our interlocutors well but also to write them well. In our attempt to illuminate the richness and complexity of people's subjective experiences, we set ourselves the task (and challenge) of composing these accounts in narrative form. Inspired by current nonfiction writing from across the region and recent social science work produced in narrative style, we aimed to produce engaging pieces of writing that would capture the texture of people's realities and the ways their lives have evolved alongside the social, political, and economic changes happening around them. The result, we hope, is a text that students as well as people outside the confines of academia will enjoy reading, that will make them think and reflect about the larger processes going on in the Latin American region through the intimate details of individuals' lives.

The Broad Picture: Inequality and Contention

Latin America is characterized by persistently high levels of social, economic, racial-ethnic, and environmental inequalities, and the structuring principles of those inequalities "are sustained by pillars as deep as they are solid" (Mora-Salas 2021, 98; see also Hoffman and Centeno 2003; Reygadas and Gootenberg 2010; Huber and Stephens 2012; Torche 2014). As such, it has long been understood and represented as a continent where poverty and luxury boom side by side, and where social exclusion plays an outsize role in shaping life outcomes. These inequalities endure: embedded in social relations, spatially inscribed into land and territory, and carried in the bodies of those who live them day to day.[2]

As these myriad forms of inequality have boomed across the region, however, so have public, oftentimes massive and disruptive gatherings in which all sorts of people loudly make their demands for inclusion and equality heard. After all, Latin America is not only characterized by durable inequalities but also by powerful movements for change—from prominent Indigenous and labor movements such as those in Ecuador, Mexico, and Bolivia to vibrant student and feminist ones such as those in Chile and Argentina. Plenty of good scholarship has dissected the origins, dynamics, and impacts of collective struggles across the region (Castells 1974; Yashar 2005; Bidegain and von Bülow 2021; Fernández Anderson 2021; García Serrano 2021; Rice 2021; Rossi 2021), noting that Latin America is as contentious as it is unequal.

The stories in this volume reflect a wide array of experiences and are situated within diverse societal contexts. Nevertheless, several broader, historically significant processes and trends span the continent and play significant roles in shaping contemporary life. Here we highlight three of those key overarching issues to offer greater context for many of the stories to come: long histories of resource extraction, the enduring presence of neoliberalism, and the rise of urban violence.

Extractivism

The Latin American region has long experienced intensive extraction of natural resources for international export, with significant social and ecological consequences. From the earliest eras of colonial domination in which European colonizers plundered its precious metals and coveted agricultural goods, to the arrival of powerful foreign-owned corporations expanding mining and energy operations in the twentieth century, to more recent examples of state-led resource extraction aimed at funding social programs and national development under leftist administrations, extractivism has profoundly influenced Latin America's place in the global hierarchy as well as development, inequality, and conflict within its territories (Riofrancos 2020).

Today, a variety of state and private actors continue to pursue new frontiers of extraction across the continent. During the first decade of the twenty-first century, the profitability of Latin American commodities (including oil, metals, and soy) soared on the global market, spurring a new period of export-oriented growth in the region. Together with the old extractive activities, new forms and scales of extraction took root, among them excavation of open-pit mega-mines, expansion of agribusiness models that employ monocropping and widespread use of GMOs, and construction of massive hydroelectric dams (Svampa 2019). When states harnessed this growth from the commodity boom to expand social safety nets—such as under recent progressive "Pink Tide" governments—poverty levels in some cases diminished, albeit modestly (Weyland, Madrid, and Hunter 2010). However, this resource-dependent growth has not necessarily translated into sustained decreases in poverty and income inequality.

Extractivism has been as ecologically devastating as it is developmentally significant, threatening biodiversity, spreading toxic contamination, and contributing to the acceleration of global warming. As various scholars have detailed, the region has also seen a multitude of socio-environmental struggles, from resistance movements against extractive industry and development models to armed conflict and violent encounters over control of land (Escobar 2008; Li 2015; Riofrancos 2020). The environmental degradation, land grabs, and conflicts that resulted from extractivism have become significant forces of dispossession and displacement across the region, with Indigenous, Afro-descendant, and peasant communities most profoundly affected (Sawyer 2004; Lapegna 2016; Svampa 2019).

Neoliberalism

In the 1970s, a series of global economic crises and transformations began to unfold that would have lasting consequences in the region. Following four decades of state-led development in Latin America, in which government intervention played a significant role in shaping national economies, neoliberalism emerged as a powerful ideology and policy program that promoted "transferring economic power and control from governments to private markets" (Centeno and Cohen 2012, 318).

Neoliberalism comprised a whole gamut of market-based economic interventions, including fiscal austerity and the dismantling of social safety nets, privatization of public infrastructure and services, establishment of free-trade agreements, deregulation of credit and labor markets, and erosion of many labor protections. As Almeida and Pérez Martín (2022) note, in the late 1980s and early 1990s, these policies came to be known as the "Washington Consensus" and were soon a mandatory condition for Latin American states to receive development loans from international financial institutions like the World Bank and the International Monetary Fund. These economic prescriptions grew to represent a veritable political common sense, a sort of unquestioned and widely shared belief that minimal government intervention allows for the most efficient and prosperous economic growth.

Over the last fifty years, the entrenchment of neoliberalism has drastically changed the relationship between citizens, markets, and the state throughout the Americas. According to Portes and Hoffman (2003, 41), a "visible increase in income inequality, a persistent concentration of wealth in the top decile of the population, a rapid expansion of the class of microentrepreneurs, and a stagnation or increase of the informal proletariat" were the direct result of neoliberal policies. In the early 2000s, left-leaning "Pink Tide" governments came to contest this political economic doctrine, putting in place a set of policies that both expanded social spending and increased consumption. However, the consequences of neoliberal policies are still felt across the region—so much so that many would argue that it is hard to understand contemporary dynamics in the Americas without understanding neoliberalism as an economic, political, and cultural project (Fridman 2010; Almeida and Pérez Martín 2022).

Urban Violence

Along with the advance of neoliberal policies, the end of the 1990s and first decades of the twenty-first century witnessed striking increases in urban violence, making Latin America the only region in the world where lethal violence (measured in homicide rates) is still growing without being at war (Cruz 2016; Santamaría and Carey 2017). Home to 8.4 percent of the world's population, Latin America accounts for 33 percent of global homicides (Muggah and Tobón 2018).

This violence concentrates in the territories where the urban poor dwell—known as favelas, *colonias*, barrios, *comunas*, or *villas* in different parts of the continent (Rodgers, Beall, and Kanbur 2012; Salahub, Gottsbacher, and de Boer 2018). A number of factors are associated with this increasingly ubiquitous character of violence in low-income neighborhoods, including poverty, unemployment, inequality, the dismantling of social safety nets, disinvestment, and the pernicious influence of the drug trade. These circumstances have had dire consequences for the most marginalized, who often have few resources to protect themselves in the face of chronic insecurity and accumulated structural disadvantage. In many contexts, this has pushed people into illegal activities such as drug dealing as a means of survival, at the same time making them dependent on violent and unpredictable actors, as well as legitimizing state-sponsored forms of exclusion, discrimination, and oppression (see, e.g., Fontes 2018; Arias and Grisaffi 2021; Jensen and Rodgers 2021).

Widespread fear of crime has also shaped the broader rhythms of city life and urban development across the region. While many of the urban poor navigate spaces affected by interpersonal violence, the informal control of the drug trade, and militarized policing in their daily routines, elites have invested in fortifying their environments and increasingly relied on the private security industry for a sense of safety. The now very familiar images of Latin American cityscapes reveal these dramatic contrasts between enclaves of abundance—opulent shopping malls, extravagant development projects, gated and heavily guarded communities—and relegated territories where citizens struggle to make ends meet in perilous terrain (Caldeira 2001; Rodgers 2004).

Together, these three historical processes play crucial roles in shaping the Latin American region. While they are certainly not the only significant dynamics structuring life across the continent, they nevertheless offer important contextual background for the stories to come. As we meet individuals from peasant communities and Indigenous nations feeling the effects of extractivism, diverse citizens who endure and navigate chronic urban violence on a daily basis, and people from various walks of life grappling with the social and economic transformations that have accompanied neoliberalization, we gain insight into not only their unique lived experiences but also these broader structural processes constituting the region's contemporary reality.

Road Map

The chapters that follow examine consequential issues of social inequality as they manifest in daily lives: precarious work, lack of good-quality health-care, asylum bureaucracy, state violence, workers' militancy, gender oppression, displacement, the workings of patronage, environmental contamination, and more. Spanning wide geographic reach—from the Southern Cone to the southern United States—they offer windows into the vast array of places, histories, cultures, and identities that together constitute the region.

The lives detailed in this book are not governed by any central or predominant set of forces. Across their different national political contexts, we find governments advancing neoliberal policies of austerity and deregulation, others expanding the state's social welfare function, and still others operating somewhere in between. While some have been part of the region's left turn toward progressive programs, or so-called twenty-first-century socialism, others face deepening polarization and a resurgence of right-wing movements—all of which shape the way people perceive, interact with, and experience the state in their daily lives.

Their economic contexts are equally varied: some countries are suffering the effects of deindustrialization and returning to a form of development that relies mostly on exports of primary products, while others have moved toward a service-based economy. Some grapple with the strains of high inflation, whereas others engage in the (usually contested) implementation of structural adjustment reforms. And underneath these broader trends are distinct lived experiences of labor—in exploitative service jobs, burgeoning informal sectors, hazardous work environments, and elite entrepreneurial firms—as well as efforts to actualize more dignified forms of work and ecologically sustainable modes of production.

Across the diversity of topics and contexts explored in these chapters, however, readers will find that each one is attuned to the question that opened our initial inquiry: How and why do people legitimize or challenge the inequities—the structural oppression, discrimination, interpersonal violence, or bureaucratic manipulation—that they experience?

The question we posed ourselves was intentionally open so as to avoid the traps that still haunt students of subjugated individuals or groups:

miserabilistic and populist interpretations (Grignon and Passeron 1992). Under the spell of the first, we are inclined to see the dominated, the excluded, as victims of an all-powerful system. Under the influence of the second, more popular these days among academics, we tend to read (project?) into every action of the subjugated an act of resistance somewhat miraculously untouched by material deprivation or symbolic domination.

The reality is more often somewhere in between, and as such, this book does not provide a definitive answer to the question we sought to address. Thinking with Ezequiel, Doris, María, and others, we hope, will illuminate the multiple, complex, and at times contradictory ways in which people cope. Their actions and experiences, readers will see, are underpinned by a range of sentiments, from angry resentment, to fatalism, to cautious and, sometimes, stubborn optimism. By paying attention to the ways intersecting inequalities land in peoples' lives, it is our hope that readers will come up with tentative answers and new, even more challenging and stimulating interrogations for themselves.

The volume begins with the story of Soraya, a manicurist and drug dealer from a poor barrio in the Nicaraguan capital of Managua. Although drug dealing in Latin America is considered a predominantly male enterprise, Soraya is one of the women who has established herself within the trade. Her involvement in dealing seems to have outwardly imbued her with confidence and strong-willed independence, but it has also brought much tragedy to her life. While Soraya challenges many gendered expectations, as Dennis Rodgers shows in this chapter, her life possibilities are also fundamentally constrained by enduring structures of *machismo* and patriarchy, which have in many ways been magnified by her involvement in drug dealing.

In the urban periphery of Rio de Janeiro, we meet Maíra, a fiercely protective mother of three. A single parent focused on her family's day-to-day needs, Maíra never imagined becoming involved in human rights activism until her teenage son became a victim of police violence and was later incarcerated. Alison Coffey's chapter follows Maíra's journey through motherhood and militancy as she finds her voice in a movement of women struggling against state violence, mass incarceration, and racial injustice in Brazil, the country with the third-largest prison population in the world.

In the next chapter we meet Rodrigo, an ambitious entrepreneur working to solve the security problems of Mexico City's elite. Armed with knowledge, networks, and surveillance technologies he previously acquired as a security contractor in Mexico and abroad, Rodrigo has established himself in a growing, globalized industry of private security provision. Tracing the extralegal networks of collaboration Rodrigo brokers between government officials and wealthy citizens, Eldad Levy illustrates in his chapter the ways Mexican elites deal with urban insecurity and the increasingly blurred lines between state and private actors that have emerged in response.

The next account introduces us to Fabio and Angélica. Along the Cauca River in rural Colombia, they grow organic coffee, cacao, and nearly everything they eat on their isolated farm. Alex Diamond's chapter tells the story of their struggles to maintain their way of life in the face of broader forces that threaten to dispossess them. With Colombia's historic peace process has come the construction of new highways, a hydroelectric dam that has destroyed local economies, and violent conflict between guerrilla and paramilitary groups. Nevertheless, Angélica and Fabio persist in working the land in ecologically sustainable ways, resisting the industrial pressures and threats of displacement mounting around them.

In Wallmapu, the ancestral homelands of the Mapuche people in what is also known as Chile, we gain a window into the life of Doris Huaiquian. A language teacher and cultural adviser, Doris performs vital work preserving the culture of the Lafkenche, or "people of the sea." In recent years, however, the ocean has encroached on Doris's home, and she must confront the prospect of relocating inland. Detailing the social and ecological transformations wrought by various waves of colonization, Cinthya E. Ammerman sheds light on the continuities that exist between colonialism and climate change, the relationship between ecological and cultural vitality for Indigenous communities, and Doris's steadfast work to preserve her people's future.

From there, we are introduced to Aurelia, living on contaminated land beside the largest oil-refining complex in Ecuador. In this informally built community along the Pacific Coast, Aurelia and her neighbors experience chronic health issues and the ever-present risk of industrial accidents. Nevertheless, they have fought for years to formalize ownership of the contested land they live on. Tracing individual and collective histories of displacement, housing insecurity, and the racialized social exclusion of Ecuador's Afrodescendant communities, Maricarmen Hernández illuminates the complex reasons why Aurelia and her community fight to remain in place despite constant exposure to toxic pollution.

Hamid is also struggling for a permanent place to call home. Born in a Palestinian refugee camp in Syria, he now lives as a refugee in Rio de Janeiro. After the Syrian conflict erupted in 2013, Brazil opened its doors to anyone from Syria who wished to come. Following Hamid as he navigates the asylum bureaucracy and attempts to rebuild his life in a new country, Katherine Jensen provides a window into the refugee experience in Latin America, highlighting the unique protections, shortcomings, and ambivalences that Hamid and others encounter with official refugee status in Brazil.

Heading north into the United States, we meet María, who left her home in Mexico to work in the grueling crawfish-peeling industry of Louisiana. Driven by family financial pressures, she takes on precarious work in an unfamiliar place, grappling with what it means to turn a move "obligated by circumstances" into the basis for a happy life. In this chapter, Jennifer Scott follows María as she pursues greater mobility by navigating the demands of an exploitative boss, a public transportation system that promises her greater independence, and, eventually, the decision of whether to stay permanently in the United States without documentation.

Ezequiel, meanwhile, labors as a skilled plasterer and electrician in one of Buenos Aires's poorest districts. In his forty years, he has seen his neighborhood transform from a thriving working-class community to one experiencing the tolls of deindustrialization. Detailing the impacts of Argentina's neoliberal reforms and economic restructuring, Marcos Pérez also reveals the tensions that emerge for Ezequiel, who has reacted to economic decline by embracing collective action in a progressive activist movement while simultaneously doubling down on his traditional value system shaped by old-school notions of masculinity, family, and labor.

The next chapter shuttles readers around the Bolivian city of La Paz, where Nelson, a taxi driver, and his partner, Celia, work hard to secure a steady income for their family. When Nelson fell ill, however, they faced a crisis: as he despaired about the mounting costs of quality care, Celia ran between hospitals, replenishing bags of blood for his transfusions. Through their struggles, Jorge Derpic illustrates what happens when labor precarity meets an overburdened social safety net. Despite socialist policies that have fostered inclusion and lifted many out of poverty in Bolivia, working majorities still struggle to stay afloat on their own.

Pancho's story brings us into the political universe of La Matera, a squatter settlement on the outskirts of Buenos Aires. As the neighborhood's main political broker, Pancho works day in and day out to secure state services for La Matera and resources for its residents as well as for himself. His labor, methods, and reputation, however, are not without controversy. Tracing the divergent opinions, relationships, and conflicts that swirl around Pancho, Javier Auyero and Sofía Servián examine the evolving practice of political brokerage and what it means for poor people's politics in Buenos Aires today.

Finally, in the halls of Buenos Aires's Bauen Hotel, we meet Alberto. After the social and economic crisis that rocked Argentina in 2001, he joined with other workers to seize control of the hotel from their employers and transform it into a democratically owned and managed enterprise. Through this story of service work, Katherine Sobering's chapter sheds light on the ways that economic restructuring has shaped experiences of labor in Argentina, while also illuminating what collective ownership and the small-scale practice of democracy can make possible in the lives of workers.

Portraits of Persistence

As should be evident, our book does not tell a "single story" (Adichie 2009) about the continent. We do not believe that it is possible or desirable to propose an overarching narrative about contemporary Latin America. Life in the region is multifaceted, and the mosaic we present seeks to reflect that. The individuals featured here are not representative of other individuals, of communities, or of countries. In fact, in a way, many are exceptions, but their stories, in the skillful hands of the authors, illustrate more general processes that shape contemporary life in Latin America.

Though we did not set out to tell stories that coalesced around a common theme, we nevertheless perceived a unifying thread as we brought these narratives together. Once readers get to know the trials and tribulations of Hamid, doubly displaced and still searching for a place where he can build the life he wants; or those of Nelson and Celia, burdened by the physical and financial fallout of illness yet focused on ensuring a comfortable life for their family; or those of Aurelia, building herself a house and a place of belonging in highly hazardous terrain; or those of Doris, laboring to preserve her people's language and cultural practices in the face of colonial violence and systemic racism, it will not be hard to see that the protagonists of our stories have something to teach us about persistence in the face of seemingly insurmountable obstacles.[3]

Suffering major life setbacks due to her involvement in the drug trade and surrounded by men who relentlessly try to bend her to their will, Soraya never loses her determination to remain independent—an obstinate quest that is even more remarkable given its context in a poor, violent, Nicaraguan barrio. In his Argentine neighborhood where once-vibrant working-class life is a distant memory and now suffused with daily violence, Ezequiel insists on carrying out a set of domestic, professional, and communal routines that seek to re-create that long-gone world. Far from there, in rural Colombia, Angélica and Fabio stubbornly rely on agroecological farming practices to stay put in a region where a multiplicity of forces—from dams and mines to armed groups—act against them.

To "persist" means to "continue firmly or obstinately in a state, opinion, purpose, or course of action, esp. despite opposition, setback, or failure" (*Oxford English Dictionary*). While we read these stories as ones of persistence, we also hold no illusions that our protagonists are at all times indefatigable, or that they possess some special, inextinguishable optimism about what they can achieve. Looking at the longer arc of our protagonists' lives, we see that they also reveal (at times fleeting, at times prolonged) seasons of doubt, resignation, and contemplation of whether their efforts are worth it. As readers accompany Maíra, dealing with the weight of her son's suffering in the Brazilian carceral system, along with her own guilt that he ended up in harm's way, they gain windows into the activism that became an outlet for her grief, but also the days when she feels she'd rather give up. As Alberto grapples with the repercussions of the COVID-19 pandemic and the collapse of the business he helped build into a democratically owned enterprise, he becomes mired in uncertainty about what will come next—new efforts to expand the workplace democracy movement or a return to precarious and exploitative service jobs.

In *The Sociological Imagination*, C. Wright Mills (1959, 7) argues that seeing the world sociologically requires "the capacity to range from the most impersonal and remote transformations to the most intimate features of the human self—and to see the relations between the two." Attentive to his call to examine these intersections of biography and history, this volume is as much about the lives of individual people as it is about broad issues such as violence, environmental assault, protest, displacement, migration, or patronage politics that have shaped the trajectory of the region.

Through these deep immersions into each person's biography, the authors of this volume illuminate not only how an individual's social location shapes their life outcomes but also how their lived experiences of inequality transform over time—be that in response to evolving external conditions or to the protagonist's own growth and development. These reconstructions of individual lives as they come together with larger social structures should, we hope, provoke readers to consider when, why, and how individuals may respond to conditions of social suffering with acquiescence, individual rebellion, collective action, or some combination.

But the stories of Nelson, Celia, Pancho, Soraya, and others are interesting not only because of what they tell us about broad processes or larger social structures. The protagonists of each chapter also teach readers a great deal about the reality, the hopes, the achievements, and the misfortunes of people living in highly unequal societies, through what Rosine Christin (1999) in "A Silent Witness" calls a language of "little things." Looking beyond the national narratives, the official histories, and the authoritative voices reveals these small anecdotes of everyday life and the predicaments of ordinary people. In sharing their stories, each of our interlocutors "talk[s] about a life saturated with collective history only through a personal language" (Christin 1999, 360), and as such must be listened to in particular and deliberate ways. The "little things"—the ways Angelica and Fabio use the mandarin flowers that grow on their land, the bus routes that María gets lost on, the laundry that Aurelia washes by hand alongside a contaminated river—allow us to see, in very concrete terms, what persistence in an unjust world is all about.

Persistence sheds light on the individual and collective actions people take in difficult circumstances, without losing sight of the objective conditions beyond their control. It allows us to look beyond the material strategies people use to subsist and survive, to understand the also-crucial ways they cultivate or maintain a sense of themselves, of their community, of meaning in their lives, and of collective purpose in the world. Thus, these portraits of persistence help us see what Clifford Geertz (2001, 43) called "the supposedly soft facts" of social existence: "What do people imagine human life to be all about, how do they think one ought to live, what grounds belief, legitimizes punishment, sustains hope, or accounts for loss." That is the reason why we pay attention not only to what our protagonists are going through in their daily lives—and how everyday predicaments illustrate larger processes at work—but also to the ways in which they imagine and strive toward their individual and collective futures.

We did not set out to emphasize the harsh reality of the continent or the pain and suffering of our protagonists. We did not, conversely, want only to focus on its positive aspects. Responding to the anthropologist Sherry Ortner's question "How can we be both realistic about the ugly realities of the world today and hopeful about the possibilities of changing them?" (2016, 60), our commitment was to dig deep into the subjects' experiences and their social (both material and symbolic) spaces, avoiding sanitizing their complex and difficult lives while also unearthing possibilities for transformation. In doing so, we hope to re-present, in the sense of presenting again, in a different, more personal, and intimate light, daily life in contemporary Latin America, with its necessities and possibilities, its suffering and joys, its hardships and hopes.

INTRODUCTION

Notes

1. The narrative model and methodological strategy of this book drew inspiration from a previous Urban Ethnography Lab collaboration, *Invisible in Austin*. *Invisible* relied on extended life history interviews and ethnographic observation to portray the predicament of people working at the bottom of Austin's social structure.
2. This book was written as the COVID-19 pandemic was ravaging the continent, deepening long-standing precarity and inequalities in the region. At the time of this writing, more than 1.5 million COVID-related deaths have been recorded in Latin America and the Caribbean. Home to 8.4 percent of the world population, Latin America has 28.4 percent of the world's total COVID-related deaths. The pandemic also produced deep economic crises (an average 8 percent contraction in GDP), crumbling labor markets, and shrinking middle classes, resulting in exponential growth of poverty and marginality (Benza and Kessler 2021).
3. We here adopt Loïc Wacquant's notion of "persistence." He suggested this notion to us in our ongoing discussions about the survival strategies of the poor (see Deckard and Auyero 2022). In Wacquant's forthcoming book, *The Zone: Making Do in the Hyperghetto*, he suggests that in order to better account for the complex economies of hypermarginality we need to move away from the notion of "strategies of subsistence" or "survival strategies," replacing them with the more accurate notion of "strategies of persistence." "Subsistence" or "survival," Wacquant persuasively argues, do not do justice to poor people's simultaneous efforts to cultivate or maintain a sense of self, meaning, and collective purpose in the world. Instead, "persistence" allows us to account for the ongoing struggle to hold on to what it means to be a social being—encompassing the many (and not merely material) dimensions of survival. In his words, persistence involves the efforts that those on the margins make to maintain "their social being and position in its manifold facets rather than just material sustenance."

References

Adichie, Chimamanda Ngozi. 2009. *The Danger of a Single Story*. TED Talk. https://www.ted.com/talks/chimamanda_ngozi_adichie_the_danger_of_a_single_story?language=en.

Almeida, Paul, and Amalia Pérez Martín. 2022. *Collective Resistance to Neoliberalism*. Cambridge: Cambridge University Press.

Arias, Enrique Desmond, and Thomas Grisaffi, eds. 2021. *Cocaine: From Coca Fields to the Streets*. Durham, NC: Duke University Press.

Auyero, Javier, ed. 2015. *Invisible in Austin: Life and Labor in an American City*. Austin: University of Texas Press.

Bada, Xóchitl, and Liliana Rivera-Sánchez, eds. 2021. *The Oxford Handbook of the Sociology of Latin America*. New York: Oxford University Press.
Benedict, Ruth. 2006. *Patterns of Culture*. Boston: Mariner Books.
Berryman, Phillip. 2016. *Latin America at 200: A New Introduction*. Austin: University of Texas Press.
Bidegain, Germán, and Marisa von Bülow. 2021. "Student Movements in Latin America." In *The Oxford Handbook of the Sociology of Latin America*, edited by Xóchitl Bada and Liliana Rivera-Sánchez, 357–372. New York: Oxford University Press.
Bourdieu, Pierre. 2000. *Pascalian Meditations*. Stanford, CA: Stanford University Press.
Bourdieu, Pierre, et al. 1999. *The Weight of the World: Social Suffering in Contemporary Society*. Oxford, UK: Polity Press.
Caldeira, Teresa P. R. 2001. *City of Walls: Crime, Segregation, and Citizenship in São Paulo*. Berkeley: University of California Press.
Castells, Manuel. 1974. *Estructura de clases y política urbana en América Latina*. Buenos Aires: Sociedad Interamericana de Planificación.
Centeno, Miguel A., and Joseph N. Cohen. 2012. "The Arc of Neoliberalism." *Annual Review of Sociology* 38 (1): 317–340.
Christin, Rosine. 1999. "A Silent Witness." In *The Weight of the World*, edited by Pierre Bourdieu et al., 354–360. Stanford, CA: Stanford University Press.
Cruz, José Miguel. 2016. "State and Criminal Violence in Latin America." *Crime, Law and Social Change* 66 (4): 375–396.
Deckard, Faith M., and Javier Auyero. 2022. "Poor People's Survival Strategies: Two Decades of Research in the Americas." *Annual Review of Sociology* 48, 373–395.
Evans, Harriet. 2020. *Beijing from Below: Stories of Marginal Lives in the Capital's Center*. Durham, NC: Duke University Press.
Fernández Anderson, Cora. 2021. "Latin American Women's Movements: A Historical Overview." In *The Oxford Handbook of the Sociology of Latin America*, edited by Xóchitl Bada and Liliana Rivera-Sánchez, 339–356. New York: Oxford University Press.
Fernández-Kelly, Patricia. 2015. *Hero's Fight: African Americans in West Baltimore and the Shadow of the State*. Princeton, NJ: Princeton University Press.
Fontes, Anthony W. 2018. *Mortal Doubt: Transnational Gangs and Social Order in Guatemala City*. Berkeley: University of California Press.
Fridman, Daniel. 2010. "A New Mentality for a New Economy: Performing the Homo Economicus in Argentina (1976–83)." *Economy and Society* 39 (2): 271–302.
García Serrano, Fernando. 2021. *Del sueño a la pesadilla: El movimiento indígena en Ecuador*. Quito: Flacso Ecuador.
Gay, Robert. 2005. *Lucia: Testimonies of a Brazilian Drug Dealer's Woman*. Philadelphia: Temple University Press.

———. 2015. *Bruno: Conversations with a Brazilian Drug Dealer*. Durham, NC: Duke University Press.

Geertz, Clifford. 2001. *Available Light: Anthropological Reflections on Philosophical Topics*. Princeton, NJ: Princeton University Press.

Ginzberg, Carlo. 2013. *The Cheese and the Worms: The Cosmos of a Sixteenth-Century Miller*. Baltimore, MD: Johns Hopkins University Press.

Green, Duncan, with Sue Branford. 2012. *Faces of Latin America*. 4th ed. New York: Monthly Review Press.

Grignon, Claude, and Jean-Claude Passeron. 1992. *Lo culto y lo popular: Miserabilismo y populismo en sociología y literatura*. Madrid: Endymion.

Gutmann, Matthew C., and Jeffery Lesser, eds. 2016. *Global Latin America: Into the Twenty-First Century*. Oakland: University of California Press.

Hellman, Judith. 1995. *Mexican Lives*. New York: The New Press.

Hoffman, Kelly, and Miguel Angel Centeno. 2003. "The Lopsided Continent: Inequality in Latin America." *Annual Review of Sociology* 29 (1): 363–390.

Huber, Evelyne, and John D. Stephens. 2012. *Democracy and the Left: Social Policy and Inequality in Latin America*. Chicago: University of Chicago Press.

James, Daniel. 2001. *Doña María's Story: Life History, Memory, and Political Identity*. Durham, NC: Duke University Press.

Jensen, Steffen, and Dennis Rodgers. 2021. "The Intimacies of Drug Dealing: Narcotics, Kinship, and Embeddedness in Nicaragua and South Africa." *Third World Quarterly* 43 (11): 2747–2756. https://doi.org/10.1080/01436597.2021.1985450.

Jesus, Carolina Maria de. 2003. *Child of the Dark: The Diary of Carolina Maria de Jesus*. Translated by David St. Clair. New York: Signet.

Kertzer, David I. 2008. *Amalia's Tale: An Impoverished Peasant Woman, an Ambitious Attorney, and a Fight for Justice*. Boston: Houghton Mifflin Harcourt.

Kirby, Peadar. 2014. *Introduction to Latin America: Twenty-First Century Challenges*. New York: SAGE.

Lapegna, Pablo. 2016. *Soybeans and Power: Genetically Modified Crops, Environmental Politics, and Social Movements in Argentina*. New York: Oxford University Press.

Lewis, Oscar. 1975. *Five Families: Mexican Case Studies in the Culture of Poverty*. New York: Basic Books.

Menchú, Rigoberta. 2010. *I, Rigoberta Menchú: An Indian Woman in Guatemala*. Edited by Elisabeth Burgos-Debray. London: Verso.

Mills, C. Wright. 1959. *The Sociological Imagination*. London: Oxford University Press.

Mora-Salas, Minor. 2021. "The Sociology of Inequality in Latin America." In *The Oxford Handbook of the Sociology of Latin America*, edited by Xóchitl Bada and Liliana Rivera-Sánchez, 96–112. New York: Oxford University Press.

Muggah, Robert, and Katherine Aguirre Tobón. 2018. "Citizen Security in Latin America: Facts and Figures." Rio de Janeiro, Brazil: Igarapé Institute.

Munck, Gerardo L., and Juan Pablo Luna. 2022. *Latin American Politics and Society: A Comparative and Historical Analysis*. New York: Cambridge University Press.

Nun, José. 2001. *Marginalidad y exclusión social*. Buenos Aires: Fondo de Cultura Económica.

Ortner, Sherry B. 2016. "Dark Anthropology and Its Others: Theory since the Eighties." *Journal of Ethnographic Theory* 6 (1): 47–73.

Perry, Keisha-Khan Y. 2013. *Black Women against the Land Grab: The Fight for Racial Justice in Brazil*. Minneapolis: University of Minnesota Press.

Portes, Alejandro, and Kelly Hoffman. 2003. "Latin American Class Structures: Their Composition and Change during the Neoliberal Era." *Latin American Research Review* 38 (1): 41–82.

Reygadas, Luis. 2008. *La apropiación: Destejiendo las redes de la desigualdad*. Barcelona; Mexico City: Anthropos.

Reygadas, Luis, and Paul Gootenberg, eds. 2010. *Indelible Inequalities in Latin America: Insights from History, Politics, and Culture*. Durham, NC: Duke University Press.

Rice, Roberta. 2021. "Indigenous Movements in Latin America: Tensions, Contradictions, Possibilities." In *The Oxford Handbook of the Sociology of Latin America*, edited by Xóchitl Bada and Liliana Rivera-Sánchez, 373–389. New York: Oxford University Press.

Riofrancos, Thea. 2020. *Resource Radicals: From Petro-Nationalism to Post-Extractivism in Ecuador*. Durham, NC: Duke University Press.

Rodgers, Dennis. 2004. "'Disembedding' the City: Crime, Insecurity, and Spatial Organization in Managua, Nicaragua." *Environment and Urbanization* 16 (2): 113–124.

Rodgers, Dennis, Jo Beall, and Ravi Kanbur, eds. 2012. *Latin American Urban Development into the Twenty-First Century: Towards a Renewed Perspective on the City*. New York: Palgrave Macmillan.

Rossi, Federico M. 2021. "Labor Movements in Latin America." In *The Oxford Handbook of the Sociology of Latin America*, edited by Xóchitl Bada and Liliana Rivera-Sánchez, 325–338. New York: Oxford University Press.

Salahub, Jennifer Erin, Markus Gottsbacher, and John de Boer, eds. 2018. *Social Theories of Urban Violence in the Global South: Towards Safe and Inclusive Cities*. 1st ed. Abingdon, UK; New York, NY: Routledge.

Santamaría, Gema, and David Carey Jr. 2017. *Violence and Crime in Latin America: Representations and Politics*. Norman: University of Oklahoma Press.

Sawyer, Suzana. 2004. *Crude Chronicles: Indigenous Politics, Multinational Oil, and Neoliberalism in Ecuador*. Durham, NC: Duke University Press.

Skidmore, Thomas E., Peter H. Smith, and James N. Green. 2013. *Modern Latin America*. 8th ed. Oxford, UK: Oxford University Press.

Svampa, Maristella. 2015. *La sociedad excluyente: La Argentina bajo el signo del neoliberalismo*. Buenos Aires: Taurus.

———. 2019. *Neo-Extractivism in Latin America: Socio-Environmental Conflicts, the Territorial Turn, and New Political Narratives*. Cambridge: Cambridge University Press.

Torche, Florencia. 2014. "Intergenerational Mobility and Inequality: The Latin American Case." *Annual Review of Sociology* 40 (1): 619–642.

Weyland, Kurt, Raúl L. Madrid, and Wendy Hunter, eds. 2010. *Leftist Governments in Latin America: Successes and Shortcomings*. New York: Cambridge University Press.

Willis, Graham Denyer. 2015. *The Killing Consensus: Police, Organized Crime, and the Regulation of Life and Death in Urban Brazil*. Oakland: University of California Press.

Yashar, Deborah J. 2005. *Contesting Citizenship in Latin America: The Rise of Indigenous Movements and the Postliberal Challenge*. Cambridge: Cambridge University Press.

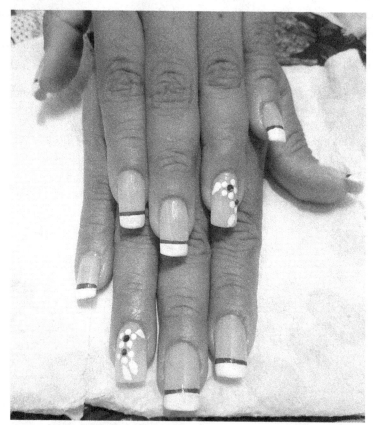

Fig. 1.1. *Wanda's nails.*

CHAPTER 1

Soraya

LA REINA DEL SUR IN NICARAGUA

Dennis Rodgers

FEBRUARY 2020:
Seated on a slightly tatty, overstuffed sofa, I watch as Soraya[1] meticulously manicures Wanda's fingernails. Her face a picture of tense concentration, she begins by carefully tracing red and white stripes along the distal bands of four out of five fingers on each hand, before then delicately dotting small flowers on each ring finger.

"I can come back to do our interview later," I say to Wanda.

"No, no, it's fine, Dennis," she replies. "Soraya's almost finished, and in any case, she's *de confianza*, so why don't we just get started? It's not as if she doesn't know about [my husband] Bismarck and his drug dealing... But you know what? If you want a female perspective on drugs, you should actually interview her, not me—I'm just the wife of an ex-drug dealer, but she's *la Reina del Sur!*"

"The Queen of the South?" I ask, throwing Soraya a querying glance. Looking up from her manicuring labors, she smirks sardonically before saying, "You know, Dennis, like in the *telenovela*, about that Mexican woman who becomes a *narcotraficante* [drug dealer]."

"Yes, I get that, I know the series, but she became a powerful drug dealer, and from what I know, you're not a big-time *narco*, are you?"

"Nah, I was just a *mulera* [street dealer], but people call me 'la Reina del Sur,' because I'm strong-willed and independent, just like the real Reina."

Chuckling, I reply, "You do know the Reina isn't real, yes?" before then asking her more earnestly, "but would you be willing to do an interview with me, though?"

"What would you ask me about?" Soraya queries.

"About your life, your family, how you got into drug dealing, manicuring, your hopes and dreams for the future, that kind of thing. But it would all be confidential and anonymous, and you would only have to talk about what you wanted to talk about. Would that be okay?"

Soraya ponders my request for a few seconds before replying brusquely, "*Dale*, but not today, I've got an errand to run. I'll meet you here at the same time tomorrow." Without waiting for an answer, Soraya then dots a final petal on Wanda's left index nail, packs up her files and polish, and leaves Wanda and me to our interview about her troubles and travails as a drug dealer's wife...

Drugs and Gender in Latin America

The drug trade has become a hot academic topic in Latin America over the past two decades. This is arguably especially true in relation to contemporary Central America. On the one hand, as the geographical bridge between drug-producing South America and drug-consuming North America, the region has always been a major transit point for drugs. On the other hand, the particular socioeconomic and political dynamics linked to the drug trade have become so endemic in Central America that many of its constituent countries are considered to be "narco-states," systemically bringing together the authorities, local elites, and criminal actors into forms of co-governance that revolve around, or are profoundly shaped by, drugs. The nature of the drug trade under such conditions has been shown to vary significantly from context to context and from time period to time period. Many excellent studies have traced drug trafficking routes, how local drug markets are collaterally and contingently created, the way that the actors involved can change over time, how control of the trade can be both diffuse and concentrated, and the profound impact that international law enforcement activities can have on its evolution, as well as the way that drugs can significantly shape local social, cultural, and economic life in both positive and negative ways.

One thing that most studies of the drug trade in Latin America—and elsewhere—tend to agree on, however, is that it is predominantly a male enterprise. Such gendered representations are clearly overly simplistic, though. Women are not only obviously often directly impacted by but also involved in the drug trade in a variety of ways. Certainly, my interviews with Wanda in Nicaragua over the years have starkly highlighted how her husband Bismarck's drug-dealing activities have fundamentally conditioned her life, and the existence of female dealers such as Soraya was apparent right from the beginning of the two and a half decades of longitudinal ethnographic research on gang dynamics that I have been carrying out in barrio Luis Fanor Hernández, a poor neighborhood in Managua, the country's capital city. They are, however, clearly less common than male dealers, and until I interviewed Soraya in February 2020, I had not actively engaged with any during the course of my research. This was largely because the particular—and gendered—nature of my connections into the local drug trade in barrio Luis Fanor Hernández had been through gang members, and for the majority of the duration of my research in the neighborhood, local gang members have always been male.

I had, however, known Soraya for thirteen years when we had the above exchange. I first met her in 2007, as a recent addition to the Gómez household with whom I stay whenever I visit barrio Luis Fanor Hernández. My first stay with them lasted a year in 1996–1997; I subsequently returned for extended periods of time in 2002, 2003, 2007, 2009, 2012, 2014, 2016, and 2020. Soraya became Elvis Gómez's partner in 2003, and although they separated in 2015, she has remained part of (some of) the Gómez family social circle, including Wanda Gómez and her husband Bismarck's in particular, so I have seen and talked to Soraya frequently over the years. Several other members of the Gómez family had mentioned to me at various points in time that Soraya was involved in the drug trade, but it was difficult to know to what extent this was just malicious gossip prompted by her family connections with known local drug dealers, on the one hand, or the often-fraught nature of her relationship with Elvis, on the other. The opportunity to ask her about this directly did not present itself until Wanda openly connected her with drug dealing in her presence, and Soraya admitted to being "la Reina del Sur."

I was immediately intrigued by Soraya's justification for her nickname, that she was "strong-willed and independent." Women involved in the drug trade generally tend to be seen through the prism of one of two tropes, either as victims who (collaterally) suffer forms of direct and indirect violence and exploitation as a result of being the mothers, wives, or girlfriends of drug dealers, or else as empowered individuals challenging gendered structures of power and inequality. In both cases, however, drug dealing is seen as something of an exceptional sphere of economic activity, one that is socially autonomous and responds to its own internal dynamics, and the negative and positive gendering inherent in the above tropes are considered to derive from drug dealing itself. My interviews with Wanda over the years had already brought home to me how the trope of the long-suffering drug dealer's wife was very much a caricature, one that divested her of agency and also obscured the way that her life was critically conditioned by other factors that had little to do with her husband's involvement in the drug trade. An obvious question was whether this was perhaps not also true of the trope of the empowered female drug dealer.

This question is particularly relevant in relation to a broader Nicaraguan context that—like much of Latin America—is profoundly marked by patriarchy, and where the once-famous progressive social gains of the left-wing Sandinista Revolution that held sway in Nicaragua between 1979 and 1990 have been unraveling continuously since the post–Cold War regime change. Certainly, there has been a steady erosion of women's rights in Nicaragua over the past quarter century, perhaps most visible in the total interdiction of abortion introduced in 2006, but also evident in the watering down of laws against gender-based violence in ways that reinforce hegemonic beliefs that enable and normalize patriarchal rule. Such beliefs are embodied more generally in the pervasive notion of "machismo" that Roger Lancaster, in his classic study of the phenomenon, *Life Is Hard* (1992), has defined as a "system of manliness" that draws together ideas about masculinity and femininity into an ideological system that provides templates for accepted and acceptable social behavior patterns on the part of both men and women. Over the years of my visiting Nicaragua, I have been able to observe how deep, enduring, and pervasive these templates are, and I wondered whether female involvement in drug dealing really challenged them.

"Let Me Tell You . . ."

I meet Soraya the following day as agreed, in front of Wanda and Bismarck's house. "Let's go to my place to talk," she says as soon as she turns up. "The walls have ears here."

"Sure, no problem," I answer, getting up from the steps I had been sitting on. "I thought you were friends with Wanda and Bismarck, though?"

"I am, but you can never be too careful," Soraya replies, before adding, "and I prefer to be in my own space if we're going to talk about me."

"No problem," I repeat. "Where do you live?"

"Not very far, on the east side of the barrio."

We walk down the potholed central avenue of the neighborhood, turning right at the end and then walking another 300 meters until reaching a ramshackle wooden house surrounded by a makeshift fence of barbed wire and corrugated zinc sheets. On the left side of the house is a cracked *lavandero* (sink and washboard), and there is an outhouse on the right. When I first arrived in barrio Luis Fanor Hernández in 1996, most of the neighborhood's houses had been similar, uniformly displaying a certain infrastructural shabbiness, but over the course of the past two and a half decades, almost half of the neighborhood's building park has been rebuilt, with cement blocks replacing wood, dirt floors being tiled, and toilets and washing facilities moved indoors. One of the major drivers of this infrastructural mutation in barrio Luis Fanor Hernández was the drug trade. Bismarck and Wanda's house, for example, had been completely transformed as a result of his almost decade-long involvement in dealing, from a rickety wooden shack to a sleekly painted concrete construction that boasted crystal chandeliers inside, while other dealers had even gone so far as to add second stories to their houses, something that is extremely rare in Managua's poor urban neighborhoods. When I mention (half-)jokingly to Soraya as we settle down on the porch to talk that her house does not look like a drug dealer's house, she gives me a dirty look, and says, "I've only moved here recently, and I don't deal anymore."

"But you did, no?" I query.

"Yes, but not everybody who deals gets rich, Dennis, let me tell you . . ."

Portrait of a Female Drug Dealer

Soraya Méndez García was born in barrio Luis Fanor Hernández in 1987. Her mother, Gladys, was from a neighborhood *familia fundadora* (founding family), while her father, Jorge, was from Villa Cuba, another neighborhood in the northeast of Managua. They had an on-and-off relationship for the first decade of Soraya's life, meaning that she moved several times between her father's home in Villa Cuba and the Méndez household in barrio Luis Fanor Hernández, which also included Soraya's grandmother, her aunt Tina, Tina's husband, and their daughter. When Soraya was eleven, she "had a problem with my aunt's husband, and my mother and I moved out to live with my father." Soraya and Gladys stayed with him for two years, "but he drank a lot, and would often hit my mother. One day I tried to stop him, and he started beating me with his belt. He beat me really hard, he was like a madman, hitting my face with the buckle, over and over again . . . There was blood everywhere, and he wouldn't stop, until my mother stabbed him in the back with a kitchen knife . . . We then quickly gathered all our things and left, and I never saw him again."

Tina had split with her husband in the intervening period, so Soraya and Gladys were able to move back into the Méndez family home in barrio Luis Fanor Hernández. Soraya's grandmother had died, and her cousin had married Ricardo, better known as Pac-man (due to his voracious appetite). According to Soraya, Pac-man was at the time the right-hand man of the main drug dealer in barrio Luis Fanor Hernández, a person known as "el Indio Viejo," and it was through him that she was first drawn into the drug trade. As she explained: "My mother and I moved back in with my aunt after we left my father. There were five of us in the house—me, my mother, my aunt, my cousin, and my cousin's husband. You know him, Dennis, he's the one they call Pac-man, so you know he's a *narcotraficante*. My aunt and my cousin would help him from time to time with his *bisnes*, but this was when the drug trade was increasing, and he had lots to do, and they started asking me to 'do them a favor,' to help them. At first it was small things, you know, moving drugs or money from one place to another, or helping them 'cook' cocaine into crack, but after a while, I started selling for him as a *mulera*, in the streets."

"How old were you then?" I asked.

"I was fourteen or fifteen at the time."

"That's young to start in that line of work!"

"I wasn't doing it so much for the money, it was because they were family, you know, they would ask me to help, and I would say, *dale pues*, of course I'll help you. 'Take this for me,' they would say, or 'Come with me,' and I'd accompany them when they went to make deliveries, because the police would be less suspicious of me, as a young girl, you know."

Soraya rapidly graduated to street selling, and even if she claimed "not to be doing it for the money," she established herself as a successful *mulera*, making around US$100 a week, a contextually significant sum of money compared to the average (non-drug-dealing) household income of around US$120 a month at the time. The way she became involved in the drug trade highlights well how the dynamics of the latter often respond to logics that not only entangle both personal and instrumental motivations but are also extremely gendered. On the one hand, her status as a young woman made her instrumentally useful for carrying out certain drug-dealing operations without attracting suspicion, while on the other hand, her familial connection made it difficult for her to refuse to help Pac-man. At the same time, however, kinship relations also led to Soraya subsequently reducing her involvement in the drug trade: "When I had my son, Ramses, in 2007, I stopped selling regularly. When my aunt or cousin needed me, I'd still help, but I no longer did it all the time, just sometimes; when I needed money, I'd sell a few *catos* [packets] here and there."

Such part-time involvement in drug dealing is by no means unusual. As Gabriel Kessler (2004) has highlighted in his book *Sociología del delito*

Fig. 1.2. *Doses of crack cocaine prepared for sale.*

amateur, (especially youth) delinquency often occurs in an "amateur" manner, that is, as a response to contingent individual consumerist desires or by taking advantage of spur-of-the-moment opportunities, rather than on the basis of carefully planned out, professional practices. The point at which Soraya decided to stop dealing drugs on a regular basis coincided more generally with a professionalization of the drug trade in barrio Luis Fanor Hernández, and the sidelining of the first generation of "amateurish" *muleros* and *muleras* by a more professional emergent *cartelito*, or "little cartel," that was still run by el Indio Viejo, but no longer drew on local youth to sell drugs, except for a few trusted individuals, and mainly involved outsiders. It was at this point that Pac-man actually became el Indio Viejo's right-hand man, helping him discipline local youth in barrio Luis Fanor Hernández who might have previously sought to sell drugs. He did so through a mixture of carrot-and-stick tactics: for example, on the one hand sponsoring the neighborhood soccer team while on the other hand hiring a couple of experienced former gang members to intimidate any youth not associated with the *cartelito* who tried to sell drugs or who made trouble for *cartelito* drug dealers. Soraya's direct connection to Pac-man is likely what allowed her to continue selling on a part-time basis during this period.

According to Soraya, she stopped dealing drugs altogether in 2012. This was a time when "the police started coming round a lot to [my aunt's] house. Although we didn't keep drugs in the house, and they'd never find anything, my aunt and my cousin were *fichados* [known], and so they kept on coming round. *Me daba nervios* [It made me nervous], and one time, in 2012, I got so annoyed with the police. They were searching my room and breaking my things, and I shouted at them, and they took me, they took my aunt, my cousin, and her husband, and we were put in the district police station jail for three days. It's horrible there, I tell you, there's no beds, nothing, only metal frames, no mattresses, and the women who are already there are treacherous, they either tell you to sit or lie down next to them or ask you to give them whatever you have, and the bathroom has no doors, no walls, it was dirty, and women would follow you in to watch... We'd sleep together for security, but it was a terrible *zancudero* [mosquito breeding ground], so you couldn't sleep... I cried the whole time, but I was not crying because I was jailed, I was crying for my son, for Ramses, thinking 'What will he think?' 'Who will take care of him?' I was crying because I thought I would never see him again, and that he would know that I'd been imprisoned... On the third day, though, the *guardias* [police] came and called my name and I was able to leave. My cousin and her husband [Pac-man] were also released, but not my aunt Tina; she was condemned to five years in prison. It made me think even more, 'What if it had been me?' 'What would happen to my son?'... *Eso no es vida andar cayendo preso* [Being imprisoned is no life], and so I decided there and then that I would stop dealing, for my son."

"What about your cousin's husband, did he continue after being released?"

"He continued, which is also why I decided to stop living with them. He still put pressure on me to continue working for him, but I don't do so like before... I don't sell for him anymore, at most I just accompany him while he's working, or when he goes and makes deliveries. I just can't continue, for my son."

Bargaining with Patriarchy

There is a revealing bias in Soraya's narrative about her involvement in drug dealing that concerns her aunt Tina, who was in fact dealing drugs long before Pac-man. Indeed, the latter became involved in the business through Tina, rather than the other way round. Tina had been one of three local marijuana sellers in barrio Luis Fanor Hernández in the mid-1990s, along with el Indio Viejo and his brother, and when el Indio Viejo "graduated" to dealing cocaine at the turn of the century, she was one of the first people to whom he "outsourced" the new commodity (also likely partly because they had been lovers in the early 1990s). Tina thus became a *púsher*, buying cocaine regularly (and exclusively) from el Indio Viejo, and then "cooking" it into crack, which she would then sell through a group of *muleros*, or street dealers, among whom was Pac-man. Pac-man took over from Tina as a *púsher* when she was first imprisoned in 2003, and they then worked together when she was released in 2008, until she was reimprisoned in 2012, at which point Tina decided to "retire" for good. Pac-man then continued to deal drugs until he was arrested and sentenced to five years in prison in 2016.

It was Tina, not Pac-man, who recruited Soraya into drug dealing around

2001–2002, although she ended up working mainly for the latter, since the former was imprisoned in 2003. Soraya's narrative, however, suggests that it was Pac-man rather than her aunt who was responsible, clearly because drug dealing is an activity imbued with significant moral ambiguity. Indeed, as Soraya herself complained during our interview, it is often difficult for individuals who choose to leave the drug trade to shake off the negative connotations associated with it, and many dealers who have turned a new leaf often actively try to conceal their drug past altogether. While Soraya did not try to deny her aunt Tina's involvement in the drug trade, her narrative made her involvement less central and dependent on Pac-man (rather than the other way round). This implicitly framed Tina's involvement as a function of machismo, effectively portraying her as a woman who was unwittingly dragged into drug dealing at the insistence of a wayward male relative. As such, Soraya's narrative can be seen as an inverse instance of what Deniz Kandiyoti famously called "bargaining with patriarchy" in an eponymous article published in the journal *Gender and Society* in 1988. Soraya drew on gendered tropes in order to minimize her aunt Tina's involvement in the drug trade and thereby protect her reputation. Such a shifting of the blame is obviously reductive of Tina's agency, but it also highlights how more general patriarchal dynamics condition the lives of female drug dealers. Certainly, my broader research on the drug trade in barrio Luis Fanor Hernández has revealed that there is a critical difference in the way that female and male dealers become involved in the drug trade, with the latter mostly drawn in as a result of having been gang members, while the former come to the business principally through familial and affective connections. This means that women's involvement in drug dealing is fundamentally enmeshed in a range of other social relations and processes, arguably making it more difficult for them to refuse to be involved.

Soraya's involvement in the drug trade over the years has also been complicated in a number of other ways by its entanglement with her relationship with Elvis Gómez. Even their initial encounter was intimately linked to drugs, as she explained: "I first met Elvis in 2001, when he would come and buy drugs from my aunt Tina. He told me that I'd immediately caught his eye, and he would flirt with me [*me venía tirando el cuento*], telling me how beautiful I was, how he couldn't stop thinking about me. I didn't know what to think, I was just fourteen, he was twenty-one, and he had his wife Yulissa and a daughter, but he said he wanted to get to know me, and so he would come and wait for me after school, and we'd go and sit in the park together and talk. I told him that he was too old for me, and that I didn't want any problems with his wife, but you know what men are like, he kept on telling me that I was beautiful, that I was special, that he loved me, that it was over with his wife and that they were going to separate . . . Eventually I said to him that if he wanted something with me, he had to do it properly and talk to my mother, as I didn't want to have to hide. He agreed, and so I went to talk to my mother to prepare things. I told her who he was, and how he was no longer with his wife, and so on. Then Elvis came to talk to my mom, and she gave him permission to visit me at home, saying that she didn't want problems, so it had to be in the house, not in the streets, and she didn't want his ex-wife to turn up. It was like an official *noviazgo* [engagement]: Elvis would come and see me every day, around 7:00–8:00 p.m., and he would stay until 10:00–11:00 p.m."

According to Soraya, Yulissa did not realize that this courtship process was going on "for a whole year," but when she found out, she left Elvis immediately, "although not before burning all of his clothes," as Soraya told me, rather amused.[2] Soraya then "began to spend nights with Elvis at his house, although I was still telling my mother that I was staying with a school friend to study together," and shortly after her sixteenth birthday in 2003, she officially moved in with him. They stayed in the Gómez household for two years, until the end of 2005, before renting a house elsewhere in the neighborhood once Elvis secured a stable job as a taxi driver, but after two years there, "the owner wanted the house back, and we had to move back in with the Gómezes" in 2007, according to Soraya. They then stayed there until 2010, in Elvis's case, and 2012, in Soraya's case.

Soraya did not provide me with much more in the way of details about the first part of this period of her life, except in two respects. Firstly, she said that one year after moving in with Elvis, she realized that he was still seeing Yulissa, and so "I told him 'I'm leaving,' and I went to stay with a cousin in another neighborhood. Elvis came to find me, he was calling me, crying, saying that he had made a mistake, that he would never see her again, that he loved me, and he asked me to come back. He came to see me every day for six days, and on the seventh day, I went back with him." She said that it was this episode that prompted them to start trying to have a child, at Elvis's insistence, and that she tragically suffered two miscarriages in the years prior to their son Ramses's birth, "which made us so happy." Secondly—and perhaps not unrelatedly—she told me that Elvis had enthusiastically embraced her drug dealing, partly because it ensured that he had continuous access to drugs, but also because of the money that it brought in, and after she moved in with him, they rapidly began to operate "as a team."

Doña Yolanda, the matriarch of the Gómez family and Elvis's grandmother, put a different spin on things. According to her, Soraya was a notorious crack addict who "corrupted" and "entrapped" Elvis. She had not been happy when they moved in together into the Gómez household, as she underscored angrily during a conversation in February 2020.

"Pah! You could smell them smoking all the time; it was horrible, disgusting. I always lived in fear that the police would come and arrest everybody in the house . . . That woman was a corruption."

"Come on, Doña Yolanda," I replied. "Elvis smoked before he met Soraya. And she was only fourteen when they got together, and he was twenty-one. Don't you think that if anybody corrupted anybody, it was he who corrupted her?"

"No, it was her," she answered categorically. "Age doesn't have anything to do with it; she was a drug dealer, everybody knew that, and she involved him in her *bisnes*. Every evening, after she moved in, I could hear them preparing packets of drugs—scratch, scratch [of the taping], whisper, whisper—and then she would leave the house in the middle of the night with a backpack to go and deliver them somewhere. After a while, I couldn't take it anymore, so I threw them out."

The fact that Doña Yolanda blames Soraya rather than her grandson Elvis for their involvement in drug dealing is not necessarily surprising (although it is likely also linked to the fact that Elvis has since emigrated to the United States and is a source of occasional remittances for her). But while it is probable that Soraya was the senior partner in the pair's involvement in drugs due to her kinship relation to her aunt Tina and Pac-man, considering the age gap between Soraya and Elvis at the time, as well as the latter's quasi-grooming of the former, there are significant grounds to suspect that other, more gendered dynamics were probably at play between them that owed little to drug dealing. Certainly, Elvis's public demeanor in his relationship with Soraya at the time generally corresponded very much to that of a (stereo) typical macho Nicaraguan man, dominating her verbally and generally acting possessively and "in charge," and one could speculate that such behavior very likely extended to Soraya's drug-dealing activities.

There is also another disjuncture between Soraya's and Doña Yolanda's narratives. The latter claimed that the reason Elvis and Soraya had to move back into the Gómez home in 2007 was because Soraya stole C$20,000—approximately US$1,100 at the time—from Pac-man, and when he came to claim it, she forced Elvis to sell his taxi. As a result, they could no longer afford to pay rent, so they had to return to live in the Gómez home. However, I learned from a drug dealer who was Pac-man's confidant at the time that he had in fact given Soraya the money to keep, as part of a strategy to spread money and drugs around trusted collaborators rather than risk keeping it all in one place, and Elvis had helped himself liberally behind Soraya's back to "loans" from this money to feed his drug habit. When Pac-man found out, he took Elvis's taxi as compensation. Soraya was apparently absolutely livid with Elvis about this, something that would tally with the palpable tension that I noted between them when I first met Soraya in July 2007 (but which I had attributed to her being in the last stages of her pregnancy), not just due to the breach of trust but also because it was as a result of this episode—rather than her motherhood—that Soraya (unwittingly) became a part-time drug dealer, as Pac-man no longer trusted her to be one of his primary street dealers.

Double Crosses and Double Standards

The tension that I observed between Elvis and Soraya in 2007 had dissipated by my 2009 visit to Nicaragua, however. Elvis had stopped smoking crack and had found another job as a courier, Soraya seemed to be a contented homemaker, and their son Ramses was a happy, bubbly, cheerful child. Many of the conversations I had with them at the time revolved around Elvis's impending emigration to the United States, sponsored by his mother, who had emigrated there in the early 1990s. Soraya later explained to me that Elvis had said that it was better if he went alone first, to establish himself and then start the administrative procedures to bring her and Ramses over under family reunification rules. Elvis ended up leaving in 2010. He lived with his mother in Miami but had rapidly taken on multiple formal and informal jobs, including working in a Taco Bell, cleaning office buildings at night, and working informally as a motorcycle mechanic and odd jobs man in his local neighborhood. Soraya described how during this period "he would send me money every month," and that on discovering that family reunification required that they be formally married, had come back to Nicaragua in 2011 to do so. He had, however, been able to initiate the procedure to bring their son Ramses over straightaway, and the latter went to live with Elvis in Miami in late 2012.

Shortly after Ramses left to join Elvis in the United States, Soraya "decided to leave the Gómez household and move back in with my mother and cousin at my aunt's, because the Señora [Doña Yolanda] began fighting with me." She said that Elvis continued sending her money, including "extra sums to improve my living space in my aunt's home, expanding it and putting *cerámica* [tiles] in the bathroom, because he would stay with me instead of with the Gómezes whenever he came back to Nicaragua." I stopped in Miami on my way to Nicaragua in February 2014, and met up with Elvis there. He talked excitedly about being able to bring Soraya over very soon and gave me a laptop computer to deliver to her (although pointedly did not have anything for me to take to other members of the Gómez family). A few months later, however, Soraya said that out of the blue, Elvis "accused me of being unfaithful to him. He said somebody had told him that they'd seen me with a man. I told him it wasn't true, but he became completely obsessive, he even sent me a photo of the guy who was supposed to be my lover, and would call me at any time, day or night, to check on me, and he would send people to look for me and keep an eye on me."

"Were you being unfaithful to him?" I queried.

"No," Soraya replied categorically. "I won't say I hadn't thought about it, it's not easy being alone, and you know what I'm like, I like to party and go out . . . I also discovered that he hadn't cut things off with Yulissa like he'd told me he had, because when he took Ramses to Miami, he also took his daughter with her with him, which he never told me about . . . But no, I wasn't being unfaithful. He didn't want to hear it, though, and he became like crazy, insulting me, telling me that I was a *puta*, and I got so sick and tired of it, I decided 'fuck it,' I'm an independent woman, if he's going to give me all this shit for nothing, I might as well get together with a guy to give him something to really complain about."

"That seems a bit . . . impulsive? What happened afterward? I'm guessing that he found out? Did somebody tell him?"

"Yes, but would you believe it, it was Ramses, the little *hijueputa*! Elvis sent him over to see me by himself, and when he went back, he told his father that another man was sleeping in his bed!"

"Ah . . . and then what happened?"

"Then Elvis stopped talking to me, and he also stopped me from communicating with Ramses."

"I'm sorry to hear that—it must have been really hard for you."

"*Sí*, I was going crazy, texting him every day, telling him to let me talk to my son, and telling him to bring him back to Nicaragua, that I wanted him to live with me. It wasn't until Elvis came back to Nicaragua a year later that we talked again. He came to see me with divorce papers, telling me that it was over between us, and that unless I signed the divorce papers and gave him custody, I'd never see Ramses again. He said that if I signed the papers, he'd allow me to communicate regularly with my son, and that he'd bring him back to Nicaragua every two to three years so that I could see him, but otherwise he was going to bring him up in Miami, and that I should be happy that he was allowing me that much contact after what I'd done to him. There was nothing I could do, so I signed the papers, and we were divorced in 2016."

"I'm sorry about that, Soraya . . . You must miss Ramses so much."

"*Claro*, of course I miss him . . . Even if we talk every few days on WhatsApp, it's not the same. *Idiay*, I gave birth to him, he's my son. Even if, as they say, I didn't give birth to him with strength [*no lo parí, como dicen, con fuerza*], I still carried him for nine months, so of course it hurts me . . . But I say to myself that it's a sacrifice that I'm making for him. It's better for my son to stay over there, because over there he has opportunities, he won't be spending his time in the streets like he would here, he's getting a good education . . . That way he'll become somebody in life, and not just a nobody here. I'm thinking about his future, not mine, although perhaps one day he'll bring me over to join him in Miami . . . He's a US citizen now, so perhaps he'll be able to sponsor me to come and live with him."

At this point in our conversation Soraya fell silent, before then adding bitterly, "And you know what's even worse? All this had nothing to do with my betrayal, but his! Within less than a year of divorcing me, Elvis remarried Yulissa, so that he could start the papers to bring her over there . . . That was the real reason he wanted to divorce . . . I don't think he ever stopped seeing her."

I have no idea who accused Soraya of being unfaithful initially, although she is persuaded that it was a member of the Gómez family, "who were jealous that he sent me money and things, and they never received anything." This would not surprise me, as Gómez family members often made snide remarks about Soraya and complained how "unfair" it was that Elvis was helping her but not them during my 2014 visit to barrio Luis Fanor Hernández. More importantly than who made the accusation, however, the Gómez family's behavior vis-à-vis Soraya contrasted strongly with that displayed in relation to another family member, Winston Gómez, whose partner Nedesca had emigrated to Spain. She regularly sent him money, which he mostly spent carousing around bars with women, something that was universally hidden from Nedesca, despite the fact that, unlike Soraya, she personally got on very well with everybody in the Gómez family. This difference starkly highlights the gendered double standards that Soraya faced. Though by no means surprising in view of the pervasive machismo that permeates Nicaraguan society, the fact that Elvis was able to browbeat Soraya, first into sharing her drug dealing, and then into divorcing him and giving up custody of Ramses, underscores how the empowerment that is often assumed to be inherent in female drug dealing is not only by no means necessarily manifest but is more often than not trumped by broader forms of gender inequality.

SORAYA

Beautician Blues

At first glance, it might seem surprising that Soraya has not returned to drug dealing in the aftermath of her separation from Elvis, as she is clearly struggling economically, and drug dealing—for those who have the connections to get involved, which Soraya does—remains one of the most attractive ways of making money quickly in a poor neighborhood such as barrio Luis Fanor Hernández (despite the obvious risks that it can entail). She has instead set herself up as a beautician, and I asked her about this at the end of our interview.

"When did you start your beauty business?" I queried.

"After the divorce," she replied. "Elvis was no longer sending me money, so I had to earn a living. I decided to study *belleza* [beauty]. I learned how to do nails, toes, and so on, manicuring, you know, and then I started going around to people's places."

"And how is business?"

"*Ahí voy*... It's growing, by word of mouth."

"You haven't considered working in a salon?"

"No, I prefer to be *independiente* [independent]. If you work in a salon, you only earn 30 córdobas [about US$1] on the 200 córdobas [US$7] that customers pay, while I do home service for 150 córdobas [US$5] and get to keep it all."

"Why don't you set up your own *salón de belleza* in your home, like [a common acquaintance called] Spencer has done for his barbering business, for example? Wouldn't it be easier than going around all the time?"

"It's too expensive. Spencer gets help from his mother in the United States, that's why he was able to set up his barber shop, buying a chair, and all the razors, and so on. I was barely able to buy my beauty tools... And in any case, I like going around to people's places, it's more interesting!"

Several drug dealers in barrio Luis Fanor Hernández have suggested to me in interviews that Soraya's home-visiting manicure business provides her with a convenient cover for drug dealing, especially in the present period of increased police patrolling and repression following the failed April 2018 popular uprising against the current Nicaraguan government that has made street dealing more difficult. The fact that Soraya seems to make, according to her, no more than US$15–$20 a week from her manicure business, yet is the sole breadwinner in a household made up of herself and her mother, and that she pays US$120 a month in rent, would certainly seem to support this contention. I, however, believe Soraya when she says that she is no longer dealing. She is clearly an extremely resourceful and resilient person, and frequently engages in a variety of odd jobs to make ends meet, including some that she would almost certainly not take on if she were still dealing drugs due to their low-paid and socially demeaning nature, such as temporarily working as a maid for Wanda and Bismarck for the two weeks that they put up a research collaborator who came to visit barrio Luis Fanor Hernández with me in February 2020. Soraya is very aware that there continue to be a lot of rumors about her, but she was adamant in our exchanges that she no longer sold drugs:

"So, you haven't gone back to dealing drugs, even part-time?" I probed.

"No. I'd tell you if I had, but those days are really behind me, I've retired," she replied firmly.

"Then why did Wanda call you 'la Reina del Sur' the other day?"

"*Pues*, people call me that because everybody knows that I used to sell, they started calling me that many years ago, and the name has stuck, even though I've stopped dealing . . . But you know what, although I've retired from that kind of *bisnes*, I still like the name and being associated with the real Reina in the *telenovela*, even if my life is nothing like hers . . . She's *tuani* [cool]," Soraya said a little wistfully.

"Did you see the second season [of the TV show]?" I asked her.

"No, why?"

"Well, in that one she's retired, but then her daughter is kidnapped, and she becomes a *narcotraficante* again to get her back . . ."

"Por siempre la Reina!!!"

Soraya's story clearly suggests that the putative trope of the empowered female drug dealer is more complicated than is frequently assumed. On the one hand, this is because drug dealing is unquestionably a highly gendered activity, but on the other hand, it is also due to the fact that it is gendered in a way that intersects with other gendered processes and practices that have little to do with drug dealing itself. This is because drug dealing is a fundamentally embedded economic activity that is inevitably conditioned by broader social structures and practices such as patriarchy and machismo. Just as Javier Auyero and María Fernanda Berti (2015) highlight in their book *In Harm's Way* how different forms of violence that are typically considered discrete and analytically distinct phenomena in fact "concatenate" together systemically across different social spheres and activities, the same is also true of gender inequalities. Ultimately, then, what Soraya's story reveals is that rather than empowering her, drug dealing more often than not traps her in a web of powerful patriarchal constraints, compounding these in ways that fundamentally limit her life possibilities and aspirations.

At the same time, however, to view Soraya solely as "trapped" is not correct either. Her life is clearly marked by constant struggle and endurance in the face of different forms of domination and oppression, but she also frequently and persistently seeks to confront and challenge her predicament. Certainly, this was evident in the WhatsApp exchange I had with Soraya on March 8, 2021, after my phone alerted me that she had updated her status. She had uploaded a picture of herself drinking at a nightclub, overlaying it with the following text: "Today is international women's day, and we celebrate the power of independent and autonomous women! We are beautiful, we are strong, and we can do whatever we want!" Such behavior on Soraya's part was by no means unusual. She frequently uploads photos of herself engaging in hedonistic activities via her WhatsApp status, often accompanied by messages celebrating her "independence" and "power." But that day's upload contrasted especially starkly with those of other women in barrio Luis Fanor Hernández with whom I am in WhatsApp contact, whose status updates all associated International Women's Day with "love," "being taken care of," or "a celebration of femininity," and whose photos showed them being kissed, hugged, or pampered by their husbands, boyfriends, or children . . . I immediately wrote to Soraya to wish her a good day, saying that I hoped that she would have fun, and also to tell her that I'd started to write this chapter "about when she was 'la Reina del Sur.'" A few minutes later she replied: "*Por siempre La Reina!!!*" ("Forever the Queen!!!").

Notes

This chapter is based on research funded by the European Research Council (ERC) under the European Union's Horizon 2020 research and innovation program (grant agreement no. 787935).

1. This name is a pseudonym, as are all the names of people and places mentioned in this chapter.
2. In retrospect, it seems improbable that Yulissa did not at the very least harbor suspicions, especially as Elvis's involvement with Soraya was frequently alluded to by other Gómez family members in rather unsubtle ways, for example, nicknaming him "el Árabe" (apparently drawing inspiration from an Egyptian *telenovela* about a sheikh and his harem being shown on Nicaraguan television at the time). Yulissa was, however, supposedly conducting an affair with another

member of the Gómez household at the time, which might explain why things did not come to a head immediately.

References

Auyero, Javier, and María Fernanda Berti. 2015. *In Harm's Way: The Dynamics of Urban Violence*. Princeton, NJ: Princeton University Press.
Kandiyoti, Deniz. 1988. "Bargaining with Patriarchy." *Gender and Society* 2 (3): 274–290.
Kessler, Gabriel. 2004. *Sociología del delito amateur*. Buenos Aires: Editorial Paidós.
Lancaster, Roger N. 1992. *Life Is Hard: Machismo, Danger, and the Intimacy of Power in Nicaragua*. Berkeley: University of California Press.

Suggested Reading

On Drug Dealing in Latin America

Gay, Robert. 2015. *Bruno: Conversations with a Brazilian Drug Dealer*. Durham, NC: Duke University Press.
Muehlmann, Shaylih. 2014. *When I Wear My Alligator Boots: Narco-Culture in the U.S.-Mexico Borderlands*. Berkeley: University of California Press.
Rodgers, Dennis. 2018. "Drug Booms and Busts: Poverty and Prosperity in a Nicaraguan Narco-*Barrio*." *Third World Quarterly* 39 (2): 261–276.

On Women and Drug Dealing in Latin America

Campbell, Howard. 2008. "Female Drug Smugglers on the U.S.-Mexico Border: Gender, Crime, and Empowerment." *Anthropological Quarterly* 81 (1): 233–267.
Carey, Elaine. 2014. *Women Drug Traffickers: Mules, Bosses, and Organized Crime*. Albuquerque: University of New Mexico Press.
Gay, Robert. 2005. *Lucia: Testimonies of a Brazilian Drug Dealer's Woman*. Philadelphia, PA: Temple University Press.

On Gender and Patriarchy in Nicaragua

Lacombe, Delphine. 2022. *Violences contre les femmes: De la révolution aux pactes pour le pouvoir (Nicaragua, 1979–2008)*. Rennes, France: Presses universitaires de Rennes.
Montoya, Rosario. 2012. *Gendered Scenarios of Revolution: Making New Men and New Women in Nicaragua, 1975–2000*. Tucson: University of Arizona Press.
Neumann, Pamela. 2018. "Gender-Based Violence and the Patrimonial State in Nicaragua: The Rise and Fall of Ley 779." *Cahiers des Amériques Latines* 87 (1): 69–90.

CHAPTER 2

Maíra

MOTHERING IN THE SHADOW OF STATE VIOLENCE

Alison Coffey

As a young woman, Maíra[1] never longed to be a mother—nor did she imagine becoming an activist. But when I meet her in 2019, a fiercely protective mother of three and a respected leader in her community, it's hard to imagine her any other way. On a weekday morning in the middle of a warm Brazilian winter, she greets me with a hug and kiss on the cheek as I step off the commuter rail platform at the Vila Belém station. In her early forties, Maíra has a light tan complexion with a few delicate freckles on her cheeks, and dark, straight hair that cuts off sharply at her shoulders. Today she wears lipstick and a touch of light-blue eye shadow, more makeup than I've seen her in before, for an activist forum on state violence and anti-Black racism she'll be speaking at that afternoon.

As the rickety train lurches forward and rattles its way farther north into the Rio de Janeiro periphery, we descend the stairs from the elevated landing onto the sidewalk below. Just beyond the entrance gate is a huddle of tents where young men sell goods to commuters coming or going from the station: bottles of water, roasted peanuts, cigarettes, and chewing gum. One of the tents belongs to Maíra's son, Jefferson. In his early twenties, Jefferson has dark brown skin, close-cropped hair, and a trim mustache that frames a shy smile. Jefferson says hello, greeting me with a handshake at his mother's prodding before turning back to arrange the goods he's selling in tidy rows on a small table. He wears bright board shorts and a waist pack for tucking away bills and change. I notice, locked above a dusty flip flop, the electronic ankle monitor that Maíra has told me much about in our interviews. Almost a year prior, Jefferson was released from prison to finish a decade-long sentence under surveillance, within a defined radius of his home.

I was introduced to Maíra a few months earlier at a local human rights organization where she works. I had known the organization's director for nearly ten years and collaborated with members of his team during my previous research endeavors focused on public security in Rio de Janeiro. Over the next several months, Maíra and I met for multiple life history interviews in a small meeting space at the back of the office, our conversations usually lasting two to three hours each. As we got to know each other, Maíra invited me to accompany her to social movement events where she was scheduled to speak, as well as to informal community gatherings in her neighborhood.

As became clear over the course of our conversations, her son's contact with the criminal justice system was a defining juncture in Maíra's life, propelling her toward a new political consciousness and identity as an activist involved in struggles against mass incarceration, inhumane prison conditions, and racial injustice in Brazil. In addition to her work at the human rights organization, Maíra spends her time attending rallies, meeting with families affected by state violence, and walking up and down the sidewalk outside the train station where she can keep a protective eye on her son, while counseling other young men from the neighborhood as they navigate their own cases in the criminal justice system. While neither were paths that she had envisioned for herself, Maíra's story has been profoundly shaped by her journeys through motherhood and militancy. They are two journeys that have been woven together, supported and sustained in community with other women involved in similar struggles.

Becoming a Mother

Maíra grew up in a small town in Brazil's Northeast, a place she described as "very *machista*, very patriarchal." From a young age, she had the sense that something was not right with the societal expectations imposed on women. Experiencing the enforcement of strict gender roles and observing the submission of women in her family, Maíra constantly asked herself why she couldn't do the things that men could. "It felt like a quiet war being waged inside of me," she said. In response, she developed a fierce sense of independence. When Maíra was eight years old, her mother broke away from the constraining mores of her small town, separated from Maíra's father, and moved their family to Rio de Janeiro. Their new city was still awash with gender inequities, Maíra admitted, but was noticeably less patriarchal than her small town in the Northeast. They settled in a favela north of Rio's city center—one of the hundreds of informally built neighborhoods housing the poor, members of the working class, and migrants arriving from the hinterlands in search of economic opportunity in Brazil's industrialized Southeast.

As an adolescent, Maíra dreamed of supporting herself to live an independent life. "I wanted to work," she told me. "I idealized a professional life and my own home. Living on my own, you know?" However, in her late teens, she began a relationship with a man she knew from work. She moved with him to a city just north of Rio de Janeiro, and soon after had her first child, a daughter. "I was eighteen when I got pregnant. My pregnancy with my daughter went very well, but with my son it wasn't so good," she explained. "Marital problems started with my second pregnancy, and it only got worse." After separating from her partner, Maíra began a new relationship and soon had a third child, another boy. But the challenge of raising children on her own continued. "My kids have fathers," she explained, "but they were never present in their lives. I was always a single mother . . . Even when I was in a relationship, it was me who did everything."

Maíra has light skin and identifies as white. But with the birth of her children, she had to grapple with the racism embedded in Brazilian society in more personal ways. "My two older children are Black, and I came to suffer discrimination through them," she explained. "Even today, people on the street don't realize I'm their mother, because they don't look like me." A long history of racial mixing among people of European, African, and Indigenous descent has contributed to the oft-recited myth of Brazil as a "racial democracy," or a society largely free from racial prejudice. As the country pursued its ambition to modernize in the early twentieth century, elites sought to leave behind the "backwardness" associated with its place in the world system, and notably, its large Indigenous, Black, and mixed-race populations. Promoting the idea of a *raça brasileira*, a single "Brazilian race"—albeit one to be whitened over time with policies encouraging European immigration—the republic bolstered an ideology of racial harmony in Brazil. Contrary to the national myth, however, discrimination and violence based on a hierarchy of skin color and phenotype have long existed in Brazil and remain widespread today.

For Maíra and her children, the difference in complexions meant misrecognition at school and with the pediatrician, racist jokes from Maíra's extended family, and, in some cases, hateful comments from strangers. On multiple occasions in their adolescence, her two oldest were pulled aside to be searched by police or security guards, while Maíra and her youngest son, similarly light-skinned, were allowed to pass untouched. "As a mother, seeing your children experience that *hurts*," Maíra told me. She never hesitated to protect them: "I would say no, you are *not* going to touch them, they're my children!" But when it came to discriminatory comments directed at her for bearing children of color, she told me, "Sometimes you stay quiet to avoid a greater aggression."

After her third child was born, Maíra turned all of her energy toward gaining the economic stability to support her family. This time of her life involved several moves between the far reaches of the metropolitan region and Rio de Janeiro. In neighboring municipalities to the north, they could live on less, but formal work opportunities were scarce. In Rio de Janeiro, where she could more easily secure an income, the higher cost of living—even in the favelas—meant it was hard to make ends meet. While working long hours to provide for her kids, Maíra also returned to her studies at night, completing high school and a degree in human resources management. Soon after, she found work at a telemarketing company, which provided just enough stability for them to settle more permanently in Rio.

Violence in the "Marvelous City"

In many ways, the neighborhood in which Maíra raised her children was similar to the one she herself grew up in: a hillside favela in the North Zone of Rio, covered in small brick houses with corrugated tin roofs, and built by the collective labor of working-class residents. Despite the difficulties that came with living in informal housing—lack of city services, precarious infrastructure—she remembered the community she grew up in as a mostly tranquil place. The Rio de Janeiro that her children were born into, however, was in many ways different from the one she experienced at their age. Since the 1990s, a highly militarized war on drugs, conflict between illicit armed groups, and heightened criminalization of favela residents have led to striking levels of violence in the urban periphery.

With the arrival of cocaine to Rio de Janeiro in the 1980s, drug trafficking became a highly profitable enterprise requiring a network of storage, repackaging, and sales points throughout the city. The favelas were seen as ideal sites for such operations, as their challenging topography and labyrinthine layouts were difficult for police to penetrate. The state was never fully absent, however. As the drug trade expanded, it came to rely on collusion between traffickers, police, and government officials, or what the anthropologist Elizabeth Leeds (1996) has referred to as the "selective presence" of the state. Despite the involvement of influential social and political actors in organized crime, it is nevertheless the favelas—home largely to low-income Black and brown residents—that have been the primary targets in the war on drugs. As drug factions became a permanent fixture in peripheral neighborhoods, media outlets, the upper classes, police, and politicians increasingly associated these communities with crime and disorder, deepening the discrimination and marginalization experienced by favela residents.

This has had dire consequences for those living at the margins. In addition to the violence exerted by drug factions, militarized responses from Rio's police have been consistently denounced by international human rights organizations for their high degree of abuse and indiscriminate use of force. In the last two decades, police violence in Rio de Janeiro, as well as across much of Brazil, has reached staggering proportions. According to the Center for the Study of Security and Citizenship, a leading research institute on violence and security in Brazil, Rio de Janeiro police killed 15,497 people between 2004 and 2019—an average of three per day. In 2019, when the number of annual police killings reached an all-time high, more than one-third of all violent deaths in the state of Rio de Janeiro were carried out by state security agents. This violence is also highly racialized: of all the individuals killed by Rio de Janeiro police in 2019, 86 percent were Black, compared to a population that is 51.7 percent Black according to the last census. As the ethnographer Graham Denyer Willis writes in *The Killing Consensus* (2015, 83), police view these killings as a necessary practice for controlling crime: they are "validated, expected, and institutionally ordained as normal."

It is in this context of territorialized and racialized state violence that Maíra's son Jefferson became the victim of police violence and entered the Brazilian prison system. Jefferson had worked as a street vendor for several years, peddling cold beverages from a Styrofoam cooler slung across his back on the city's famous beaches. More recently, he had decided to vend closer to home; as a dark-skinned Black man doing informal work in the wealthy, whiter beach neighborhoods, he often faced surveillance and harassment from police, and he preferred working somewhere he didn't stand out. One morning in 2016, Jefferson woke early and set out through the winding streets of Vila Belém to begin the day's work selling water and soda at a transit hub in the North Zone of the city. At the same moment, Maíra told me, military police entered the community in a violent drug bust operation. Caught in an outbreak of gunfire, Jefferson was shot in the torso. A passerby found him on the ground and helped him into a nearby house. Maíra, who was living with a partner in a different neighborhood at the time, awoke to a phone call with the news. She jumped from her bed and raced to find her son.

Maíra described that morning in Vila Belém "like a scene of terror." Not familiar with the neighborhood, she wound her way through the streets and alleyways, asking strangers for help in finding Jefferson. Eventually, someone brought her to the house where he was sheltered. Maíra explained that getting him out of Vila Belém and to the hospital was not a simple matter: "If the police saw him shot, they wouldn't assume he was a person on his way to work, especially being a young Black man. Anyone who saw him like that would say he was a drug trafficker. That's how it works here."

Eventually, Maíra found a car to drive them to a hospital. Knowing that her son was still in danger, Maíra lied to the hospital staff. She reported that he had been shot while working on the main thoroughfare, the victim of a robbery, and not in the favela. Later, upon being questioned by the police, she was caught in her lie, arrested, and subjected to nearly twelve hours of humiliating interrogation. While there was no proof that her son was involved in the drug trade, Maíra explained that her lie was used against him in court as an indication that he had something to hide. Upon his release from the hospital eighteen days later, Jefferson was transferred directly to prison, and would eventually receive a ten-year, seven-month sentence for drug trafficking. After serving three of those years behind bars, he was released with an ankle monitor to finish his sentence from home, under curfew and surveillance.

Steep sentences based on ambiguous or tenuous evidence are not uncommon in these cases. While Brazilian drug law imposes a mandatory minimum penalty of five years, the biases of judges and structural discrimination in the court system often mean harsher outcomes for low-income and racialized individuals. As the ethnographers Adriana Vianna and Juliana Farias (2011) observe in court proceedings, opposing counsel will commonly associate young men from marginalized territories with the drug trade, drawing on racialized stereotypes in their choice of clothing and accessories, for example. In response, family members must go to great lengths to "morally cleanse" their children, offering photos of them in their school uniforms, providing copies of their report cards, and presenting legal work documents in an effort to show them as "honest" young men.

"I Couldn't Tell Anyone My Son Was in Prison"

Reflecting on the time before Jefferson was incarcerated, Maíra confessed, "I lived in my own bubble. You have your life, you go to work, you study, you have kids. You aren't fixated twenty-four hours a day on what's happening in the community." With her son's arrest, Maíra began the consuming task of learning to navigate the criminal justice system, following the details of his case, and making arduous visits to see Jefferson in prison.

"Visiting is really difficult," she told me. "You have to really steel yourself." For Maíra, getting to the prison meant an hour-long train ride, followed by another thirty minutes of travel in a ten-passenger van, a common form of informal transit in underserved areas of the city. The volume of visitors was so high, and the visitation window so small, that Maíra had to arrive a full day beforehand—sometimes two—to secure a spot in line. Family members would spend the night in line, dozing in and out of a restless half-sleep on the ground. "To visit my son—the visit was on a Thursday—I had to arrive on Tuesday," she explained. "I would spend Tuesday, Wednesday, and Thursday in line to be able to visit him. I slept on the ground . . . If you get out of the line, you lose your chance."

The lengthy trip and wait time for visitation meant that to see her son, Maíra had to request time off work. At the time, she was working seven days a week doing phone support at a large telecommunications company, and her requests were denied. Because of the stigma that comes with having a family member behind bars, explaining the reason she needed to miss work felt too risky. "Many people work in private companies, and there no one can know they have a relative who is incarcerated. We're already criminalized just for living in a favela," she explained. "When you have a family member in the system, this discrimination gets even stronger, you know? They think you're going to steal from them, or that you're going to do something wrong just because you have a relative who's incarcerated. So I hid it. I couldn't tell anyone my son was in prison."

The social stigma associated with incarceration and the inflexibility of her work situation would mean personal and professional consequences for Maíra. "I had to go six months without seeing him," she told me. "It made me feel awful. During that time, only my daughter was able to go see him . . . But even if someone tells you he's okay, it's not enough. As a mother, you have to see him, you have to touch him, to hug him. You're his source of strength." During this time, she left the place she rented in a favela near the city center and moved to Vila Belém to be closer to her daughter. After several months, the emotional toll of not being able to see Jefferson became so overwhelming that Maíra quit her job, giving her more flexibility to make the trip to prison but also plummeting her into new financial precarity.

Maíra is one of the many women navigating the incarceration of a loved one in Brazil. After rapid growth of the carceral system over the last four decades, Brazil today has the third-largest prison population in the world, behind the United States and China. In 1990, 90,000 individuals were incarcerated in Brazil. Since then, an increase in pretrial detainment and the expansion of Brazil's war on drugs have produced a crisis of mass incarceration that disproportionately targets poor young men of color. In 2020, the Ministry of Justice and Public Security reported that 773,151 individuals were incarcerated in Brazil, 33 percent of whom were being held in pretrial detention. This does not include those serving or finishing sentences under house arrest, like Jefferson, meaning that the actual number of individuals in the system is even higher. In addition to the life-altering impacts this has for incarcerated people themselves, the sheer number of people behind bars in Brazil means significant social and economic consequences ripple outward through their family networks and communities.

"A Home-Cooked Meal Is Everything"

Through the multiday endeavors required to visit the prison, Maíra came to know many women—mothers, partners, daughters—facing similar struggles. While men make up the vast majority of the prison population, it is most often the women in their lives who circulate through the visitation lines, fulfilling a caretaking role for their loved ones in the small ways they can. For Maíra, one of the most important parts of the visit was bringing home-cooked food for Jefferson. She recalls the smells filling the train cars on the trip out to the prison: rice and beans, noodles, perhaps beef with onions if there was enough money that month. "When I see women with those bags of food on the train," she shared, "I know they are going to visitation. When we see each other, we'll say, 'Freedom will come!' We always say this to each other. It's a way of giving each other strength."

Bringing a home-cooked meal was one of the few ways Maíra could offer material care and nourishment to her son. "The conditions in there are so precarious," she told me, "that when someone brings a cake, a different type of pasta, beans with seasoning . . . for them, a home-cooked meal is everything. And I'll tell you this," she added with a small smile, "I was *so* proud of my son, because he always shared with his friends. As soon as we finished eating lunch, he'd say, 'Mom, wait, I have to take some to them,' the ones who didn't have visitors, you know?"

But with unstable employment, Maíra explained, "there were times when I didn't have enough in my house. I would have just enough food to take to the visit and I would go the week without. I'd eat at my daughter's house or at a friend's. But I was happy because I was bringing him food. There were many times I had to rely on the help of friends, who knew it was visitation day but that I didn't have the money to get there." For families already living at the margins, these additional costs—lost wages from missing work, transit fares, food and toiletries for visitation—can quickly push finances to the limit. For many, this comes on top of the household crisis produced when an incarcerated family member had been a main income earner.

For Maíra, these sacrifices felt necessary in the context of the abysmal prison conditions she watched her son and many others endure. Across Brazil, the rapid rise in incarceration rates has contributed to extreme overcrowding, perpetual health crises among the inmate population, and regular use of violence to impose social control. In 2015, a Human Rights Watch investigation found that in some states, prisons held four to five times more inmates than they had capacity for. These overcrowded facilities regularly lack adequate ventilation and access to restrooms, running water, and medical care, making them especially conducive to the spread of illness and disease, from tuberculosis and scabies to meningitis and HIV. Furthermore, the presence of powerful criminal factions in Brazilian prisons has meant that life inside is jointly governed by guards and gangs—a volatile state of affairs that can quickly erupt in outbursts of violence. During one of my visits with Maíra in 2019, I would later see on the news that a five-hour riot was unfolding at the Altamira prison in the state of Pará that left sixty-two people dead. It was not the only lethal riot to occur on such a scale that year: two months prior, fifty-five people were killed in prisons in the neighboring state of Amazonas.

By bringing home-cooked food and sharing a meal together, Maíra and many other women carved out a small domestic space in the visitation room with reminders of home. As much as they would like, however, none of these efforts were immune to the intervention of prison guards and the racist structuring of prison operations. As scholars studying the familial impacts of incarceration have shown, incarcerated individuals and their loved ones are often, in the words of the sociologist Megan Comfort (2008), "doing time together." In the process of visitation, as family members pass through the prison gates into heavily controlled spaces of surveillance and confinement, they come to experience the status of being "quasi-inmates" themselves.

Maíra's light skin conferred upon her a number of privileges during these visits. She noted that she was spared the humiliating strip searches that women with darker complexions were frequently subjected to. The food she brought for Jefferson was almost always allowed in, whereas she often saw the food of other women denied. Throughout our many conversations about racism in the prison system, Maíra came back to one story again and again. A woman she had befriended during the long waits in line planned to bake a birthday cake for her son, and Maíra contributed to the cost of ingredients so that the woman could bake a second cake for Jefferson as well. "It was the same cake she made for her son—the same shape, the same ingredients, she baked it in the same oven. But when we pass through the security line, her cake isn't approved to go through, but mine is. She's Black. How come my cake goes through and hers doesn't?" she stressed, her voice rising in exasperation. "It was the same person who made it!"

The Mothers of Vila Belém

The events of the day that Jefferson was shot generated an inner struggle for Maíra about her worth as a mother: "I thought that everything that happened to my son was my fault. That I hadn't been a good mother, that I didn't care for him enough, that I didn't prevent this from happening. I blamed myself all the time. I thought the person who should be in prison was me, not him, because I didn't know how to tell the police what had happened, because *I* lied and said he had been shot in the street. He didn't do anything."

This feeling of responsibility and guilt is shared by many mothers bringing up children in challenging environments. The gendered nature of care work means that the task of raising and keeping children safe falls disproportionately to women, and it is often mothers—rather than fathers—who are considered at fault if children stray from the accepted path or fall into harm's way. As the sociologists Javier Auyero and Kristine Kilanski (2015) show in their work on caretaking in an Argentine shantytown, a commonly heard explanation for these outcomes is "bad mothering." For Maíra and others, this gendered double standard produces a hard-to-shake sense of self-blame for the hardships their children endure.

Other women have been the most significant source of support and motivation throughout Maíra's personal struggle and subsequently in her trajectory to activism. After bearing the burden of her son's incarceration largely on her own, Maíra was introduced to the Mothers of Vila Belém, a small group of women from the neighborhood whose sons had been killed by police. "As soon as I met them," she said, "they embraced me."

The Mothers of Vila Belém came together in the early 2010s. At the time, a new public security policy in Rio de Janeiro was attempting to bring a permanent police presence to informal neighborhoods that had long been under the control of drug factions. Conceived as a strategy to reduce violent crime, reattract investment, and reestablish the state's monopoly over violence, it gained urgency and momentum with the desire to remedy Rio's violent image ahead of the 2014 World Cup and 2016 Olympics. Termed "pacification," this process often involved initial violent incursions in which military police, at times with the support of the army, rooted out local gangs from the city's poorest neighborhoods.

One day, during the turbulent period of pacification in Vila Belém, a group of teenage boys began throwing rocks at police, who retaliated, in turn, with bullets. One of the young men was killed. Refusing to accept her son's killing and the state's subsequent attempt to assassinate his character by labeling him a drug dealer, his mother began fighting for accountability. With time, Maíra explained, more women who had experienced similar tragedies joined, "and we became a movement." While Maíra had not experienced the same loss as the other women—her son, unlike theirs, had survived—they nevertheless felt an affinity as mothers of children who were victims of violence at the hand of the state. Over time, the affective bond they shared would also translate into the platform of their collective struggle, linking police violence against Black youth in the urban periphery to the brutalities of incarceration in a burgeoning carceral system.

As she told me about the history of the Mothers, Maíra reached across her desk for a framed photo of the women holding their banner, which featured the faces of ten young men from Vila Belém whose lives were interrupted by police violence. She went one by one, naming each of them and telling me about their mothers. The Mothers of Vila Belém focus their fight on preserving the memory of their sons and fighting for justice and accountability. They speak publicly about state violence, participate in citywide and national protests, and support a wider network of mothers in Vila Belém and other communities. They are not alone in their efforts: the Mothers are just one of many local collectives of *familiares de vítimas* (family members whose loved ones have been killed or maimed by police) that form a broader social movement network across the country.

"When I Want to Speak, I Will Speak"

For Maíra, finding her voice in the movement was a gradual process. Burdened by fear that speaking out could harm her son's case in the courts, she spent the early days of her involvement staying quiet, supporting from the sidelines, and avoiding photographs that might make their way onto social media or the news. Eventually something shifted. As Maíra spent more time in these spaces, she explained, "I came to understand that I wasn't going to hurt his case because he's not a high-profile person. He's just another number in the system." Along with the other mothers of the movement, she began to take on a more visible and vocal role as she attended national convenings, protests outside the public prosecutor's office, and university panels on state violence and incarceration.

Maíra remembers that one of the first times she spoke publicly about her experience, the emotions were overwhelming: "The talk that impacted me the most was with the State Committee against Torture. And what I went through [being interrogated by the police] was a form of torture. I didn't understand that's what it was until then, but it was psychological torture. I went to the panel not really knowing what I was going to say, but when I started to speak, I broke down crying." She remembered that the audience treated her with respect and allowed her space for her emotion. She continued: "For me, it was very important to tell what had happened to me. Because normally people don't want to hear it."

In her work with the Mothers, Maíra became acquainted with a wider circle of activists who helped develop her political consciousness and bolstered her resolve to speak out. Through these networks, she was alerted to a job opening at a local human rights center that was launching a project focused on reducing mass incarceration and pretrial detainment. The organization sought someone who had lived experience with the criminal justice system—either formerly incarcerated themselves or the immediate family member of someone in the system. Maíra was unemployed at the time and decided to apply. "When they chose me, I couldn't believe it," she told me with a laugh. Since then, Maíra has worked with a team of lawyers, psychologists, and researchers, helping educate criminal justice administrators about the consequences of prolonged pretrial detention, raising awareness about prison conditions in the public debate, and building coalitions among social movements, NGOs, academics, and families affected by contact with the criminal justice system.

After years of bouncing between jobs in human resources, sales, and service work, moving into a professional, paid position in the human rights field represented an important shift for Maíra in her personal life and her community activism. It proved a more stable and flexible work arrangement; she no longer needed to hide her son's status and was given time off to visit Jefferson in prison and to attend hearings with him after his release. She also gained a fuller understanding of how the system functioned, learning the ins and outs of a complex bureaucracy that once seemed opaque and unintelligible. Armed with this knowledge, Maíra became better equipped to advocate for her son and eventually to share that knowledge with other young men and families in similar situations.

In part, pushing herself to speak is a means of resisting against the pervasive stigma and exclusion she has experienced as the mother of an incarcerated son and as a resident of the favela. The denial of basic rights for people living in communities like Vila Belém produces a struggle for personhood, what Janice Perlman (2010, 316), in *Favela: Four Decades of Living on the Edge in Rio de Janeiro*, calls "the importance of being *gente*." This same fight for recognition is reflected in Maíra's accounts of speaking out. For one of our interviews, Maíra and I planned to meet early in the morning at her office, but we had to push back our conversation by several hours when military police entered Vila Belém in yet another violent operation, forcing Maíra to stay sheltered inside until it was over. It would not be the only time we had to reschedule for that reason over the course of our meetings. I proposed that we reschedule for later that week, not wanting her to feel pressure to sit down for an interview after such an event. But the routinization of police incursions means that life goes on amid the persistent assaults. She insisted that we still meet; she would need to go in to work anyway.

As we talked later that afternoon about what moves her to speak out, she recalled that morning, telling me, "I'm silenced all the time by this racist, classist, fascist state. I was silenced this morning. I was silenced when two armored tanks entered Vila Belém . . . My right to come here this morning was denied because of a police action. So I decide that when I want to speak, I will speak, that's it. I won't use my voice to tell a pretty story to people, we have to speak the truth. We have to talk about what's really happening . . . So even when I go to spaces where people try to silence me, even if I leave hurt, I will leave knowing I spoke, and that they were obligated to listen to me."

As Maíra found stronger footing in the movement, she helped expand the platform of the Mothers from a focus on accountability for police killings to include the question of mass incarceration. At the start, she told me, "the Mothers of Vila Belém didn't have an understanding of the prison system. They lived their children being killed, but they didn't live the prison . . . but the oppressors are the same, the people who fabricate these stigmas against our children are the same. And when you realize this, it all comes together." With more time spent alongside one another, the Mothers came to see the struggles against police violence and incarceration as closely intertwined, and they added the demand of "freedom" to their fight for "memory and justice." "The prison is a machine that grinds people up," I heard Maíra say more than once; "it's just another way of killing people."

As in other parts of the Americas, the foundations of mass incarceration can be traced back through historical legacies of slavery, and today are perpetuated through continuities of structural racism that treat Black people as disposable. After becoming the last country in the hemisphere to abolish slavery, in 1888, Brazil (unlike the United States) never inscribed racial segregation or antimiscegenation measures into law. Nevertheless, other laws established in the years following abolition, such as those restricting free movement at night and outlawing Afro-Brazilian religions, worked to criminalize formerly enslaved people. Moreover, de facto segregation has long been inscribed into the landscape, with darker-skinned Brazilians relegated to underserved territories in the urban periphery. While many legal and policy advances have since made strides toward racial inclusion, Brazil's systems of punishment have nevertheless carried a racialized logic of criminalization into the twenty-first century. In the 1990s, as neoliberalization generated new crises of unemployment and rising crime, politicians responded by expanding the repressive arm of the state, investing in a prison-building boom, and in the years that followed, passing new drug laws with more severe sentences and mandatory minimums.

The demographics of mass incarceration illustrate the racist nature of the prison system in Brazil today. While just half of Brazilians identified as nonwhite in the last census, the Ministry of Justice and Public Security reports that as of 2017, 64 percent of Brazil's prison population was *preta* (Black) or *parda* (mixed race). In the state of Rio de Janeiro, this rate is reported at 73 percent. Today's high rates of police violence and incarceration affecting Black and mixed-race Brazilians represents just one chapter in a long history of racial subjugation. As Maíra told me the first time we met, "It's no use talking about the prison system if you don't talk about racism. Prisons are today's slave ships."

In speaking with people across various social classes, Maíra regularly challenges beliefs in the legitimacy of the prison as an institution. "The idea that prison is the solution," she explained, "is something we have to deconstruct." She recalled one conversation with a woman from a neighboring favela, who suggested the answer was to improve prisons, to humanize them. While Maíra advocates for better conditions in the near term, she never misses an opportunity to raise consciousness about the deeper logics that structure the carceral system. "The struggle can't only be about 'improving' prisons," she responded. "It doesn't matter if the prison is shiny and new. None of that will change who ends up there—they will still be locking up Black people, poor people, *favelados*. In this racist, classist society, prisons aren't a solution."

New Meanings of Motherhood

Through her activism, Maíra's identity as a mother has taken on new dimensions. Her motherhood is no longer defined solely in relation to her three biological children. "In Vila Belém," she told me, "we say that we're not just mothers to our own children, but mothers of all of Vila Belém." Most days she spends her free time at Jefferson's tent. As he sells goods to passersby, she offers guidance to young men with cases open in the criminal justice system. "Other boys will come around," she explained, "and I'll sit there and talk with them." Maíra makes clear that she has no formal training in the law, but that she is offering this advice as a mother who learned to navigate the system for her son. Her job in the human rights field has, arguably, given her unique access to knowledge that many other affected families cannot easily obtain. "I can't say no to a boy asking me to help him with his case," she shared. "I see it as something of an obligation, since there were many people who offered me help to get through this, you understand? I can't see myself doing anything else. This is how I'm giving back—by helping to guide others through it."

"Come see," Maíra offered, leading me across the office to her desk. It was scattered with reports and pamphlets that read "Prison isn't a solution" and "More schools, fewer prisons." From her purse she pulled a handwritten list of cases she had promised to check up on, and powering on the computer monitor, opened a web browser to the justice system's website. "I have five cases I'm looking into today," she said. Typing in the case numbers assigned to young men who requested her help, she showed me their files in the online system, detailing their sentences, time served, and future court dates they would need to attend. Scrolling through, she printed out a series of updates to take back to Vila Belém; she would go over them with the young men the next time they stopped by the tent.

While much of her work involves speaking on panels, attending protests, and traveling to national convenings, she sees these community-level efforts as the most important base of her activism: filling her off-hours at Jefferson's tent, talking to people about public security policies, human rights, and the criminal justice system. "I have to start here, in my favela," she explained. "First, I have to take care of my own house, my own backyard, my own neighbors. And afterward, if I feel I can, I take the fight to other places." While she feels a responsibility to her community, she also feels the strain of dedicating so many waking hours to it: "It's difficult to sustain because it takes resources to set up your little table, sit there and educate people about their rights . . . but you still have to eat, pay your rent, take care of your children."

Importantly, as a mother of "all of Vila Belém," Maíra's activism is imbued with emotional care work that extends not only to young people in the neighborhood but, crucially, to other mothers whose children have experienced state violence. Maíra provides solace, urges them to see that what happened was not their fault, and tries to show them that they can stand up and fight for their children. For the past several years, Maíra has traveled to states across Brazil, supporting the struggles of mothers elsewhere to hold the state accountable for abuses and working to build a broader movement. This socialized meaning of motherhood extends an ethic of motherly care beyond the nuclear family and the home and into the community realm. But Maíra is clear that this was a role she was thrust into by circumstance. "It was imposed on me," she stated. "I didn't choose it."

At the same time that the Mothers of Vila Belém invoke dominant images of a woman's role as maternal caretaker, they simultaneously challenge traditional ideas of a woman's place by taking to the streets, confronting armed state actors, and working to build collective power. Through contentious collective action, their maternal identity is reconfigured in not just social but also political terms—an expression of what the political scientist Sonia Alvarez (1990) has called "militant motherhood." These efforts recall movements in other parts of the Americas as well, most notably the Mothers of the Plaza de Mayo, who since 1977 have gathered in front of the Argentine presidential palace to protest the disappearances of their children under the country's dictatorship.

Across various contexts, this militant motherhood has carried unique moral authority. As the anthropologist Márcia Leite (2004) discusses in her work on mother's movements in Brazil, maternal grief has translated into special standing to demand justice. In particular, the primordial relationship between mother and child, along with allusions to the suffering of Mary, mother of Jesus, becomes a form of "symbolic capital" that lends legitimacy to their struggles. The weight of what these mothers have endured elicits deference, and in some spaces, tribute. At each community gathering I attended with Maíra and the Mothers—from formal activist forums to a late-night poetry slam organized by young artists in their neighborhood—their collective was publicly acknowledged, honored, and applauded by others in attendance.

At the same time, this moral standing remains ambiguous. Their difficulty in successfully holding police accountable reveals how the figure of the grieving mother is not sufficient to absolve their sons of purported crimes or themselves of the stigma that comes with being considered a *mãe de bandido* (mother of a criminal). As Maíra's need to hide her son's incarceration from previous employers and acquaintances shows, this becomes all the more difficult for the mothers of children in prison, who have been formally tried and convicted of crimes by the justice system.

The intensity of an activist role that centers motherly care and militant action demands emotional strength. For Maíra, assuming the fights of other women, along with her own, doesn't come without a real toll. "It's not easy being a mother to everyone," she said. "It's not easy seeing women crying. What can I do? We embrace them, we encourage them to stand up and fight for their sons. Or if they can't, if they can't bear it, we say, 'We will fight for you.'" Despite the difficulties, Maíra affirmed that she also draws purpose from those relationships: "Seeing them fight gives me strength as well."

"A False Freedom"

Becoming part of a collective struggle and a community of activists has offered Maíra an important source of support and motivation. During one of our interviews that took place three years after Jefferson's incarceration, she said that she had largely moved past her feeling of self-blame for what had happened. She attributed this largely to the support of the Mothers, to spending time in social movement spaces where she developed a more structural analysis of carceral violence, and recently, to seeking out therapy to cope with the trauma she has been living with.

Nevertheless, she still felt unable to escape the grasp of the carceral system, experiencing her own loss of freedom through her son's incarceration. "For the family, it's like being imprisoned along with him," she explained. "How are you going to savor a meal knowing that your son has nothing to eat? How can you go to the beach and enjoy yourself knowing he's locked up? How do you sleep knowing that at any moment there could be a riot inside the prison? And going out to have some fun, I end up thinking, 'Oh, my son really likes that, my son loves this dish, my son would love these clothes.' To say that he's incarcerated and I'm not—I can't."

Maíra still felt that sense of imprisonment, despite the fact that Jefferson had been out for eight months at the time, finishing his sentence at home with an ankle monitor. She accompanies him to every check-in and court hearing, worrying before each one that they will have found some reason to send him back to prison. "I feel like we live eternally imprisoned," she explained. "I thought that when he got out I would feel better, but I'll tell you, since then, if I hear any noise, I wake up and have to check that he's still next to me. I don't know if they're coming to take my son... After all this, you can never feel, 'Oh, I'm free.' I don't think anyone can."

This takes a significant psychological toll. Since her son's shooting and incarceration, Maíra has dealt with insomnia, panic attacks, and depression. "As a mother," she explained, "sometimes I blame myself, sometimes I feel despair, sometimes I just try to forget. It's a battle every day." At times, these anxieties give way to a sense of resignation. When I asked her how she thinks her life will change once Jefferson finishes his sentence, she told me that she doesn't think it will. "In Brazil, they don't see a Black person as a person, as a subject with rights. They only see him as a criminal," she tells me. "The issue isn't the ankle monitor... because even once it comes off, he's still a target all the time. It's really hard to be a mother when your child is constantly at risk."

For Maíra, being on the outside is nothing more than what she calls a "false freedom," an illusion that one's rights will be guaranteed. While Maíra's effort to add "freedom" to the platform of the Mothers of Vila Belém speaks to a specific fight to end mass incarceration, it also represents a broader struggle for liberation in the context of racial, gendered, and class-based oppression curtailing life chances at the margins.

"It's These Women Who Inspire Me Most"

When contemplating her future, Maíra thinks about going back to school for a degree in social work or law but often feels constrained by her circumstances. "I could dedicate myself," she told me, "but there are so many external things that get in my way." She imagines police operations in Vila Belém preventing her from studying for the entrance exams or keeping her from getting to class: "If I'm at the university and something starts happening back home, I'm leaving right away to check on my son." What Maíra hopes for herself most, however, is to be able to move out of the rented studio apartment she shares with her two sons and to buy her own home. She described something modest, a little house with a porch and a window she can look out of. It recalls the same hope she had as a young woman nurturing her dreams of an independent life, before finding herself journeying through motherhood and militancy.

For now, however, Maíra is focused on pushing ahead in the arduous struggle for decarceration and prison abolition in Brazil. When I asked Maíra where her courage to denounce the state comes from, when many other women are afraid or unable to, she told me, "The first thing that keeps me pushing forward is my son, the conditions he still has to live with. As a mother, I don't accept that he was criminalized by the state, that he is still a target of the state all the time. There have been times when I've wanted to give up and say, you know what, I don't want anything to do with this. Because it's awful to have to relive your pain all the time. Sometimes I want to forget, to just erase what's happened in my life."

Despite this, being in community with other women helps, in part, to carry her forward. When I asked Maíra about the women who have most inspired her, she named several prominent human rights defenders and activist mothers from across Brazil. But what really keeps her going, she professed, "are the mothers that can't be in the fight." While Jefferson's incarceration politicized Maíra and set her on a journey into activism, this pathway was by no means inevitable. For many women facing similar struggles, a multitude of circumstances keep them from participating in collective struggle: the demands of daily life and basic subsistence, caretaking responsibilities, a lack of access to social movement networks, or the overwhelming nature of grief.

"Many times, we go somewhere," Maíra continued, "and there is always a mother who comes to us, saying, 'This happened to my son, but I don't have the strength to fight.' Many mothers believe what happened to their sons is their own fault, or that because their sons are guilty they can't stand up for them. I believe that I have to be their voice as well. More than for the other women who are already in the fight. I need to show these women that yes, they can shout their son's name. It doesn't matter if her son was involved with drugs or not. She *can* shout his name, she *can* fight for him. It's these women who inspire me most to continue, that push me to keep going . . . I know a mother who buried two of her sons, and she doesn't feel capable of fighting. I tell her, 'It's okay, I will fight for you. I'll take your son's name wherever I go.' . . . I know that I have to be there for them, you understand? I *need* to be."

Note

1. The names of people and neighborhoods in this chapter are pseudonyms.

References

Alvarez, Sonia E. 1990. *Engendering Democracy in Brazil: Women's Movements in Transition Politics*. Princeton, NJ: Princeton University Press.

Auyero, Javier, and Kristine Kilanski. 2015. "From 'Making Toast' to 'Splitting Apples': Dissecting 'Care' in the Midst of Chronic Violence." *Theory and Society* 44 (5): 393–414.

Comfort, Megan. 2008. *Doing Time Together: Love and Family in the Shadow of the Prison*. Chicago: University of Chicago Press.

Human Rights Watch. 2015. *The State Let Evil Take Over: The Prison Crisis in the Brazilian State of Pernambuco*. https://www.hrw.org/report/2015/10/19/state-let-evil-take-over/prison-crisis-brazilian-state-pernambuco.

Leeds, Elizabeth. 1996. "Cocaine and Parallel Polities in the Brazilian Urban Periphery: Constraints on Local-Level Democratization." *Latin American Research Review* 31 (3): 47–83.

Leite, Márcia Pereira. 2004. "As Mães em movimento." In *Um mural para a dor: Movimentos cívico-religiosos por justiça e paz*, edited by Patricia Birman and Márcia Pereira Leite, 141–190. Porto Alegre: Universidade Federal do Rio Grande do Sul.

Musumeci, Leonarda. 2020. "Letalidade policial e pessoas desaparecidas no estado do Rio de Janeiro, segundo os dados oficiais (2006–2018)." *Boletim Segurança e cidadania* 25 (Centro de Estudos de Segurança e Cidadania). https://cesecseguranca.com.br/boletim/letalidade-policial-e-pessoas-desaparecidas-no-estado-do-rio-de-janeiro-segundo-os-dados-oficiais-2006-2018/.

Perlman, Janice. 2010. *Favela: Four Decades of Living on the Edge in Rio de Janeiro*. New York: Oxford University Press.

Ramos, Silvia. 2020. *A cor da violência policial: A bala não erra o alvo*. Rio de Janeiro: Rede de Observatórios da Segurança/Centro de Estudos de Segurança e Cidadania. https://cesecseguranca.com.br/textodownload/a-cor-da-violencia-policial-a-bala-nao-erra-o-alvo/.

Vianna, Adriana, and Juliana Farias. 2011. "A guerra das mães: Dor e política em situações de violência institucional." *Cadernos Pagu* (37): 79–116.

Willis, Graham Denyer. 2015. *The Killing Consensus: Police, Organized Crime, and the Regulation of Life and Death in Urban Brazil*. Oakland: University of California Press.

Suggested Reading

Alves, Jaime Amparo. 2018. *The Anti-Black City: Police Terror and Black Urban Life in Brazil*. Minneapolis: University of Minnesota Press.

Lago, Natália Bouças do. 2020. "Nem mãezinha, nem mãezona: Mães, familiares e ativismo nos arredores da prisão." *Sexualidad, salud y sociedad* (36): 231–254.

Leu, Lorraine. 2020. *Defiant Geographies: Race and Urban Space in 1920s Rio de Janeiro*. Pittsburgh: University of Pittsburgh Press.

CHAPTER 3

Rodrigo
"MANY SECRETS, NOTHING TO HIDE"— SECURITY ENTREPRENEURSHIP IN MEXICO CITY

Eldad J. Levy

Rodrigo[1] peers out the back window of the SUV, his eyes flickering as he scans the streets of Ecatepec on the outskirts of Mexico City. He is dressed in sleek business casual and seated directly behind his driver-bodyguard, Julio, who doesn't need to say a word to make his presence felt. Rodrigo doesn't like having an escort but has found it increasingly necessary when he travels. In the past couple of years, Rodrigo has become one of the most sought-after security entrepreneurs providing protection and intelligence services for the Mexican elite.

Ecatepec blurs as we pass. The neighborhood is one of the most impoverished in Mexico City, the kind with a name that has become a euphemism for the crime and violence that plagues the capital city. We approach a large steel sculpture alongside the highway, and Rodrigo's eyes fix on it: it depicts a winged man, kneeling, overlooking the sprawling northern boroughs. The statue is called *El Vigilante* (*The Watchman*), crafted by the famous sculptor Jorge Marín.

"What a joke," Rodrigo scoffs as we pass by it. "Look at this! You think the people in this neighborhood need a fancy sculpture?" he asks me, eyes still directed out the window, leaning back in his seat. "They need new roads. They need schools. They need a public library!"

"So why did they get a winged-man sculpture instead?" I ask.

"For the same reason everything happens in this country. Probably a local *politiquillo* [little politician] cut a deal somehow to have this *chingadera* [piece of shit] here."

Rodrigo is no *politiquillo*, but he converses with them regularly. Rodrigo and I are on our way to a *fiscalía regional*[2] where he has put his team to work to help a local official crack down on a gang of loan sharks in a state outside Mexico City.

His work is not simple. Against the backdrop of pervasive corruption in the Mexican justice system, Rodrigo has positioned himself as a security entrepreneur, offering his high-tech surveillance and intelligence services both to an ailing state bureaucracy and to the needs and ambitions of some of Mexico's wealthiest denizens.

"You should know this business has two façades," Rodrigo explains in our first meeting in a small coffee shop outside his private security office. "There's the visible business, the business of private security." He continues, and a subtle smile spreads slowly on his face. "And then, there's the other side. A business that is not evident and that occurs behind the scenes. But you need to know that sometimes it's a gray legal area. I'm happy to show you. I have many secrets but nothing to hide."

Cracking Open the Mexican Security Apparatus

Rodrigo has carved this career for himself out of an existential problem in Mexico: the intractable violence and corruption that has plagued the country for decades, a crisis that has only been exacerbated in recent years. From 2017 to 2020, every year was crowned the most violent in Mexico's history, as the country again and again broke its own annual record of homicides, peaking with over 36,000 victims in 2020.

Outside Mexico these problems are often framed as revolving around Mexico's infamous drug cartels; the international press rushes to report gruesome gang-related murders. But Mexico's struggles with crime go much deeper than sensational headlines suggest. The very institutions of law and justice lack the resources, training, and autonomy to do their jobs effectively, and they have long been skewed by clientelistic pressures and corruption. As a result of these, and an impunity rate that is over 95 percent, most Mexicans have little faith in the ability and impartiality of the police and the judiciary. A 2021 report by the Mexican National Institute of Statistics and Geography (INEGI)[3] estimated that over 90 percent of serious offenses, such as robbery and house burglary, either went unreported or were not investigated. In the cases of kidnappings and extortions, the rate was over 98 percent, suggesting that many Mexicans are dealing with security crises in ways other than going to the police.

One of the major challenges of doing justice in Mexico is anchored in the general weakness of the police and the judiciary. In 2018, a reporting team from Mexico's media outlet *Animal Político* reviewed the steps taken in homicide investigations in Mexico. The team pointed out the causes that weaken the Mexican justice system: low salaries for public servants, lack of funding and supplies to conduct proper investigations, and acute shortages in manpower and training—all of which ensure that victims and their families will rarely see justice unless they can incentivize officials to prioritize their cases. Additionally, these shortcomings occur in a justice system that is inundated with criminal cases.

Yet, settling for merely institutional weakness as an explanation to the insecurity crisis that Mexico lives would be shortsighted. The rise of powerful crime organizations and drug cartels since the 1990s is often invoked to explain the deep corruption of the criminal justice system, as kingpins buy their way out of scrutiny. However, the long tentacles of organized crime are only the present manifestation of an issue rooted in institutional permeability, that is, the ability of elites to meddle in the work of the Mexican justice system.

In Mexico, a longed-for yet elusive "rule of law" has always been applied selectively, reflecting social and political positions in Mexican society. Throughout the seventy-year rule of the Partido Revolucionario Institucional (PRI), Mexican governance was based on a powerful system of loyalty to the party. The police were no exception: throughout the twentieth century, party elites used the police as a political arm to deter opposition and stipulated favors and resources in return for loyalty. As the urban scholar Diane Davis (2006) argues, as the modern Mexican state consolidated through development, urbanization, and industrialization projects, the Mexican police became key to protecting the interests of business, industrial, and political elites that needed to be harnessed to a massive project of state building.

In the late 1990s, when the PRI saw a gradual decline in its power, new and varied political and financial elites were able to create patronage relations of their own with high officials. New, and often competing, political and economic constellations emerged, splitting the loyalty of the security apparatus once monopolized by the PRI. In *Votes, Drugs and Violence*, Trejo and Ley (2020) talk about informal gray zones, in which new political, economic, security, and criminal elites collude with state officials to advance mutual interests and enjoy state protection or impunity. One result is an often taken-for-granted impunity for white-collar criminals and anyone else who can mobilize powerful contacts within the police. Now this new and fragmented system needs new brokers who can hook you up with the right official. It is in this context that Rodrigo has created a unique position for himself: part broker, part specialist troubleshooter, part security profiteer.

I first met Rodrigo in 2006, when he was in his early twenties and studying at the Institute for Counterterrorism in Israel as an international student from Mexico. He was studying International Relations at a prestigious private university in Mexico City when a mutual friend invited him to visit Israel. When I first met Rodrigo, I was already beginning my undergraduate degree in sociology in Haifa, where he and our mutual friend sometimes visited me. Despite knowing little about Israel before that visit, Rodrigo was fascinated with the country, and he soon relocated to Israel and began advanced studies in security and intelligence at the Israeli institute. After Rodrigo finished his studies and left Israel, we lost contact almost completely, aside from brief updates through social media and our mutual friend.

When Rodrigo came back from Israel in 2009, he became involved in the Mérida Initiative—a 2007 security cooperation accord between the United States and Mexico aimed at strengthening the southern border of Mexico and creating a second line of defense against drug trafficking and organized crime. Through the Mérida Initiative, the US government transferred some US$1.6 billion to various Mexican law enforcement agencies to provide training, technical assistance, and equipment, with the declared goal of disrupting the capacities of organized crime. Rodrigo was never fully comfortable with the role Mexico played for the American security apparatus, but the influx of dollars gave him a chance to apply his newly acquired security skills—and make a pretty penny doing so.

But getting into business with the government in Mexico requires more than the right paperwork or the best offer. Rodrigo grew up in an upper-class family, long involved in local politics in the south of Mexico and powerful establishments in the capital. When the Mérida Initiative money first started flowing, some of his family members had taken influential positions in state governments in the South. With some start-up cash, family contacts, and his new credentials, Rodrigo soon found his way into security provision for state governments participating in the initiative.

With his acquaintances in local governments, Rodrigo developed several projects financed by the Mérida Initiative. To mention a few, he supplied armored trucks to one of the states and helped train their special forces units. For other projects, Rodrigo's résumé of training in Israel helped him into a position consulting with local commanders in newly formed Sensitive Investigative Units (SIU). These units specialized in the collection of intelligence and the operation of undercover agents to build cases against organized crime leaders and worked in tandem with the Federal Bureau of Investigation (FBI) and the Drug Enforcement Administration (DEA).

Rodrigo prospered immensely from his work in the Mérida Initiative, but he remains critical of the entire project, in which Mexican units essentially worked for American agencies and fed them the intelligence the Mexicans generated. He becomes visibly upset when he talks about this, his eyes narrowing in on mine as he describes the Mérida Initiative as another manifestation of the new arm of American imperialism. "That's the reality, that's what the Mérida Plan was about," he says, shaking his head. "American control over Mexican interests. We weren't working to figure out our own interests, only theirs."

Rodrigo formally worked in the Mérida Initiative until 2013. His disillusionment with the project and frustration with the government, he says, pushed him into the private sector, taking his developed security expertise—including his high-profile network of government contacts and cutting-edge surveillance technologies—to market. He founded Titanium Security in 2014, offering at first only security guards to elite schools and luxury condominiums, but he soon began employing his skill set and contacts for those who could afford something more.

"I take care of them personally," he says of his new clients, a smattering of Mexican elites. "This has helped me protect our key clients—to give them something extra and situate us as trusted providers who have access to services that not all security companies have."

Rodrigo can offer his clients several layers of protection: a variety of security personnel, consultation about their security needs, and, most importantly, an immediate contact in case of emergencies such as kidnapping and extortion attempts.

"These services often involve extralegal means, and I got to be in touch with everybody—the good guys and the bad guys." Rodrigo smiles mischievously when he hints at this work, a sign of his mastery in the backend of the Mexican criminal justice system.

The irony in Rodrigo's professional formation is palpable. To a great extent, Rodrigo is the product of an American intervention in the Mexican security apparatus that aimed to enhance the state's capabilities against organized crime. But the result of this dubious attempt has been quite the opposite. By creating a cluster of knowledge, training, technology, and contacts between private and public actors, the Mérida Initiative forged private security actors who took advantage of the fragmentation of the security apparatus and accessed it for the benefit of their clients. This insidious consequence is not unusual. In *The Politics of Drug Violence*, Durán-Martínez (2017) argues that the recurring American interventions seeking to strengthen the security apparatuses of Mexico and Colombia resulted in their further fragmentation, enabling a variety of nonstate actors to crack them open.

The Israeli nexus is also inescapable. Israel has positioned itself as a major exporter of security expertise, and former officials of the Israeli security apparatus are often employed as consultants for private enterprises around the world. However, most famously, Israel has become a renowned exporter of surveillance technology and spyware, prompting criticism for using these technologies to suppress civil rights for authoritarian governments around the world. Although Rodrigo was not an alumnus of any Israeli security agency, his studies in counterterrorism enabled him to capitalize on the Israeli images of security.

Just as Rodrigo shares his own professional formation, his phone rings and interrupts our conversation. It's a video call from Sofía, his wife. She has been living for the past two years outside Mexico, in her home country. Rodrigo presses his lips as he tells me they lived happily together in Mexico for several years.

"She was enamored with the culture of Mexico and the kindness of the people," he tells me in a resigned tone. But Sofía left Mexico with their child within months of his birth, according to him, unwilling to raise him in Mexico's current security climate.

The Works

When I first learned of Rodrigo's work, I assumed it was primarily about the severe problem of phone extortions in Mexico. This is how extortions work in Mexico: The extortionist places a phone call, often to a wealthy target, falsely claiming they have kidnapped a family member. When a child is claimed to have been kidnapped, predators often use a strategy called *el chillón* (the cry-baby) and play the recording of a screaming child in the background to add to the victim's agony. While surveilling targets is still common practice, social media has dramatically facilitated the acquisition of valuable information on targets and their family, which is later employed to make the abduction seem real. Talented extortionists will manipulate the target, extracting more information from the victims in real time and pushing for a hasty transfer.

Phone extortions have increased by 90 percent in the past six years, and according to the Secretary of Security and Civilian Protection, they have become one of the most popular crimes committed by organized crime in

Mexico, second only to aggravated robbery. These recurring extortions are a big problem for the upper class, and the Mexican police can't be trusted to do their job faithfully. Knowing someone like Rodrigo provides a more effective alternative.

Take, for example, the elite high school that Titanium Security offers security services to, a school Rodrigo himself attended almost twenty years ago. The wealthy parents are occasional victims of these extortion attempts. Parents then inform the school about the extortion attempts and request that the staff show increased alertness. In response, the school principal often puts the concerned parents in contact with Rodrigo to consult on their security concerns: "The parents provide the numbers that have been calling them. Sometimes we recommend they hire additional security personnel at home. We do this in a dissuasive manner, working so the kidnapping never actually occurs. In some cases, we check the phone's account statement to see if it belongs to someone, and if not, we turn to geolocation to see if it yields a place to start investigating." Based on his application of geolocation technologies, Rodrigo estimates that over 90 percent of fraudulent extortion calls originate from inmates within penal facilities in Mexico City affiliated with criminal organizations.

Geolocation technologies track the location of cellphones in real time. They send stealthy periodic pulses to the target's cellphone, which return to the sender and indicate their exact location on a map. These technologies are normally reserved for the use of law enforcement or intelligence agencies, given their ability to invade individual privacy. Thus, they often require warrants, justified with evidence as part of an ongoing investigation. Rodrigo became familiar with geolocation technologies as part of the Mérida Initiative, but an illegal market of intelligence technologies and services abounds in Mexico.

"What happens when the client finally finds out who's been harassing them?"

"It's up to the client. Sometimes we send the police. Sometimes they just want to *desquitarse* [get back at them], so they send someone to beat the shit out of the guy. Sometimes they even want to do it themselves."

"And you can set that up?" I ask tentatively, with eyes wide open.

"If the client wants," he answers, visibly amused by my reaction. "You need to understand how desperate some people are when they get to me, how frustrated they are from the way the police handle their problems."

In some cases, Rodrigo's services are activated as live extortion attempts are taking place. In one incident, he recalls, the extortionists took advantage of a school bus running late, placing their call during a critical window in which a daughter should have been home but wasn't. Unable to locate the girl, the school principal contacted Rodrigo, who was able to geolocate her and the origin of the call. He deployed his own men within minutes to the place, only to discover the girl was locked out of her house. Many times, "his own men" are police officers who work under a chief associated with Rodrigo or draw a parallel salary from him and are thus incentivized to respond quickly and efficiently.

"Who paid for the service in this case?" I ask.

"The school did," Rodrigo responds. "The ransom was not delivered because we acted swiftly. But this is an example of an extortion of our clients that also implicates responsibilities for the family, the school, the bus company. Our quick reaction frustrated the attempt," he says matter-of-factly. "See what I mean? They get the proper security service and the additional access to technology and contacts . . . things that not every company can provide."

For the upper class in Mexico, Rodrigo's contacts provide a valuable alternative route to public security services, especially in emergencies. Almost all branches of the Mexican police are severely underpaid, undertrained, and thus acutely inefficient. Perhaps worse still, the police force is often swayed by political interests and in some cases deeply infiltrated by organized crime. Mexicans with means will shell out tens of thousands of pesos for Rodrigo's protection rather than take a chance by going to the local police.

But "reactive" intelligence is only a minor part of Rodrigo's daily routine. A few days later, we met on the second floor of his office to talk "more discreetly of other aspects of his work," as he puts it. Rodrigo's clients are predominantly members of the Mexican elite and have a much more intricate set of interests. The Mexicans that make up his clientele—wealthy businessmen, prominent lawyers, and such—often have ambitions beyond protecting their children.

Despite recent celebratory attempts to reform the justice system in Mexico—to enhance institutional autonomy and eradicate bribery—corruption in the judiciary remains prevalent. Among the Mexican elite, buying off officials, prosecutors, and even judges is normal: giving *mordidas* (bribes, literally "bites") or using personal contacts and kickbacks to expedite any official process (from evading a ticket from a cop to obtaining the desired result in a bureaucratic procedure) is common practice. In the 2018 Transparency International Global Ranking, Mexico ranked 138 out of 180 countries, placing it among the governments most perceived as corrupt.

But when both parties in a legal dispute—say, estranged business partners—are equally monied and connected, the "expedited justice" they seek can turn into a bribery arms race. In this situation, a tedious, prolonged judicial process is unleashed, entrenching both sides for years as more money is poured into the system. In these situations, Rodrigo's services become extremely valuable as a kind of extralegal means of "discovery." In addition to his geolocation systems and regular field agents employed to surveil targets, Rodrigo employs a cell of hackers who can crack emails, phones, messaging apps, calendars, and other files. The goal, Rodrigo explains, is sometimes to uncover the legal strategy of the rival, but more often to obtain potentially incriminating or embarrassing information that can provide leverage for a settlement. On some occasions, Rodrigo maps the target's patterns of life and their social networks by analyzing stolen cell data. These can be used to apply pressure by threatening to expose discreet relationships or shady business partnerships.

In most investigations, however, technology alone cannot yield the results clients need. I discovered that Rodrigo had forged a network of what he called "moles" in virtually every state institution and many private companies of interest. For example, to obtain call records, Rodrigo has recruited contacts in every mobile phone company in Mexico, and in contrast to the notoriously bureaucratic state offices, he can pull birth certificates, social security records, and bank accounts in hours.

"Your informants . . . do they know each other?" I ask Rodrigo on one occasion.

"Rarely," Rodrigo tells me. "I always prefer concentrating all the streams of information. I have more control when information only goes up. So far, I've given them smaller tasks and I do the analysis myself. But recently, with the workload I have, I'm less able to do things myself."

If Rodrigo doesn't have the right contact in a given ministry, he has enough contacts in adjacent offices to recruit a new informant in the office of interest. These are often lone workers who supplement their absurdly low salaries by extracting documents, photographing databases, and exporting other information for money. This form of blackmail becomes vital when clients are ultimately fed up with the judicial process and opt to end their dispute through extralegal means, agreements, or sheer violence. By piecing together and controlling these contacts from above, Rodrigo constructs a sort of arm with which to control Mexican state agents.

Business is good. He tells me that, at any given time, he is handling six to eight operations simultaneously and that a large-scale operation could pay as much as 300,000 pesos (US$15,000). As with any enterprise for profit, Rodrigo has his eye on expansion—more and larger investors and operations.

"Do you ever meet your collaborators in person?"

"It depends. With some I do, with others never. Why? To know as little as possible about each other."

He smiles and adds: "Ignorance is a blessing for us."

Scaling Up the Security Business

Rodrigo and I are having lunch in a small *comida corrida* restaurant when he gets a call from his friend Marcos, who is furious at a recent appeal a judge had granted his estranged cousins. I can clearly hear Marcos screaming from the other line.

"That's it! I don't care what it costs! I just want to know where they are and go there myself and *madrearlos yo mismo* [fuck them up myself]. You can do that, right now, right, Rodrigo? Tell me where they are. How much will it be to find them now?"

"Calm down, Marquitos," Rodrigo answers. "We can do many things, but let's not do something hasty. There are much better ways to get those *cabrones* . . . I can walk you through some options." These "options" represent a second prong of Rodrigo's security operations. Alongside private protection, Rodrigo also offers his intelligence services to "grease" the wheels of Mexico's judicial system.

Marcos and Rodrigo met at university in Mexico City. Marcos was a friend, later a client, and currently he is in the process of becoming an associate in Rodrigo's business. Despite the years that have passed since college, Marcos still has a cheeky attitude that reminds me of American fraternity boys, strikingly different from Rodrigo's serious demeanor. Marcos enjoys parties, traveling abroad, sports, and the thrill of stepping into Rodrigo's professional world.

Marcos is part of the third generation of a profitable family business in Mexico: a well-known apparel store chain with dozens of stores throughout the country. But struggles over the family business tore the family apart when Marcos's cousins were thrown out of the company for embezzlement. The cousins later opened a long and exhausting legal battle against the rest of the family.

A couple of days later, I ask Rodrigo if I could meet Marcos to talk about his own perspective as a client. "Absolutely," he tells me, "and now that I'm partnering with Marcos, you can see where this business is heading to with his investment."

We arrive at an old commercial borough near the Centro Histórico, and the SUV pulls up in front of the original apparel store. Marcos greets us with enthusiasm and hugs. "Why don't we talk first and then we can show him what we've got going on here?" Marcos suggests to Rodrigo, leading us to a conference room.

"My cousins . . . I don't know what got into them, but back in 2011, we noticed that they were embezzling money from the company . . . They began acting like this whole place belongs to them."

When the conflict escalated, Marcos and his brother physically threw the cousins out of the very office in which we are sitting. When the grandmother refused to compensate them as they saw fit, they started suing.

"From 2011 to 2014 they filed over twenty civil suits. Sixteen out of the nineteen suits were against my grandmother, the owner of the brand. They just wanted to screw with us." According to Marcos, the cousins were bribing judges but hadn't just taken legal action: they were harassing their grandmother and intimidating family members with thugs. Facing the tension of possible prison time, Marcos's grandmother suffered a stroke.

"That's when things got personal!" Marcos says, pointing his index finger forward. "When they messed with her health, they crossed the line, and now anything goes. When they moved from the civil to the criminal game with *cochinadas* [tricks], they moved to a whole other ball game—a game that if we start playing, we can all come out very wounded, because we all have contacts . . . You know very well how it is in Mexico: They buy off a judge? We buy off his boss."

"So, when do you decide that you're resorting to Rodrigo?" I ask.

"Well, the problem is that paying judges takes a lot of time, and it's very expensive . . . That's when we turned to our buddy here." Marcos grinned mischievously at Rodrigo. "The point is not to expose them with legal evidence. What we find would be inadmissible and would only mean trouble for us." Marcos wants to either find embarrassing information and blackmail them to end the quarrel or simply remain one step ahead of their legal strategy.

After the interview, when I have a moment alone with Rodrigo in the conference room, I ask him how much he intends to charge Marcos for his service. He replies: "My intention is not to profit from Marcos's situation. I help Marcos and his brother because I've witnessed with my own eyes the horrible things that their cousins have done to the family . . . Marcos's family has tried to get justice for years and dealt with corrupted judges. You tell me, do you think it's fair, Eldad? Is it fair that people agonize over their pursuit for justice in a rotten system?"

Rodrigo and I alone hop back into his SUV. We drive north on the scenic

Paseo de la Reforma, heading to Rodrigo and Marcos's new office in one of Mexico city's ritziest neighborhoods north of Chapultepec Park.

After a few minutes of relative silence, I take advantage of the fact that we're finally alone: "Rodrigo, why are you telling me all this? Secrecy is imperative in your work."

"You promised confidentiality, and I trust you," he answers succinctly.

"Still, why show me all this? Why take me with you and introduce me to your clients? What interest could you possibly have in letting a nosy researcher go around asking questions?"

"Why? Because I want people to know how rotten things are in Mexico, *mi querido* Eldad. I want people to read what you're writing and understand how corrupt the Mexican elite is and how a bunch of *mamones* [arrogant jerks] abuse the system. How we're dominated by a political leadership that just serves American foreign interests and leaves us in complete chaos, so we keep killing each other instead of articulating our own interests. I've seen it myself. They just want us to keep being the best show on Netflix," Rodrigo says with fervor.

"Chaos is probably a good thing in your business," I push back. "Chaos means more *mamones* need your service, right? More corruption and more insecurity mean more business coming through the door."

"That's true. Chaos means good money. But I would infinitely prefer to make much less money and live in a country under the rule of law. A country that provides security to all of us and owns its national intelligence instead of forcing citizens to resort to people like me. I would much rather have my son living here with me in my own country, something that, with how bad insecurity is here, neither I nor his mother are willing to do."

"Rodrigo, forgive me for insisting, but you work for these guys."

"Yeah, I do. But I don't work for drug lords, and I don't work for organized crime as many others do. I only work for people who I've learned their case and think they've been wronged."

We arrive at the new office. It's a beautiful, sunny day in a gorgeous neighborhood full of gardens, carefully designed homes, and fashionable coffee shops. I look up, and we're standing in front of a tall, red office building. Marcos is already waiting for us. We climb the stairs to the third floor to an office of a distinguished architectural firm, responsible for several well-known projects throughout Mexico City. A young man with carefully trimmed stubble opens the door.

"Good!" he says. "Let me grab the keys and I can show you how things are advancing."

The architect opens an adjacent door to an empty office space, similar in size to his own, ready to be renovated. Buckets of paint dot the floor, and orange plastic cables are coiled, waiting to be installed. I open one of the windows, and a fresh breeze comes through.

"I was thinking you could have one office room here," the architect says, indicating by lifting and dropping a straight arm with his extended hand, "and another one here. Depends on how big you want the foyer to be."

Rodrigo is visibly thoughtful, clutching a folder with the design plans and standing close to the architect. Marcos, by contrast, is roaming the room and inspecting walls and windows with a big, satisfied smile.

"¡Está poca madre! [It's fucking awesome!]," Marcos shouts from the back.

"It looks good," Rodrigo concurs briefly while nodding his head.

"And look, Rodri, here we're going to have an awesome bar, fully equipped with the best booze, in case we want to party." Marcos laughs while pointing at one of the corners. "And here there's going to be a huge chaise longue! And I want a receptionist, but she has to be super hot. Right?"

"Why the two offices? Why not work from Marcos's office?" I ask Rodrigo on our way out.

"One for high-profile business. One for the operations. I like to separate the security consulting and handshaking from the actual work."

I soon learn that Rodrigo has "security consulting" contracts of similar sorts with a wide variety of Mexican elites. When clients are interested in discretion, Rodrigo can issue the clients receipts from the numerous front companies he owns in a variety of industries.

We spend the rest of the day in a marathon of meetings in the garden of a classy Mediterranean seafood restaurant. A parade of clients come and go as we dine on grilled fish and fine pasta and drink good wine and several *carajillos*. The place is brand-new, Marcos tells me as he surveys other tables with his look, and anyone who is anyone can be spotted here: actors, politicians, and sports stars.

Whenever a new client arrives, I'm always introduced as a researcher from the University of Texas at Austin, studying insecurity in Mexico City. Despite my constant concern about the meaning of secrecy in this business, rarely does anyone seem surprised by my presence or reluctant to speak about their cases. Some attorneys were an interesting exception, but usually it didn't matter if the clients were high-ranking company executives, entrepreneurs, or one side in a messy divorce.

One of the clients we meet today is a pharmaceutical corporation CFO accompanied by his lawyer. For a long time, he has been chasing a former employee, who allegedly stole hundreds of thousands of pesos from the company. The employee, a senior accountant with links to organized crime, skillfully evaded both the law and the private surveillance offered by previous providers. The lawyer, a partner in a firm that routinely contracts Rodrigo's service, seems silent and nervous. The CFO, an older man in a suit with an affinity for details, remains tranquil and polite but is clearly losing patience, as one of Rodrigo's field agents has failed repeatedly to make an arrest: "It just cannot be, gentlemen," he says as he clears some crumbs from his white mustache with a napkin. "We've been after this guy for . . . (he quickly flips the pages on a small leather-covered notebook) three months now. May 23. I have it right here. It's enough already."

"We know where he is," Rodrigo answers in a reassuring tone. "He's hiding at his extended family's house in that nasty neighborhood. But we need to remember, this bastard is not your regular accountant. He has done it before and knows other criminals. If we crack down on him without caution, we're risking a *turba* [mob] lynching the agents. Regardless, I'm not here to make excuses. It's my commitment to you, sir, that we'll have him by next week."

Accessing the State

As we pass the statue *El Vigilante* in his black SUV and slowly move away from Ecatepec, Rodrigo tells me softly, "I'm excited about you meeting Ignacio. I want you to see how hard it is for good people in the system to deal with inefficiency and corruption."

Ignacio is a senior attorney in one of the *fiscalías regionales* in a state outside Mexico City. *Fiscalías regionales* are similar to district attorney offices, and they are the agencies charged with prosecuting local crimes.

"He's busting his ass trying to do good stuff," Rodrigo explains. "You know, putting away criminals who prey on hard-working people. I want you to see how hard it is for him to get what he needs to do his job. He can't get the warrants he needs on time, he doesn't have immediate access to databases and technology, he is forced to work with colleagues paid off by organized crime or pressured by *políticos*. It's very rough, *mi querido* Eldad. You'll see many things."

We drive several more hours until we arrive at a rural town, the seat of a regional *fiscalía* in one of Mexico's most violent states. There's nothing majestic about the small *fiscalía* building, which is surrounded by cornfields at one end and a narrow road with various food stands along it. It's nothing like the colossal state buildings in the capital.

The courtyard of the *fiscalía* is crowded with people: whole families with children, young couples, lonely men, and groups of teenagers. They are waiting for appointments with local officials to press charges, give testimonies, and identify aggressors in lineups, among many other procedures. Many are holding papers while talking on their cellphone. Others seem visibly worried. Whether victims, suspects, or witnesses, everyone in the courtyard would be considered, in local parlance, *gente humilde* (humble people): people of the working, rural, and Indigenous classes. The courtyard is so full that street vendors sell *tacos de canasta* to cater to those waiting for their cases to be reviewed. The place is also manned by several police officers in combat uniforms, some wearing caps and others helmets, but all with bulletproof vests and assault rifles.

Rodrigo and I hop out of the vehicle and walk swiftly to an adjacent building. We don't wait in any lines. We're waved into the building and directed up the stairs. After climbing to the third floor, Ignacio's secretary shows us in. Ignacio is still on the phone when we enter his office, but he conveniently finishes the conversation as we walk in.

"¡Pásenle por favor! [Come in, please!]" Ignacio speaks quickly, and he smiles as he approaches to shake our hand. "It was from the state attorney general's office. So sick of their *chingaderas* [bullshit] . . . Carmelita, bring me my coffee and a bottle of sparkling water, will you? Gentlemen, what can we get you?"

There's something misleading about Ignacio's appearance. Slightly overweight and wearing a flamboyant tie, he could be a caricature of a state bureaucrat, what Mexicans derogatorily call a *godínez*. The reality is vastly different: a brief Google search shows that in recent years, Ignacio was involved in the investigation and prosecution of several drug lords and later led the case against a high-profile politician, accused and later convicted of corruption. Rodrigo tells me that Ignacio was posted in this regional *fiscalía* to cool him off, because things were getting "way too hot for him."

We are here, I learn, because Ignacio is working on a new investigation. And this time, he wants Rodrigo's help.

Rodrigo introduces me and my interest in security in Mexico. Ignacio nods at me and immediately picks up the conversation "So . . . you want to hear about organized crime and kingpins? What do you want to hear about? Just ask."

"Thank you!" I say excitedly. "Let me just get set with my equipment." It is so natural from all my previous encounters with Rodrigo's stakeholders; I immediately pull out the recorder and notebook from my backpack. It instantly becomes evident I've trespassed with Ignacio, and he wears a serious face as he looks at Rodrigo.

"Perhaps . . . ," Rodrigo says in a somewhat embarrassed tone, "you can take notes of Ignacio, instead of recording him?"

"I have a better idea," Ignacio says and calls his secretary. "Carmelita, get me Óscar here, will you? Why doesn't my deputy show you around, and he can answer all of your questions."

Óscar is a polite, yet reserved, attorney, second in command after Ignacio. We return to the main building, where his office is located. As we walk, he introduces me nonchalantly to clerks, prosecutors, investigators, and police officers. He shows me the reception desks, the interrogation rooms, and even the prison cells, carefully explaining about the work in each room. When we enter the latter, a putrid smell is so overwhelming I can hardly concentrate on what Óscar is saying. These old, decayed, crowded cells each house approximately fifteen men. Some of the detainees are asleep on the floor, covered with wool blankets as we enter. All of them lift their heads and look at us when we enter, as if expecting news on their cases.

When we are finally by ourselves in Óscar's humble office, I ask if he'd agree to an interview about the bureaucratic and legal challenges that hamper his daily job. Óscar doesn't reply immediately. He takes a seat behind his desk and asks if I mind if he smokes.

"Adelante [Go ahead]," I answer as I sit in front of him.

Noticing the previous dynamic with Ignacio, I remind Óscar I can simply take notes, or he is free to decline all together. Óscar agrees to be interviewed, but when we finally begin the interview, he deflects most of my questions, giving diplomatic responses like a spokesperson answering reporters. Óscar talks vaguely about issues of organizational capacity, funding, and facilities.

I figure I'm pushing the line with the trust I thought I was given. I'm about to give up on the interview altogether when Óscar says: "When the interview is over, I'd like to tell you other things." I turn off the recorder and meet a whole different Óscar. Not only the content changes but also Óscar's attitude, now chatty and inviting.

We talk about the investigation team's difficulties accessing surveilling technology or even getting warrants for pressing cases. He talks about the lack of capacity of most of his personnel and the heavy mistrust among public servants within the judiciary. Óscar's account corroborates what Marcos had told me before: many public servants, including judges, were subjected to external pressures either by organized crime or by powerful individuals, sometimes politicians and sometimes the wealthy elite and their associates.

"You need to understand that we're infested with police officers who are informants of organized crime. It's a cancer, not only in the police but in all institutions and all levels of government in this country," he says.

"In this institution as well?"

"Everywhere. These guys will tip off criminals before raids, will leak information, or hamper investigations. But that's not even our main problem." He pauses for a few seconds, looks at the ceiling, organizing his thoughts.

"In this country, the political question is always heavier than the legal question." Óscar proceeds and finally makes eye contact. "In many instances, cases must be resolved according to instructions from above rather than by what the law dictates."

"Can you give me an example?" I ask. "It can even be a hypothetical example if it makes it easier."

"Hypothetical. . . . Yes." Óscar seems pleased by the framing of my question. "Let's imagine we're in a regional *fiscalía* and we have arrested the mayor of a small town . . . not in this state, but in a remote one, right? Now, let's assume this individual has a close relation with the governor of the state. This suspect is arrested for using a firearm or something of this sort, and we even have a victim. However, because this suspect is friends with the governor, the governor drops orders, and the orders will be . . . [Óscar pauses to build up suspense] to release the suspect and not to pursue the investigation. Even if the suspect should be held in custody for the crime he has allegedly committed. So, the public servant is obliged to build the case in such a way that it will justify the suspect's release to follow the political instructions."

"What consequences are there if the attorney refuses to follow orders?"

"What happens if the public servant refuses to follow instructions?" Óscar smiles cunningly at the naïveté of my question. "Well, two things: First, the case will be taken away from you because you don't prosecute as you are told. Second, this form of disobedience could have criminal implications. Needless to say, your employment, at the very least, is on the line. So how much does the political weigh and how much does the judicial weigh? Or better said, the judicial is at the orders of the political."

"So, if I'm a powerful person, if I have political associates, if I have a contact up there, I can eschew the legal system and even bend it as I please?"

"Absolutely. In primitive times, it was 'the rule of the strongest.' In Mexico today, we have the rule of the best positioned: the one with the best contacts." When Marcos told me this before, I thought he was perhaps exaggerating. But my stomach turns when a public official uses the same description.

"And we can't separate the political interventions from the legal procedures?"

"Separating the legal from the political is a fallacy. The legal is for the poor, the political is for the rich, and that's it." Óscar puts out his cigarette and leans back comfortably on his chair, putting both hands on the back of his head. I'm in awe from our conversation, and Óscar seems pleased by this.

Óscar and I return to Ignacio's office, where he and Rodrigo are still talking.

"So? Did you learn something?" Ignacio asks with satisfaction as we walk into his office.

"Plenty," I reply with an embarrassed smile, wondering to myself what Ignacio is looking so smug about.

As we are talking, the secretary knocks at the door, peeks into the office, and announces that "everyone is ready."

We are taken to a side room, where a presentation is set up around a conference table with laptops and a projector. I'm surprised when I realize that we're not invited to a presentation, but that in fact the presentation is made for Rodrigo. There are four of us around the table: Ignacio, Rodrigo, me, and a bespectacled young man in a gray suit. The latter is a criminal analyst, a public servant working under Ignacio in the *fiscalía* on criminal investigations. He leads the presentation and gives a briefing about the case.

The team is looking to bring down an illegal lending-and-extortion regime run by well-organized gangs that is called *gota a gota* (drop by drop). *Gota a gota* is a relatively new form of loan shark scheme perpetrated by Colombian criminal organizations operating in Mexico and many other Latin American countries. The loan shark model involves lending relatively small sums at exorbitant interest rates, usually between 20 and 25 percent, to individuals who have trouble obtaining credit from the official banking system. Most commonly, these are temporary hired workers or street vendors living in extreme precarity, who are going through a financial emergency and need immediate cash. The name *gota a gota* is the term used by the Colombian gang and refers to the supposedly easy and slow payment of a loan. Naturally, when borrowers struggle to return the rapidly inflating loan, the lenders resort to severe violence to extract the money or confiscate the street vendor's merchandise, which often means taking away their whole livelihood.

As the analyst talks, a full network analysis mapping the gang's organizational structure appears on the screen: orange lines stretch across the screen, connecting circles that encompass photographs of about twenty men. Those in the center of the screen have six or seven lines coming off them, indicating their seniority in the gang; those at the margins, significantly fewer. Names of members, dates of birth, nationalities, addresses, close associates, and places of operation all appear on the screen. Rodrigo pays close attention to the presentation, leaning forward in his chair, and putting his crossed fingers together on his lips.

"This would have taken us months without you," Ignacio tells Rodrigo with satisfaction. "But we had it in . . . how long?" Ignacio turns to the analyst.

"Three days, sir," the analyst replies, pushing his slipping glasses back up the bridge of his nose.

For Ignacio, there are two ways to crack down on the Colombian gang. First, the legal and bureaucratic way—collecting enough evidence to demonstrate the organizational structure of the gang, and then properly asking for a warrant to wiretap the calls of the suspects, geolocate their phones, and possibly obtain some call records. If this process goes smoothly (i.e., if all officials do their job properly, no one leaks information from the investigation to the gang, and no judges are bribed to hinder or deny the warrants, among many other concerns), it would take several weeks, perhaps months, from the moment the petition was made to the actual granting of access to the meager intelligence and technological means at the disposal of this regional *fiscalía*. The fact that the victims of these predatory loans were primarily poor street vendors did not make Ignacio any more optimistic about the chances that the police would be incentivized to work diligently on this matter.

The problem certainly isn't that the Mexican state is, or has ever been, reluctant to infringe on the privacy of its citizens. Throughout its long rule, the Mexican PRI routinely used its intelligence and surveillance agencies internally to deter potential political opposition and thwart popular mobilization efforts. To this day, political elites use intelligence to achieve political gains. In fact, just in 2017, the Mexican government was embroiled in a major scandal when it was revealed that it had been spying on journalists and political activists with the aid of Pegasus, Israeli spyware.

Mexico has even officially been gradually relaxing the often-ignored legal impediments to surveillance. For example, since 2012 mobile phone geolocations no longer require a warrant in cases of imminent danger or organized crime activity. Moreover, according to records published in the media, the state *fiscalía* to which Ignacio belongs had submitted thousands of requests for lawful interceptions during 2017.

Nevertheless, Ignacio opted for the second route: drawing on Rodrigo, his technology, and his expertise to get a complete network analysis of the gang within only a few days. By turning to Rodrigo, the official bypassed the cumbersome procedures of the legal system. With the analysis in hand, he is now ready to act against the gang.

"We can't use any of this of course," Ignacio tells Rodrigo, "so we're going to nail them with their migratory statuses. We checked, and they're all overstaying their visas in Mexico and can now be legally deported from the country. I'm going to put these *hijos de puta* on a plane back to Medellín. There's nothing else to do."

As we're finishing our visit with Ignacio, the young analyst meets Rodrigo and me on our way, next to the elevator. He's clumsily balancing three long rolled-up sheets of paper in one hand, his laptop bag in the other, and a backpack on his shoulder. He almost drops them all when he tries to reach for the elevator. Rodrigo presses it instead and asks him, "Are you ready?," to which the analyst replies, "Yes, sir, ready to go."

To my surprise, we drive all the way back to Mexico City, fighting the infamous traffic of the capital, with the analyst, in what is an awfully silent, awkward, and long drive. I have so many questions for Rodrigo on his relationship with Ignacio, but they all must wait until we have time to talk alone. I read my fieldnotes on the way, and I realize their sensitivity after everything I heard and saw today.

We arrive at Roma in the early evening. One of the most emblematic neighborhoods in Mexico City, Roma has European-style architecture, a hipster subculture, and a big culinary scene. Rodrigo, the analyst, and I climb out of the SUV and enter a beautiful neocolonial-style building. The entrance of the house is narrow but carefully adorned. This is a remarkable house, even from within, resembling an aristocratic Mexican house of the 1920s. I realize we are at a boutique law firm only when I see that the family foyer is in fact a cozy lobby with a small reception desk and the back wall is covered with a law firm cliché: shelves stacked with brown law books.

"Mikel is a client of mine. He is a partner in this firm, which deals with a lot of high-profile companies. We have a presentation for him here, so maybe you can interview him shortly before we start?" Rodrigo suggests.

"What's the presentation about? Why is the analyst here?" I ask, almost whispering.

"This is just a little something Mikel is interested in. Maybe I'll tell you later," he responds in a hushed tone, speaking very close to my ear.

Mikel comes to meet us in the lobby, and we move into the conference room next to the lobby. Mikel is blond and thin, and even though he is about Rodrigo's age, he looks boyish in appearance. He is dressed casually but elegantly.

"So? You live in Austin?" Mikel asks me after Rodrigo introduces me. "I love that place. Such a nice city. Have you been to the ACL music festival?"

Mikel pulls out an electronic cigarette and begins vaping while we sit at the corner of the table. We're making conversation, but I have one eye on the long sheets of paper being unfolded by the analyst on the conference table, trying to figure out why a criminal analyst from a regional *fiscalía* is at this exclusive law firm. The conversation is friendly, but Mikel is clearly hesitant about my unexpected presence in their meeting.

"I was wondering if you'd like to be interviewed for my research," I finally ask Mikel. I pull out my recorder and place it on a table. "Or if you mind if I stay to observe the presentation Rodrigo is about to give."

"Oh, unfortunately this isn't a good time for an interview." Mikel shuts down my intentions immediately, "and observing would be getting us too close to the particularities of clients and their attorney-client privilege. Right? I'm sorry!" Mikel answers with a regretful smile.

Rodrigo intervenes almost instantly. "Mikel, let me just show Eldad how to get back to his apartment from here."

Rodrigo walks me down the wooden stairs. It's getting late, and after making sure I know how to get back to my apartment, Rodrigo tells me: "You're probably starving. We haven't eaten all day, and I thought we'd have dinner after this. I'm so sorry! But don't worry, there's a great sandwich place you've got to try! It's like two blocks from here." I shake hands with Rodrigo and thank him for the day. I decide it has indeed been a long day to go without lunch and begin walking toward the famous sandwich place recommended by Rodrigo.

Only as I am leaving Mikel's office do I realize how inadequately I have understood Rodrigo's web of collaborators. Rodrigo has woven a network of moles in almost every government ministry, stealthily leaking information for a fee. However, the gray zones of collaboration are so widespread that they require little to no cover-up. I'm suddenly reminded of what he had told me on one of our first meetings. In a place where state agents and private actors collaborate so openly, Rodrigo had many secrets but nothing to hide.

If officials have enough authority and subordinates, they can place whole departments of staff at the disposal of private entrepreneurs. But unlike Rodrigo's exchange with his lone moles, which was transactional, his relationship with high-ranking officials involves all sorts of favors, such as protection, overlooking illegal activities, information, and even swift deployment of forces. Sometimes the public servants reap their own benefits, sometimes they expedite bureaucratic processes that should in theory be accomplished within state institutions.

I never found out what was in the presentation the analyst gave to Mikel. Considering he was an attorney in private practice, exclusively representing corporations and members of the Mexican social elite, I'm willing to bet it was valuable information collected by a state agency that could serve the interests of one of Mikel's clients. Rodrigo was able to provide this to Mikel thanks to the relations he had fostered with Ignacio. This relation is facilitated, first, by the low salaries earned by law enforcement and justice officials, who are constantly looking to supplement their income; second, by the inability of many public servants to perform their duties in an unwieldy bureaucracy; and last, by the permeability of the system that allows political and financial interests to meddle in the justice processes. None of this is truly new. Rodrigo is just a new actor, belonging to the burgeoning private security sector, a sector that has been gaining primacy in Mexico and increasingly enjoys access to officials in the Mexican security apparatus. In Rodrigo's eyes, his service is an imperative of a dysfunctional system, but as Jenny Pearce (2010) argues in "Perverse State Formation," Latin American elites have hampered the formation of strong and autonomous state institutions to preserve their own interests. Even if we agree with Rodrigo that he manipulates the system for a greater good, many other actors do the same with much less benevolent pretense.

After meeting Rodrigo and his clients, I came to believe that secrecy in this business is often performed. Rodrigo's attempt to enact secrecy is often contrasted with the pervasiveness and openness of gray practices in Mexico. People will certainly try to be discreet about the questionable legality of this business, but in the end, "knowing someone" is such a common practice for those well positioned that the questionable practices have become normalized.

Despite walking through the colorful and mostly safe Roma neighborhood, I think to myself, what would happen if I were to be mugged on the street right now? If they took my recorder and my notebook, so many people would immediately be made vulnerable if that data were to make it into the wrong hands. I suddenly realize that despite all my doubts about what constitutes secrecy in Mexico, I'm walking around with something way more valuable than all the money I have in my pockets: Rodrigo and his clients' secrets, those he supposedly doesn't need to hide, but that I, nevertheless, worry about. I decide to give up on the sandwich, get an Uber, and go straight to my apartment.

Notes

1. All the names of individuals, entities, and locations in this chapter have been altered to ensure the confidentiality of participants.
2. This is similar to a district attorney's office in the Mexican justice system.

3. Encuesta Nacional de Victimización y Percepción sobre Seguridad Pública (ENVIPE) 2021.

References

Abrahamsen, Rita, and Michael C. Williams. 2010. *Security Beyond the State: Private Security in International Politics*. New York: Cambridge University Press.

Davis, Diane E. 2006. "Undermining the Rule of Law: Democratization and the Dark Side of Police Reform in Mexico." *Latin American Politics and Society* 48 (1): 55–86. doi.org/10.1111/j.1548-2456.2006.tb00338.x.

Durán-Martínez, Angélica. 2017. *The Politics of Drug Violence: Criminals, Cops, and Politicians in Colombia and Mexico*. New York: Oxford University Press.

Pearce, Jenny. 2010. "Perverse State Formation and Securitized Democracy in Latin America." *Democratization* 17 (2): 286–306. doi.org/10.1080/13510341003588716.

Trejo, Guillermo, and Sandra Ley. 2020. *Votes, Drugs, and Violence: The Political Logic of Criminal Wars in Mexico*. New York: Cambridge University Press.

Suggested Reading

Arias, Enrique Desmond, and Daniel M. Goldstein, eds. 2010. *Violent Democracies in Latin America*. Durham, NC: Duke University Press.

Auyero, Javier. 2007. *Routine Politics and Violence in Argentina: The Gray Zone of State Power*. New York: Cambridge University Press.

Müller, Markus-Michael. 2012. *Public Security in the Negotiated State: Policing in Latin America and Beyond*. New York: Palgrave Macmillan.

CHAPTER 4

Fabio and Angélica
THE RESISTANCE OF STAYING PUT

Alex Diamond

On one of the rare days I wake up before him, Fabio gets up just after six to examine the avocado tree that rises above his modest home in the rural Colombian village of Briceño.[1]

"The *marteja* kept me up making a tremendous scandal," he says to explain why he slept in, referring to a nocturnal monkey that crashes loudly through the jungle, jumping between the taller tree branches that stretch out over their coffee plants and cacao trees below.

"It didn't leave a single avocado," his wife Angélica bemoans. I share her pain. It's May 2020, and I've been staying with them for nearly two months, isolated from the outside world as the global pandemic spreads through Colombia. We've been hungrily eyeing the avocados for weeks as they've grown on the tree.

Fabio walks by a pepper plant growing just outside their outdoor kitchen. "Ahh, those animals, look how they damaged it," he says. The plant has been stripped of the tiny bright yellow peppers that Angélica uses to spice up her homemade *ají picante*, a sauce they sell at markets organized by and for campesinos, the word and identity that Latin American farmers embrace with pride.

"The *marteja* again?" I ask.

"No, this was an insect." Fabio loops a machete into his belt and grabs a small bag of corn kernels he'll plant on a steep hillside five minutes away. The family's chestnut-colored dog, Niña, jumps up, excited to tag along.

Fabio and Niña are barely out of sight before he calls back: "The mandarins are flowering."

"The flowers of the mandarin have a marvelous scent," Angélica explains to me enthusiastically, accenting the first three syllables of the Spanish word for marvelous as if it were each its own word: *MA-RA-VI-llo-so*. You can dry the flowers or put them in alcohol or oil, she says, explaining that they work to either scent a bathroom or flavor a cake.

I follow Angélica as she grabs several large black mesh sacks and walks up to two mandarin trees that have already begun to cover the ground with white and yellow blossoms. She lays the sacks below. Flower petals begin settling on them immediately, forming a satisfying contrast against the black mesh netting.

"Who says," Angélica asks rhetorically as she gathers the blossoms a few hours later to make a kind of potpourri, "that everything in life has to be bought? We can invent things as well."

For Fabio and Angélica, this inventiveness fits within their adoption of agroecology, a global movement that has been described by the ecologist Steve Gliessman (2018) as encompassing scientific research to create sustainable agroecosystems, Indigenous and campesino practices to cultivate in harmony with nature, and social change to transform power relations and inequalities related to food distribution. As agroecological farmers, they renounce the use of a range of agro-industrial products that seek to bring nature under human dominion: chemical sprays to protect crops from insects, herbicides to clear brush for planting, and genetically modified seeds that promise to increase harvests. But the insects and monkeys that share their farm and occasionally their crops are far from the greatest threat to their livelihood. Instead, they and other campesinos in the area confront human forces causing irreversible changes in the region: Colombia's largest hydroelectric dam, Hidroituango, which has cut off their access to the Cauca River and destroyed traditional fishing and gold-panning economies; and a peace process that seeks to reverse a long-standing violent conflict but also to pacify the region surrounding the dam. In this context, their social movement activism and agroecological farming practices combine to offer an alternative vision.

I originally came to Briceño because it was a key site for Colombia's 2016 peace agreement with the Revolutionary Armed Forces of Colombia (FARC), a guerrilla group that had mounted a half-century insurrection during which they grew to control large swathes of the countryside. The conflict pitted the Marxist guerrillas against both the army and illegal right-wing paramilitary groups, though most casualties and suffering have been borne by rural civilians. Of Colombia's fifty million people, over nine million have been displaced by the violence. Angélica is one. The conflict intensified beginning in the 1980s, as both the FARC and the paramilitaries funded their operations with profits from cocaine, which is extracted from the light-green leaves of the coca plant. The landmark peace agreement thus included a substitution program designed to help coca farmers transition to licit crops. Briceño, whose economy was dominated by coca and where FARC and paramilitary groups had long fought for control of the region and its drug trade, was named a "Peace Laboratory," the site of the first pilot coca substitution program. With the hydroelectric dam under construction, it was also a strategic site from which to explore the unfolding relationship between peace and capitalist development. I planned to root my research in the lives of village residents to learn how the community was experiencing and influencing this period of wholesale transformation.

I first met Angélica in June 2018 during a female empowerment forum in Briceño. Fifty-six years old, with graying hair and animated speech patterns, Angélica stood out for her sharp analysis and critical perspective. When she gets excited, she sprinkles religious exclamations into her speech: "¡Ave María!, some men spend 50,000 pesos [US$20] on beer, and make their women beg them for 1,000 pesos for a coffee." "*Gracias a Dios*, my husband and I share our profits." Before she left town, she invited me to visit their farm in El Orejón, a two-hour motorcycle ride from where I lived in the village center.

Living in El Orejón

Fabio and Angélica live on a 48-hectare (119-acre) property on the steep walls of the Cauca River valley, around 1,000 meters above and slightly upstream from the Hidroituango dam project. Most of their property is jungle, impossibly green slopes covered with ferns and broad-leafed tropical trees that are home to thieving monkeys, tarantulas, and a variety of colorful songbirds. Even the coffee plants and cacao trees that they cultivate around their house seem to come out of the jungle, interspersed among their mango, mandarin, and lime trees. These agroecological farming practices contrast sharply with most farms in the area, where farmers use chemical fertilizers and herbicides to create orderly rows of single crops or bare pasture for grazing cattle. Although their cultivation isn't the regional norm, they never tire of trying to convince their neighbors to adopt agroecological practices.

Fabio, also fifty-six and lanky with a prominent mole on one cheek, does most of the agricultural work on their farm. As he plants and harvests their crops and clears underbrush, he wears rubber galoshes, a threadbare button-down shirt, and a full-brimmed hat from Machu Picchu that someone brought him as a souvenir. Angélica transforms their crops into products for

Fig. 4.1. *Fabio picks mandarin oranges on land that once held coca.*

sale: toasting their cacao and coffee beans on their outdoor wood stove before grinding and packing them; mixing fresh-ground cacao paste and honey to make delicious artisanal chocolate candies; and drying and pulverizing turmeric root. Once a month, they load their motorcycle with all the products it will carry and take them to an organic market in Medellín. Angélica is the salesperson. She draws in prospective customers, offering samples and explaining the virtue of their products. Everyone who tries the chocolate candies, she says, ends up taking some home. With the money they make, they buy rice, cooking oil, and an occasional birthday gift for their grandchildren. Nearly everything else they eat—eggs, beans, yuca, peanuts, avocados, plantains, corn, fruit, chicken, fish, and more—comes from their farm.

Ironically, for a couple who share a passion for organic agriculture, they were brought together by technology. In 1985, Fabio, who was born in a rural community on Colombia's northern coast and had grown up farming before training as an electrical technician, had his own electronics workshop on the rural outskirts of Medellín. One day, Angélica showed up at his shop. "I brought him a tape recorder to fix, and he couldn't fix it for me," she says.

"I fixed *her* up, though," he says mischievously as they share a flirtatious laugh.

Fig. 4.2. *Fabio on the path that leads to his and Angélica's home, with the Cauca River below.*

They each had two children from previous relationships; they had a fifth child together in 1990. Although in the first years of their relationship they owned and ran a succession of small urban businesses together—a fruit and vegetable store, a bar, and finally a restaurant—they shared an affinity for farm life that dated back to their respective childhoods. Angélica was raised near Briceño in the village of San Andrés on a large farm that produced both subsistence for her seventeen brothers and sisters as well as milk, coffee, and *panela* (unrefined cane sugar) for sale. Fabio grew up helping his father grow flowers for sale. Each stresses that their family's cultivation was chemical-free. "I had no idea that people spread poisons on their crops," Angélica says.

In 2006, they visited one of Angélica's brothers in Pueblo Nuevo, the hamlet that neighbors El Orejón. After a ten-hour bus trip to a nearby village, they embarked on the six-hour hike to Pueblo Nuevo. The house they live in now was the first they encountered halfway along the mule path. The trail cuts through dense jungle roughly two-thirds of the way up the Cauca River valley's walls, crossing various streams that flow down to the river. When they passed by their current home, an old man sat at the gate. He greeted them and gave them water, eventually asking them to buy his farm.

Angélica lights up at the memory, emphasizing how much she didn't want the property: "Inside I thought to myself, *Dios bendito*, is this man crazy or what? So I responded, 'No, we're not buying land.'"

Nonetheless, they left their phone number. Two weeks later, the man met them at their home outside Medellín. He told them his asking price, Angélica remembers. "And I said, '*Por Dios*, that's an exaggeration!' And I told him, 'No, that property is so far from everything.' And he asked how much we would give him, and when I told him, he said, 'Okay, give it to me.'"

Fabio and Angélica paid $11,000 for the farm. With their kids all graduated from high school, they saw this as an opportunity to return to the rural lifestyle that both remembered so fondly. The farm's coffee plants and cacao trees were overgrown, but because it had been years since anyone had sprayed herbicides or insecticides on them, it was perfect for launching an agroecological farm. In moving back to the countryside, they were defying a long trend of rural-to-urban migration that has filled the peripheries of Latin American cities with former farmers. Even more unusually, however, they were moving into an active conflict zone—the only reason they could afford the farm.

The Rural Frontier: Guerrillas, Coca, and Conflict

In 2006, El Orejón seemed worlds away from a massive dam, the peace process, or the gaze of state power. When Fabio and Angélica arrived, their first move was not to register the sale with government officials but rather to visit the FARC. The guerrillas had acted as the local authority since 1981, resolving disputes, keeping law and order, and organizing collective labor. The guerrillas informed them of the rules: no one could leave their home at night; they had to participate in communal work groups to fix local paths; those who fought or stole would be made to leave; and finally, all the coca had to be sold to FARC-approved buyers.

Coca, Fabio explains to me as we sit at the handmade wooden table of their outdoor kitchen, dominated the local economy. "Coca supported the *raspachines* [mostly young men who picked the coca leaves by hand]; the women who made food for them; the people who delivered supplies on mules; those who sold chemicals [both to grow the coca leaves and to transform them into coca paste]; those who sold gasoline [for processing the coca]. It was an immense chain."

Although Fabio and Angélica planned to grow healthy and organic food crops, they inherited a plot of coca near their home. They tended it for almost two years, hiring Angélica's nephews to help pick the leaves and paying a neighbor to soak them in gasoline and then extract coca paste with a noxious mix of chemicals. Each harvest they produced up to a kilo and a half of coca paste, which they sold to nearby buyers for about $1,500, a lot of money compared to traditional agricultural goods. But they replaced their plot of coca with turmeric and mandarin trees, Fabio says, because it contradicted their personal ethics. "I said to myself one day, 'I don't feel good administering this.' I have grandchildren."

Fabio and Angélica objected to coca because of the chemicals used in its production and the fact that Briceño's coca was used to make cocaine, a highly addictive drug strongly associated with violence. But even more important to their everyday reality, they recognized that along with the dam, Briceño's coca economy was the major driver of a violent conflict for local territorial control between the FARC and right-wing paramilitary groups.

Fabio and Angélica say that most members of the community grew coca out of a lack of alternatives. "Why did people cultivate coca here?" Angélica asks rhetorically. "Because we didn't have roads. There was lots of plantain, lots of mango and oranges, a huge amount of yuca, corn, but how were we going to take it out to sell it? Look, for me to take goods from this farm to the valley, they charged me 50,000 pesos [US$23] for a mule, a freight charge. But on the other hand, two kilos of coca, you could put that in a small backpack and take off walking."

Every two months or so, FARC-approved buyers would spread the word that they were coming to buy coca paste. "Everyone went in a parade with their mules, or with their coca under their arm or in a backpack," says Fabio.

"They would come back with their three or four million pesos [US$1,400 to $1,800]," says Angélica.

"For you to take out a *carga* [125 kilos] of coffee, which at that time was worth 500,000 pesos [US$230]," says Fabio, "you had to work all year, and additionally, you had to pay someone to take it out for you. So people saw that growing coca was a much easier option." Before the village filled with coca in 2000, local fields were covered with coffee plants. However, a precipitous decline in coffee's global prices throughout the 1990s and early 2000s meant that once farmers figured in the costs of transport, labor, and goods, they were lucky to break even. Coca, for all the violence it brought, saved their economic fortunes.

Living in a Conflict Zone

While the FARC controlled El Orejón and its coca trade, right-wing paramilitaries had dominion over much of Briceño. These paramilitary groups were founded by wealthy Colombian landowners in the 1980s to protect themselves from guerrillas like the FARC. By the time they arrived in Briceño in the late 1990s, they had become private armies that not only fought guerrillas but used violence to traffic cocaine, attack left-wing organizations, and displace campesinos from resource-rich lands. In much of the village, their arrival followed and encouraged the spread of coca cultivation through the territory. However, in El Orejón and areas that were close to the hydroelectric dam, many interpret paramilitary violence as the first step toward enabling Hidroituango. "That was to clear out the canyon," Fabio says, referring to a rash of violence from the late 1990s to early 2000s that occurred in the area surrounding the proposed dam site. In the municipalities surrounding the Hidroituango project, fifteen massacres of innocent farmers occurred from 1996 to 1998 alone, including some of the most notorious in Colombian history.

In 2007, just after Fabio and Angélica moved in, the Colombian military entered the region in force, occupying the area around the pending Hidroituango dam project. The FARC were pushed farther up the valley walls, including as far as Fabio and Angélica's farm. They tell me about that period on a beautiful morning, as we drink *agua de panela con limón* (a drink made from unrefined cane sugar and lime juice) and look out over their sun-drenched yard. As we talk, their chickens roam free in the garden, pecking at food scraps. Their two dogs play, the mother fending off the playful attacks of her mischievous puppy and nipping at her throat to discipline her. By their gate, one of their mules, gray with black spots, rolls back and forth in the grass, scratching an itch. The tranquility of the scene contrasts with their description of the area just a few years earlier.

"There were battles at all times of day," Fabio says, mimicking the sounds of shooting and explosions. "Pam, pam, pam. There were shots, bombs. It was a delicate situation between the army that was taking care of the [Hidroituango] project and the guerrillas who wanted to take care of the territory."

"Look," says Angélica, pointing to the ridge far above their farm. "That's the Alto del Oso; there were some battles up there, when a helicopter arrived to bring goods to the soldiers. *¡Por Dios!* It was like the apocalypse, they dropped some [bombs] that even split the trees. And I was so scared I couldn't sleep. And sometimes you would be sleeping, and when you least expected it, you heard 'bubububu,' and that sound came like it was echoing from inside a pipe."

To stop the army from advancing, the FARC planted land mines, hundreds in El Orejón alone. The guerrillas informed the local community where they couldn't go, closing off large parts of the territory, many of which are still restricted to this day. In other areas, they warned locals not to stray off the path: even if they had to relieve themselves, they should do it in the middle of the trail.

While many of the mines were permanent, the FARC also laid temporary mines on paths after 6:00 p.m. and removed them by 5:00 a.m., a dangerously effective way to enforce their curfew and prevent the soldiers from advancing at night to take them unawares. But this practice led to accidents.

One night in 2013, at 9:00 p.m., Fabio and Angélica heard a loud explosion. It turned out that a mine had exploded while three guerrillas were setting it up. One had died, with the other two badly injured. But the tragedy didn't end there. The community went at dawn to see what had happened, gathering around the guerrilla's mangled corpse. What they didn't know was that before the accident, he had planted another mine nearby. When it exploded, it injured ten community members and killed a young woman.

After the accident, Angélica couldn't sleep. She thought of the photos she'd seen of the dead bodies and one of her injured neighbors whose backside "looked like seared meat." She thought of the opposing guerrilla and army forces, neither far from their farm. She thought of their grandchildren. Finally, she couldn't bear any more. "I was getting sick. I told Fabio, 'Let's go.'" They still had their home on the outskirts of Medellín, now occupied by their daughter. "But Fabio said, 'What are we going to eat there? What are we going to live on?'"

Six days after the explosion, Angélica left Fabio tending the farm and traveled to Medellín with a sack of fruits and vegetables. It was more than a year before she felt safe enough to permanently return.

The Dam Project (and Resistance) Advances

As violence raged on in the valley walls above, the dam project below advanced. Angélica, who grew up in nearby San Andrés de Cuerquia, says people had spoken since the 1970s of a planned hydroelectric dam. But a crucial moment came when Public Enterprises of Medellín (EPM), the public-private partnership that operates Hidroituango, arrived to conduct a census of the people who would be affected. The census fulfilled EPM's legal obligation to identify and compensate anyone whose economic activity would be harmed by the project. This should have been a long list of people. If coca was the primary driver of the economy, the Cauca River was the second. Locals referred to the river as their *patrón*, meaning both sponsor and provider. It offered them fish, sand for construction projects, and, most importantly, silty riverbanks filled with gold nuggets for the taking. Even before coca arrived in 1999, gold panning offered locals a lucrative and easily transportable source of income to supplement their subsistence farming.

Angélica has fond memories of gold panning on the banks of the Cauca River with her father. They would stay for days, even weeks on end, sleeping under a plastic tarp stretched across four tree branches they drove into the sand. While the gold itself was important, she reminisces more about how gold panning brought together people who spent much of their time on isolated farms. On the beaches of the Cauca River, they sifted through the silt in search of gold nuggets, shared stew made from fresh-caught fish, and traded with each other.

One day in 2008, a group of people rushed by Fabio and Angélica's home. "'Hurry up,' they told us. 'They're doing a census in Chirí from one to two,'" Angélica says. It was already eleven in the morning. They briefly considered going but didn't want to waste their day chasing a rumor. But it wasn't just a rumor. EPM was performing the census to determine who would be compensated for lost economic activity based on construction of the dam, which would close off the river to the local community. They had just announced the census that same day, by radio, which made it impossible for workers on the beaches to be included. Angélica continues: "It was the worst that could happen, because they didn't do the census in the site on the beaches where people were working." Of roughly one hundred people in El Orejón, all of whom depended on the river in some way for their livelihood, only nine were able to participate in the census. Those who missed their chance never got another one.

In 2011, EPM officially banned local access to the river. Rather than preventing the community from continuing to gold pan, however, this prohibition turned a traditional livelihood into contentious politics. People from Briceño and surrounding communities started planning to meet on the riverbanks, figuring that coordinated occupations would both give them safety in numbers and pressure EPM to include them in the census. "It looked like a city," Angélica says, describing agglomerations of plastic tarp huts that more than one hundred people in all quickly erected. During the day, they would fish and pan for gold. At night they held *tertulias*, informational discussions at which they spoke about their struggle.

In response, EPM sent in a special battalion composed of private security and the army, who repeatedly used violence to remove them from the beaches. Soldiers pulled down their tents, often throwing them in the river, and forcibly dragged people from the beaches. The campesinos dispersed, only to reorganize themselves and move to another beach. This pattern of occupation and forced eviction repeated itself several times. "It started as our normal economic activity," Angélica says. "From there, they started to remove us, and we decided to stay as an act of resistance."

Locals never resisted violently, but they did use, in Fabio's words, "a strategy that nature gave us." Campesinos in the area learn early in their lives to avoid a plant that is known locally as *pica pica* (literally "sting sting"), a shrub with curved seed pods that are covered with toxic light-brown hairs. Just brushing up against the plant causes a severe rash and a nasty combination of itching and stinging. One of the beach occupiers had the idea of shaking the plant out when the soldiers were downwind, unleashing highly toxic flurries of nearly invisible hairs on the unsuspecting battalion. Fabio chortles as he remembers it: "We were on the beach when we heard 'The soldiers are coming!' So we already knew what [their comrade] was going to do. There were ten or twelve soldiers. They started shaking out their clothes like they had animals stuck to their bodies. It made us laugh really hard because they didn't know what was happening."

As dam construction started, Fabio heard a woman on the radio talking about the dam project: how it was responsible for the violence in the community and its potential for destroying the environment and local livelihoods. "So I said, 'I'm going to call this person,' because I'm also affected here in El Orejón, so we started coming together and telling each other our experiences."

The woman was from Ituango, across the river from Briceño. She was part of Ríos Vivos (Living Rivers), a new organization seeking to organize local resistance into a more concerted movement against the dam. Along with many others in the community, Fabio and Angélica joined the movement.

In late 2012, supported by Ríos Vivos, the community organized a protest in Chirí over the issue of the paths and the compensation of those who had been left out of the census. They used the most common strategy of disgruntled Colombian campesinos, a road blockage. With eighty to one hundred people, they blocked the road and stalled construction for four days, forcing EPM to negotiate with them. EPM met with a community representative from El Orejón, promising to invest in the community and expand the census to include those who had been left out. But with no coordination between the other participating hamlets, different groups started arguing, and the protest dissolved. "That was EPM's strategy," Fabio says. They never lived up to their promises.

Fabio says, "We weren't prepared—we were completely raw." But through

Ríos Vivos, they continued meeting with people from other affected communities, and in March of 2013 planned an action that would not be so easily defeated. This time, around five hundred campesinos gathered together to block the highway in a municipality just upstream from Briceño.

The Colombian riot police attacked the protesters with nightsticks, arresting twelve people they identified as leaders and taking them south to Santa Rosa. The campesinos again occupied the road, and again the police attacked them. At this time, seeing the futility of their attempts to block the highway, they took off walking toward Santa Rosa, 100 kilometers down the road, to demand the release of their comrades. They carried signs to bring visibility to their cause: "No to Hidroituango"; "We're displaced by Hidroituango"; "EPM has kicked us out of the territory." As they walked, people gave them food, and they told their story.

By the time they arrived in Santa Rosa, the movement leaders had already been released. Already halfway there, the group decided to continue to the big city of Medellín, site of EPM's headquarters. It took them ten days. Radical students sympathetic to their cause invited them to take up residence in the University of Antioquia coliseum. Telling the story, Fabio and Angélica relive the triumph of the moment.

"We made ID cards to enter and leave," Fabio says, laughing. "And we controlled the entry to the university."

"Why did they let you do that?" I ask.

"We controlled our own entrance because no one controlled us," Fabio says defiantly.

"But why didn't the police come in?"

"One time they did want to come in and get rid of us," Angélica says. "But a fight started. Those students armed themselves with *papas bombas* [homemade potato-shaped bombs that shoot out scraps of metal and have long been the weapon of choice of the University of Antioquia's radical student body]."

"So it was because of the support of the students?"

"Yes, they said, 'You're not going to touch our campesinos,' and they threw *papas bombas* at them."

Every day they organized demonstrations against Hidroituango in different parts of Medellín and managed the logistics of providing for four hundred people. Fabio lists the committees they formed to organize their time there: cleaning, security, finance, logistics, health, food, and communications to meet with the press.

Feeding everyone was particularly challenging. They shared everything but didn't have money. Local unions donated firewood to allow them to cook, and the food committee visited wherever they could think of to ask for donations.

"One day we had five sacks of carrots," says Angélica. "Because we didn't have anything else, we started cooking carrots in a pot, and we just had carrot water, what a disgusting thing!"

"Pure carrot water?" I ask.

"Yes, carrots with water. Another day someone brought a truck with cabbage, and we didn't have rice, or anything else. So we started to cut heads of cabbage with machetes, like you do for mules. And we threw them in the pots with salt, so we were eating cabbage with water. We ate like this many days."

Fabio adds: "One time a man arrived with a truck full of papayas. So it was, 'Everyone take your papaya and eat it,' and that was it."

As the local government continued to ignore them, as they tired of the food and discomfort, and as the hydroelectric project continued unabated back home, their numbers thinned. When the group finally broke up after eight months of living in the university, they were down to two hundred people.

Despite the hardship, Fabio and Angélica look back at that experience as one of the most meaningful of their lives. They had developed what Jocelyn Viterna (2013) in *Women in War* calls an "activist identity," a role that is shaped by a mixture of individual conceptions and external recognition, given meaning through both symbolic understandings and their interactions with others. It is still central to their lives, friendships, and values.

Ríos Vivos Continues and Expands

Concurrent with Fabio and Angelica's commitment to it, the movement itself was growing. The occupation of the coliseum had drawn significant national and international attention, bringing support from organizations in other parts of the world. Shortly after the occupation, Fabio had the opportunity, as a delegate of Ríos Vivos, to attend an international gathering in Guatemala of groups resisting megaprojects like Hidroituango.

Fabio says hearing about struggles all over the Americas helped him understand how Hidroituango fit into a much greater phenomenon of capitalist development and dispossession: "People from Peru talked about their problems with mining . . . how they took the mountain and left a sterile hole. So the experience was about enriching my understanding with all the other experiences of people from the Americas ... Who is going to benefit? The people, or is it going to benefit the big capitalists? ... There I started to understand that the problem isn't just in Orejón, in Hidroituango, in Colombia. It's in the whole continent, and really the whole world."

The broader problem that Fabio saw embodied in the struggles of the activists he met in Guatemala has been identified by scholars as the "global land grab," involving the capture of control over large pieces of land and natural resources. Large-scale land acquisitions are often the first step in massive development projects, including commercial food production as well as hydroelectric dams and mines. Fabio and Angélica started connecting their struggle to that of thousands of communities across the world who fight to defend their territories against large-scale capitalist development and dispossession.

In addition to sharpening their critique of global capitalism, Fabio and Angélica's meetings with campesino and Indigenous activists from all over the Americas helped them learn about alternatives, primarily through agroecology. They participated in trainings that taught them how to make organic fertilizer and educated them about soil's beneficial microorganisms. They participated in seed exchanges, through which they acquired a variety of hot peppers, nuts, and vegetables that still grow on their farm to this day.

Back in Colombia, resistance to the dam continued. The community organized road blockades to protest specific grievances: a military control post to protect the dam that limited local mobility and exposed community members to harassment; a family whose land had been seized with compensation only to the parents, not their sixteen children and grandchildren who also lived on and from their farm; the closure of a road leading to a dock where many locals kept fishing boats. In each case, they were able to pressure EPM to accede to their demands. Dam construction continued, however.

Movement participation entailed significant risks, no great surprise in Colombia, the world's most dangerous place to be a social leader. The first member of Ríos Vivos assassinated was Nelson Giraldo, who died in 2013 during the occupation of the University of Antioquia. He had left his wife and two kids to return home to Ituango to pan for gold to raise some money. He was found on the beach, shot in his legs and chest and with his throat slit.

When they heard the news, says Fabio, "We were filled with fear in the coliseum. We didn't even want to return to the territory, because we thought they were going to kill us. So you didn't know, you told yourself: if you keep doing this, you're going to die. However, we've continued, with some precautions."

Five movement members have been murdered, with countless others threatened. With authorities far away, Fabio says he has to depend on his knowledge of the territory to stay safe: "In all the years I've been here, twelve years, I've never seen a police officer. I've always believed more in this territory to protect me, in having my own means. How I know the paths, how I have dogs who let me know [if anyone is coming]."

The Demining Program

In 2012, the FARC and the Colombian government initiated peace talks in Havana, Cuba. In 2015, the two sides engaged in their first collaboration: a demining program that doubled as a confidence-building measure to push peace negotiations forward. El Orejón was chosen to host it. Fabio and Angélica say that the community was skeptical at first, unsure of what to make of the sight of FARC leaders working alongside the Colombian military under the direction of Norwegian People's Aid, an international NGO.

By now seasoned activists used to advocating for their community's interests, Fabio and Angélica worked with their neighbors to use the demining program to push for development that had long been lacking in El Orejón. "We said as a community, 'We accept the demining program, but what social investment is there going to be?' At first they told us that there was none, so we were going to oppose the demining and stop it."

Facing the threat of blockades, the leadership of the program agreed to see what they could do. The community wrote a list of eighteen demands, sending it to the Havana peace negotiations. In the end, Norwegian People's Aid funded a new community meeting house and fixed up the local soccer field, the Turkish government paid for a new school, and a government agency built a nearby bridge that connected El Orejón to the village center.

Meanwhile, Angélica was hired to cook for the demining program, which was headquartered an hour-and-a-half walk from their house. After several months, a soldier working with the demining program died when he stepped on a mine. The explosion was so strong that Fabio heard it down on their farm. He called Angélica to ask her what had happened.

Angélica's boss overheard the conversation, and after the story of the soldier's death made it onto the national news, blamed her for the information leak. They cut her pay and eventually fired her. As Angélica recalls, her boss told her, "You were taking a lot of information to Ríos Vivos, so we decided to have you leave the camp."

Jorge, a former state official who had lived in El Orejón for two years while working for the demining program, confirmed that Angélica was fired for giving information to Ríos Vivos. "We were working to generate trust with the community," he told me. "And Ríos Vivos came up with the rumor that the demining was for Hidroituango."

Was the rumor true? The community had participated in the demining program by giving information on the potential location of land mines. However, as Fabio says, "After we gave information about all the sites where there were possible mines, they decided to demine . . ."

"In another area," Angélica finishes his sentence.

Fabio continues: "Where they demined were the lands that Hidroituango had bought, land we barely used."

The community had requested that the program target a strategic and heavily mined point on the top of the ridge that allows access to many neighboring communities. Instead, they demined largely on EPM property below, including areas the community was barred from entering. In 2018, the program ended, with headlines in national newspapers proclaiming, "El Orejón, free of mines."

"The demining program was for Hidroituango, not the community," Fabio says. "Because if it had been for the community, they would have demined all the area that we told them about, an area that is now abandoned. But it's still mined and is going to stay that way for life."

Jorge said his bosses never told him why Briceño was chosen to host the program. "But you obviously knew there was interest in pacifying a zone that was so close to a strategic project for the country," he told me, referring to Hidroituango. Nevertheless, he insisted that dam officials never had any input into the areas they chose to demine in El Orejón.

Whether or not Hidroituango officials had directly influenced the area to be demined, it is not surprising that locals like Fabio and Angélica question the motivations for a "gesture of peace" that disingenuously proclaimed the area was "free of mines." The demining and new buildings that came with it were not, however, the last consequential gesture of peace made in El Orejón.

The Promises and Failures of Coca Substitution

After fifty-two years of insurrection, the FARC signed a peace agreement with the Colombian state in late 2016. The document included provisions for major investment in rural communities like Briceño that have long borne the brunt of the conflict, seeking to address the poverty and inequality that are at the roots of the violence. Recognizing the role of coca in funding the conflict, one part of the accords established a crop substitution program meant to help campesinos transition to legal crops. Building off the demining program in El Orejón, Briceño was designated as the place to launch the pilot coca substitution program and dubbed Colombia's Peace Laboratory.

The community welcomed the promised investment. The substitution program promised three levels of productive projects worth US$7,000 total per household that were supposed to be distributed within the first two years to let beneficiaries develop legal agricultural activities. Though Fabio and Angélica no longer had their own coca crop, they were still allowed to enter the program as part of a policy that recognized that money from coca was ultimately funding even legal economic activity in the area.

The program launched in June 2017, when beneficiaries received the first of a year's worth of subsidy payments designed to feed their families in the absence of coca (US$700 every two months), pulled out their coca, and waited for the productive projects. More than five years later, most of them are still waiting. Fabio and Angélica chose to request goods that would help increase and diversify their production of food for subsistence, including fish, pigs, and the supplies needed to sustain them. A still-empty corral Fabio built years ago to house the pigs they expected to arrive is testament to the program's broken promises. However, given that they were already producing and selling organic goods at campesino markets, Fabio and Angélica are fortunate compared to their neighbors who lived off coca and counted on the productive projects to develop an alternative.

Angélica points out that the disappearance of coca has combined with the elimination of gold panning: "Before, you had some time when you couldn't pick coca, but you went down to the Cauca. So now that we don't have coca, we could be sustaining ourselves with the river [gold panning]. [But] now there's no other option but to leave the area."

Just a few years ago, eighty-eight people lived in El Orejón. The number is now forty-eight. Economic collapse has displaced more people than violence ever did. However, the unstated element in Angélica's attribution of displacement to the disappearance of coca and gold-panning economies is that, beginning with Colombia's 1990 economic opening that represented the first salvo in a wave of neoliberal reforms, traditional agriculture has steadily become less and less of a viable option for rural farmers. Economic liberalization has pushed campesinos into competition with internationally produced food crops that benefit from highly industrialized production. "We grow corn to eat," Angélica tells me, "because we want to make sure it's free of chemicals. But it's much cheaper to buy than to produce."

FABIO AND ANGÉLICA

Fig. 4.3. *Fabio and Angélica in front of their farm's waterfall.*

The cheap corn she refers to is grown on massive farms in the midwestern United States, which, subsidized by federal tax dollars, have found a lucrative market in recently liberalized Latin American countries that used to produce their own corn. In the four years after Colombia's 2012 Free Trade Agreement with the United States eliminated tariffs on agricultural goods, US food exports to Colombia increased by a factor of five, including traditional Colombian products like corn, beans, rice, and milk. Colombia now imports 30 percent of its food. Meanwhile, Fabio and Angélica's neighbors often can't sell their food crops for more than the cost of production. While locals usually blame the broken promises of coca substitution for the region's economic collapse, even productive farms offer little in the way of profits.

An Environmental Catastrophe

Where Fabio and Angélica's agroecological farming seeks to live in harmony with the environment, the hydroelectric dam has turned into an ecological disaster. In April 2018, a few months before the dam was supposed to begin operating, a landslide just upriver from the project blocked a tunnel meant to divert the river's flow while the dam was under construction. With no way to pass through the massive retention wall, the river below Fabio and

Angélica's farm rose steadily. The impending catastrophe dominated nightly news in Colombia. If the river rose high enough, it could destroy the entire project. And if it forced its way through the dam, heavily populated downstream areas would flood.

However, the problem was no surprise to Ríos Vivos, whose members had warned as early as 2013 that construction was loosening the mountainsides' porous rocks. Fabio says, "We told them our mountains have fragile rocks, that water filters through. We warned them, in our campesino way of speaking, of what was going to happen with that megaproject. They said we were speaking nonsense, that for that they had geologists with degrees, and who would believe the words of some poor *montañeros* [a disparaging term for the rural poor, similar to "country bumpkins"]? And they laughed at us."

As the river was ominously rising, Fabio ran into one of the head engineers of the project. Fabio recounted telling him: "'The river has said that we were right, hasn't it? Look what's happening to you.' I said that to his face. And he responded, 'You must be happy with everything that's happening.' And I told him, 'No, never, because people live below, people like us, and if the river goes, it takes them with it.'"

Fabio's words were prophetic. On May 12, 2018, the river burst its confines. Entire downstream communities were destroyed, and 25,000 people were displaced. The dam has turned into an expensive disaster. It was more than four years after the flood before the dam entered into partial operation, and it has yet to be completed. And with the retention wall built, the river's higher, slower-moving waters below Fabio and Angélica's farm have become permanent. The effects are tangible: more (and stagnant) water below means more evaporation. Not only does this manifest itself in the form of clouds that cover the river every morning, but the increased humidity has negative effects on their crops. Fabio says the coffee and cacao are developing new kinds of fungi that never existed here before. Their coffee beans often fall off the bush before they've matured.

The area has also become warmer. Fabio and Angélica have put away the heavy blankets they used to sleep with at night. But the hot, humid weather has brought an increased quantity of insects, particularly mosquitoes. One evening, as we record an interview about the history of Ríos Vivos, I refuse the insect repellent that Fabio and Angélica offer me. By the time we finish, my ankles are covered with itchy bites. At night, they sleep in beds ensconced within mosquito netting. Before, they say, these measures were unnecessary. Beyond the discomfort, in the last few years the dangerous mosquito-borne illness dengue has arrived in El Orejón. Fabio and Angélica have both contracted it, and Fabio has had it twice. Each time they've needed to be hospitalized, involving a long and difficult journey. Once, Fabio's illness advanced to the life-threatening critical hemorrhagic stage. The fever, and changes in the microclimate, seem to be part of the territory's new normal.

Agroecology: "A Way to Resist"

One sunny afternoon as the post-lunch laziness sets in, I sit with Fabio, Angélica, and their twelve-year-old nephew David, who is visiting from Medellín during his school vacation. Just before darkness falls, we will walk to a neighbor's house to watch the Colombia-Chile soccer game in the quarterfinals of the Copa América; Fabio and Angélica's television doesn't get a signal.

David's weeklong stay with them is coming to an end. In that time, we've received an education on rural life. We've climbed high into trees to knock down mangos; tried and failed to chase down unruly chickens for a stew; accompanied Fabio as he cleared brush with a machete; and helped Angélica as she toasted, hand-ground, and packed their coffee into containers for sale. Now, as I record, Fabio and Angélica take the chance to finish their tutorial on agroecology, a word they have repurposed to describe the underlying logic and values behind everything they do. They speak to David, who, like many young people in a country where people are gradually abandoning the countryside, is a city kid born to rural parents.

"I want to say something, and I want David to hear." Angélica draws her nephew in. "What is agroecology? Agro means cultivate, and ecology is to take care of, protect."

"What we do," Fabio interjects.

"Yes, what we do," Angélica continues. "Agroecology is the art of cultivating without damaging. Because I don't gain anything if I start to remove the weeds from around these coffee plants with a chemical. Those poisons don't just kill the weeds that attack the coffee, but they kill worms, beetles, ladybugs, which are beneficial to the earth. But agroecology is also working with the whole family." Angélica talks about a woman in El Orejón who has to beg her husband whenever she needs money. "For me, agroecology is also the whole family participating, not just in the work but in how to spend the money."

"The other thing we can say," Fabio adds, "is that agroecology is a lifestyle, a way of living in harmony. With what? With nature, with ourselves, with our neighbors."

"With our surroundings," says Angélica. "And not just those who live

Fig. 4.4. *Angélica takes a break from planting organic soybeans. In the background, on the opposing wall of the river canyon, one of the camps for the workers of Hidroituango is visible.*

here in El Orejón, but I also think, how are we going to make this chocolate, thinking that it's for people who are going to go buy from us, who are supporting our economy?"

"It's sharing knowledge," Fabio says, turning to David. "Come, let's plant peanuts, come let's cut with a machete, those are things we can transmit, so that the tradition is never lost, as long as someone learns it."

Angélica continues: "And agroecology isn't only cultivating and selling, it's also telling the youth, 'Don't abandon the countryside.'"

"Agroecology is also understanding why things happen," Fabio picks up. "And the power of those who rule, the multinational [corporations]. It's to raise awareness about what they're doing to us, and who's doing it, and how. And stopping them. So we look, there are guerrillas here, there are paramilitaries. But there's also community. So who are we? What do we do?" He pauses before concluding the lesson. "It's a way to resist."

As I leave Fabio and Angélica's farm, following the valley downstream with the bloated and stagnant river below, I wonder about the future of rural Colombia, embodied in the talkative twelve-year-old who trails behind me. David, extolling the virtues of consuming agroecologically grown products from the land rather than processed foods from the store, seems enchanted by their lifestyle and personal philosophy. But when it comes time for him to chart out his adult life, will he imagine himself in the countryside?

The forces arrayed against Colombia's rural poor are many: economic policy regimes that have eliminated protections for smallholding farmers and privileged extraction; a peace process that has increasingly been captured by elite interests; and the corporations, politicians, and armed groups that seek to exploit natural resources in campesino territories. It is not surprising that rural populations are waning. But Fabio and Angélica embody another important element in struggles over the Latin American countryside: the campesino and Indigenous communities that offer distinct models of how to live and produce with nature. In the face of violence, extraction, and elite-centered development to which they are little more than an obstacle, they perform perhaps the greatest act of resistance available: they stay put.

Note

1. Fabio and Angélica both chose to be identified by their real names, and place-names are also accurate. Other names are pseudonyms.

References

Gliessman, Steve. 2018. "Defining Agroecology." *Agroecology and Sustainable Food Systems* 42 (6): 599–600.

Viterna, Jocelyn. 2013. *Women in War: The Micro-processes of Mobilization in El Salvador*. New York: Oxford University Press.

Suggested Reading

Ballvé, Teo. 2020. *The Frontier Effect: State Formation and Violence in Colombia*. Ithaca, NY: Cornell University Press.

Ciro Rodríguez, Estefanía. 2019. *Levantados de la selva: Vidas y legitimidades en los territorios cocaleros del Caquetá*. Bogotá: Ediciones Uniandes.

Lapegna, Pablo. 2016. *Soybeans and Power: Genetically Modified Crops, Environmental Politics, and Social Movements in Argentina*. New York: Oxford University Press.

Lyons, Kristina M. 2020. *Vital Decomposition: Soil Practitioners and Life Politics*. Durham, NC: Duke University Press.

Ramírez, María Clemencia. 2011. *Between the Guerrillas and the State: The Cocalero Movement, Citizenship, and Identity in the Colombian Amazon*. Durham, NC: Duke University Press.

Wolford, Wendy. 2010. *This Land Is Ours Now: Social Mobilization and the Meanings of Land in Brazil*. Durham, NC: Duke University Press.

CHAPTER 5

Doris Huaiquian
NEWEN, TENACITY OF SPIRIT

Cinthya E. Ammerman

Introduction

The one-lane highway to Nüyü is lined with flowering prairies, farms, and small patches of forest. It's summer in Chile; dogs sunbathe in the blinding sun beside the roadside food stands. Every few kilometers an old wooden bus stop appears with graffiti spray-painted on the side: "territorio Mapuche" (Mapuche territory) and "fuera forestales" (timber plantations get out), and drawings of the *meli wixan mapu* (the four directions) are ubiquitous. We are in Wallmapu, Indigenous Mapuche homelands, currently known as the region of La Araucanía in southern Chile. My family and I are traveling from my hometown an hour away to visit a lifelong family friend, Doris Huaiquian.[1] Doris is Lafkenche (person of the sea), Indigenous to the Pacific coast on what is now southern Chile. Her family has lived here for countless generations, but she will soon have to relocate due to the rising ocean that threatens to take her home.

The entrance to the small coastal village of Nüyü[2] is breathtaking. The Pacific Ocean stretches to our right, its vigorous, frothing waves dispersing over the warm black volcanic sands. To our left are a handful of humble wooden houses and shacks scattered on a moor, a blue lagoon surrounded by feathery beach grass, and soft green hills. Doris's small three-room cottage comes into view; she lives here with her eldest daughter, Margarita, and grandchildren, two-year-old Lucas and seven-year-old Matías. In front of her house is Margarita's roadside food stand, where she sells homemade snacks to the summer tourists. Atop the food stand, a Mapuche flag flies beside a Chilean flag. The dirt road that leads to their house is lined with pine trees. Every year the rows of pine grow thinner: "The ocean is taking

Fig. 5.1. *Doris and Margarita beside Margarita's roadside food stand in Nüyü.*

the trees," Doris tells me. I mention that the road also looks thinner than I remember from my last visit. "The ocean is eating the road, too," she says.

For over a decade, Doris has been receiving signs of an impending disaster. She recalls seeing sea lions traveling inland, moving far from the ocean into a place they wouldn't normally reside. "It was a sign," she said, that she, too, should move away from the coast. In 2010, she dreamed of a massive earthquake and tsunami four days before it happened. Doris's house was miraculously spared, but she doesn't think it will survive the next disaster. She has recurring dreams of flooding, as the ocean creeps closer to her house every year—"every day," she corrects me. Over the next year she will be relocating inland, to a rural parcel approximately an hour away from her ancestral homeland. Doris's impending resettlement has as much to do with the history of colonialism in Wallmapu as it does with the rising ocean .

The Lafkenche are part of a much larger Indigenous Mapuche nation whose vast ancestral territory, Wallmapu, spans central-south Chile and Argentina. Like many other Indigenous nations throughout the Americas, the Mapuche have cultivated reciprocal relationships with their homelands since time immemorial. These relationships were interrupted by the arrival of Spanish colonizers and missionaries in the 1600s, through invasion by European settlers in the 1800s, and by extractive industries and climate change.

Climate change is a consequence of the violent dispossession, extractivism, ecocide, and genocide that accompanied European settlement of Indigenous homelands. Indigenous and rural peoples are more vulnerable to the effects of climate change, yet they are not passive victims. In her personal account of these injustices, Doris weaves a narrative of resilience, adaptation, and cultural continuity akin to what Gerald Vizenor (1994) calls "survivance." Survivance is the act of moving beyond basic survival to create spaces of synthesis and renewal in the face of genocide.

Doris demonstrates survivance through her role as culture-bearer and language teacher to her children, grandchildren, and community; through her faith in *Chaudios* (a synthesis of the Mapudungun and Spanish words for God, *chau* and *dios*); and in the persistence and adaptation she demonstrates in securing a new home for relocation. She has *newen*, she asserts emphatically; "*Newen* is one's spirit, the desire to do something and to carry it out. That's *newen!*" Doris's tenacity of spirit is the primary root of her story of survivance, anchoring and nourishing her through the many challenges she has faced.

Mapudungun: "Language Is Life"

Doris affirms that she was born to transmit *kimün* (ancestral knowledge) and Mapudungun (Mapuche language). She taught Mapudungun to her daughters and is now teaching it to her grandchildren. She also works as a language teacher and cultural adviser to rural communities who wish to reclaim what was lost through colonization. She continually expresses joy in her language and tradition, speaking to me in Spanish mixed with Mapudungun.

> I love my *kimün*, I am happy when I speak Mapudungun . . . I like to get dressed with my *trarilonko* [headband], *trapelakucha* [silver brooch], my *ikülla* [shawl]. I feel decent when I dress like that, I feel very happy when I put my tools, my jewels on, *ayuwin ñi piuke* [my heart rejoices]. I am filled with *newen*, I feel like God's prize."

This chapter was written following two years of phone and in-person conversations with Doris. My family has known the Huaiquians for over fifty years; my mom's family used to spend the summers on the coast, in a small two-room shack a short walk from the Huaiquian family home. My grandmother, known to the Huaiquians as *chiñura comerciante* (merchant lady), would bring clothes, shoes, sugar, and other items from town to trade for eggs, cheese, chickens, and seafood with Doris's mom. In those years, the trip to Nüyü on the unpaved roads took many hours. My family would stay for three months at a time in that sparsely populated area, regularly sharing with the Huaiquian family. My mom and Doris remember those days fondly, playing in the tide pools, foraging for *ngalka* (a rhubarb-like plant) and *nüyü* (the fruit of a flowering bromeliad and the namesake of the beach). When recounting their stories of mischief and adventure, they seem to leave out the fact that for several years they couldn't communicate verbally—Doris did not speak Spanish, and my mom did not speak Mapudungun.

Doris started attending school and learning Spanish at eight years old. The first thing she told me about school is "I didn't have shoes like the other kids." Her father told her to wash her feet well and scrub them with pumice stone, so she could go to school *con los pies bien limpiecitos* (with really clean feet). The teachers at her rural school did not speak Mapudungun, and they didn't give her special lessons to learn Spanish. She taught herself by listening closely to the sounds: "I learned on my own, I paid attention and learned." The first thing she learned to say was "Can I use the bathroom?" She often repeats this story in our conversations about language, and you can sense the urgency she must have felt as a child who couldn't get permission to go. Yet she tells me she never felt discriminated against at school and even expresses empathy for her teachers: "It must have been hard for them to teach me, not knowing Mapudungun."

For Doris and her family, learning Spanish was a matter of survival. "My great-grandfather told me that when the Spanish arrived, they killed many, many Mapuche. Since the Mapuche didn't speak Spanish, they couldn't defend themselves." As one of the youngest children in her family, Doris was tormented by her older brothers for not speaking Spanish. "They would hit me, yell at me, call me names . . . I think I learned to speak Spanish *a varillasos* [by getting whipped with a branch]; it was terrible. That's why I taught my two daughters both languages at the same time . . ." Nevertheless, she reflects on her brothers' behavior with compassion: "[My brothers] were forced to learn to speak Spanish, same as me. They became embarrassed to speak Mapudungun . . . They didn't maintain the language like I did . . . I love my language, I never put it aside."

Nearly two million people, approximately 10 percent of the population in Chile, identify as Mapuche according to the Chilean National Institute of Statistics (INE). Despite the increasing number of people who are reclaiming their Mapuche identity, a 2017 study by Fernando Zúñiga and Aldo Olate revealed that Mapudungun is losing speakers, particularly in rural areas. Indigenous peoples throughout the Americas learned the language of the

Fig. 5.2. *Doris teaches her grandchildren to speak in Mapudungun from an early age.*

colonizer out of necessity and often through force, as in the case of mission boarding schools during the first half of the twentieth century and, later, in public schools. Over the past couple of decades, however, there has been a boom in Mapudungun revitalization projects that hint at an upward turn of language vitality. The everyday work of mothers and grandmothers like Doris is crucial to the transmission of language and culture. The urgency of her life's work is not lost on her: "Language is important for knowledge, it has *newen*. . . . Without [Mapudungun] there is no Mapuche. There is no life. Language is life."

Newen: Tenacity of Spirit

Doris describes herself as someone who has *newen*: "*Newen* is one's spirit, the desire to do something and to carry it out. That's *newen!*" She also uses the word to denote life energy, strength, vitality. She has demonstrated *newen* through every phase of her life.

In elementary school, after she had learned Spanish, she would volunteer to recite poetry or sing at school functions because the teachers would give her clothes and food as a reward:

I always got prizes like that. I liked performing, but it was also out of necessity. When I won a box of cookies, I would bring them home, we would have something to eat. It's not like it is now; before, [the poverty] was dire... We never ate sweets.

The youngest of three children, Doris was raised in a troubled home. At fourteen years old, she decided to leave her house because her mom and dad were always fighting. She says, "I got tired of seeing them break up and get back together." She later revealed that her dad, fueled by a drinking problem and a bad temper, also mistreated her because she was born with light-colored hair, and he assumed she was not his daughter.

Her father was the manager of a nearby farm, where he lived during the weekdays. On weekends, he would return to the house and kick Doris out, so she would have to sleep in the outhouse. Doris was often forced to help him at the farm where he worked. "I was raised as a man... my father denied that I was his daughter, he treated me like a man, he taught me to yoke oxen, he taught me to saddle horses, he taught me to tie lumber," and if she didn't do her work, he would come after her. "He could never catch me because I was fast! And I was barefoot, without shoes or even sandals." He made her tame oxen, putting her in front of the animals and letting them run at her.

I was skinny then, so I hid behind trees and tried everything so the animals didn't get me... He would put me in front of the animals, maybe because he wanted me dead, I don't know what the hell he was doing... and my mom kept forcing me to go work for him.

He also made her tame horses, because, according to him, only young girls could break horses. He would tie her to the saddle, and the untamed horse would run amok with her on top. "I ran horses all up and down that beach," she says, gesturing out the window. "I was frightened, it was incredibly dangerous!" She thanks *Chaudios* that she was never bucked off a horse or kicked.

Her older brother and sister had jobs as a baker and a housemaid, respectively, in Santiago, the capital city of Chile. These low-wage, service-industry jobs were commonly held by Mapuche who migrated to the cities. When her brother came home to visit the family one day in 1979, Doris decided to go back to Santiago with him. She had no shoes at the time, so she borrowed her mother's, which were too big for her, and filled them with wool to make them fit. She had never had shoes until then.

Her sister helped her find a job working as a maid for a family in the upper-class Santiago neighborhood of Vitacura. She arrived at the house with her "little bag and shoes full of wool . . . I was a skinny fourteen-year-old, I was a little girl." They didn't want to hire her at first because she was too young, but Doris was determined not to return to the hard labor that awaited her in Nüyü, so she insisted they give her a trial. Three months into her new job, she bought herself her first new pair of shoes. She remained with the family for fourteen years.

When reflecting on her experience working for a family in Santiago, she says she felt welcomed, never discriminated against. "I was respected, treated well." However, as she describes her working conditions, she acknowledges that she was exploited. Her day started at 5:00 a.m. and continued late into the night. If she wasn't up in time to prepare breakfast for her employers, they would ring a bell that was strategically placed next to her bed until she woke up: "At 5:45 a.m. I had to be at their bedside, with a mug of warm milk and buttered bread on a tray." She often fell asleep on the bus after running errands; the driver took pity on her and would let her sleep through the entire route. She attributes her labor conditions as motivating her to become interested in politics.

In 1988, Chile held a plebiscite vote to determine whether the military dictator, Augusto Pinochet, would remain in power. Doris's employers—staunch Pinochet supporters—attempted to thwart her attempt to vote. Her employer told her, "If you go vote for someone else, you will have to leave your employment here." The newly elected democratic president, Patricio Aylwin, would assume office a year later. Doris organized the neighborhood maids to visit the presidential palace dressed in their maid uniforms on his inauguration day. Doris got his attention during the moment when Aylwin was greeting the public. She told him, "I like my employers, they are nice to me, but I want fair pay and a fair schedule because we are exploited." Doris's request coincided with Aylwin's planned labor reform, which promised the protection of workers' rights and the strengthening of labor organizations. When Doris returned to her employer's house after Aylwin's inauguration, she promptly packed her bags and said good-bye to them. She continued to work for their eldest daughter for a few more years, until she married in 1993.

Her ex-husband, Juan, was also Lafkenche from Puerto Saavedra, a town north of Nüyü. Doris met him in Santiago, and they were friends for years, but he changed when they got married. He became irate, jealous, and he liked to drink. "He reminded me of my father," she lamented. She had her first daughter, Margarita, the same year she got married. The three of them bounced around from Santiago to Puerto Saavedra for six years. In 1999, she gave birth to her second daughter, María, and that same year, she decided to leave Juan and return to Nüyü to be with her mom. Doris doesn't share much about those years with Juan, except that he was abusive. After she left him, she said he would occasionally show up in Nüyü, threatening to kill her. The local police would come to her aid, and later gifted her two dogs to protect her.

Back in Nüyü, she began harvesting and selling seafood in the streets of nearby towns to provide for her daughters. Margarita would nap on a blanket on the beach while Doris collected seafood, and she would ride on her shoulders while Doris sold her harvest around town. As one of the few fluent Mapudungun speakers in her locality, Doris was recruited by an elementary school to teach the language. Shortly after, in 2006, she was awarded a scholarship for a certificate program through a prominent university, where she learned to read and write Mapudungun. Although she no longer works at the school, Doris continues to teach in communities that have lost the language. She also works as a cultural liaison. She is not a traditional authority, unlike her older brother who is a *lonko* (head of a community), but she is well known and respected by local government officials, regularly receives visitors from neighboring towns who seek her advice on cultural matters, and is often asked to serve as a translator in local government meetings with Mapuche communities.

Her role as cultural adviser is often voluntary, so she continues to supplement her income by harvesting and selling seafood. She is one of the few in the area who still sells seaweed like *ulte, piure*, and *luche*. "I've raised the price, because the seafood is scarce now, it's harder to find, but my clients never complain." She sells most seafood fresh, except for *luche*, a type of sea lettuce. She sells it cooked because "few people have the knowledge of how to prepare it anymore." She harvests according to her traditional knowledge, every fifteen days. "I work with the moon. I harvest when the moon is full and when the moon is new." She also gives offerings to "the living water," according to her traditional knowledge.

> When [the ancestors] took seafood, they gave offerings; the ocean gave to them, and they gave to the ocean. They would give it potatoes or toasted flour and they would thank the *ngen lafken* [guardian of the ocean]. There are few people who do that now, but I still do. That's why the ocean gives me its offerings. I offer *muday* [a fermented corn drink], small things. One feels so happy when one gives offerings. When I offer in Mapudungun, I say, "I bring you this to thank you—for all that you give me, all that you have given me. *Mañum mew.*" *Mañum* means to be grateful deep in your soul, when you are brimming with gratitude.

Fig. 5.3. *Doris during our last visit in January of 2022.*

Mapu: The Multidimensionality of Place

"Mapuche" (people of the land) is an umbrella term for several identities that denote specific relationships to a territory, for example, the Pehuenche (people of the Pehuén tree in the Andes) and Williche (people of the South). Doris identifies as Lafkenche (person of the ocean) from the Lafkenmapu (Pacific coast in southern Chile). *Mapu* is both a physical and a metaphysical concept that is often used interchangeably with the words "place," "territory," "land," "landscape," and "homelands." *Mapu* alludes to a multitude of tangible and intangible dimensions; beyond the physical land, there are worlds above and below that are unseen by humans.

Physically, the ancestral territory expanded from the 30th parallel north to the 44th parallel south in South America, spanning the border between Chile and Argentina. Mapuche have inhabited their ancestral territory since 500–600 BC and controlled the largest territory of any ethnic group in Latin America prior to European invasion. Furthermore, they were the only known Indigenous group in Latin America to have successfully resisted the Spanish invasion after the Hundred Years' War, from 1550 to 1656. The Parliament of Quillín, signed by the Spanish in 1641, officially recognized Mapuche sovereignty and autonomy, consolidating their territory into what later became known as La Araucanía.

Though Mapuche territory was sovereign, it was irreversibly changed through the introduction of non-native plants and animals brought by the Spanish. "Back then [before the Spanish invasion] there were a lot of foods that grew on their own. There were a lot of native foods . . . They began to disappear when [the Spanish] brought foreign animals." Before the Spanish, Doris tells me, there were no domestic animals:

> When the ancestors wanted to eat meat, they would create a *minga* [work party], and they would have to hunt an animal down . . . They would hunt two or three animals for all the communities, and they ate them. Nobody owned animals. Nobody was an owner. But when the Spanish arrived, they brought foreign animals, and their animals ate the native plants.

The loss of territory and native species parallels the loss of language, because Indigenous languages are deeply rooted in the land. For Doris, learning Mapudungun centered around being outside, taking care of the farm animals, "goats, lambs, sheep, geese, chickens, ducks—in the midst of all those little animals we were raised." She spent a lot of time playing barefoot in the ocean and sand dunes, "We never got cold, we never got sick." Doris tells me that Mapudungun transmits *newen de mapu* (energy of the land) because, according to the teachings from her great-grandfather, the language emerged from the *mapu*, from the land:

> The ancestors invented the language from sounds they heard. . . . In the past, they took time to listen to the earth. *Ponían su pilún hacia el mapu* [they put their ear to the earth]. This language is not foreign, this language is native. The same as a native tree, it's incomparable to pine and eucalyptus.

Doris is referring to the non-native pine and eucalyptus plantations that were introduced in the early 1900s. These exotic species are currently taking over the region, threatening Mapuche lifeways and intensifying the effects of climate change in Wallmapu.

Colonialism and Capitalism

For many Mapuche, the timber industry in Wallmapu is a continuation of colonialism. Colonialism in the Americas is an ongoing structure of domination that is foundational to contemporary nation-states; Chile, like the United States, was built on colonialism. Colonialism grants settlers power over political, economic, and social systems. European settlers throughout the Americas employed diverse strategies to usurp and establish control over Indigenous lands and lives. In the course of five hundred years in Wallmapu, settlers have sought to missionize Indigenous peoples, exploit their labor, and eliminate and replace them through forced relocation and genocide. For many Indigenous communities, capitalism is a colonial structure that enables the continued exploitation of land and life for profit, and it is in direct opposition to Indigenous value systems of respect and reciprocity.

Chile claimed its independence from Spain in 1812 and shortly thereafter waged war on Mapuche through the ill-named "Pacification of La Araucanía." By the 1880s, Mapuche territory was under Chilean control. In the eyes of Chileans, La Araucanía was valuable arable land that would ideally be inhabited and developed by new settlers from what Chilean government officials considered "superior" cultures. The Chilean government established "agencies of colonization" in Germany and other European countries, recruiting colonists with the promise of free land. New settlers were deeded approximately 70 hectares or more of stolen land, and their male offspring received an additional 30 hectares. Meanwhile, throughout La Araucanía the surviving Mapuche were forced into *reducciones* (reservations) with approximately 6.1 hectares of land per person.

Doris recounts the disturbing story of settlers who killed her great-great-grandparents in Nüyü so they could usurp their land. "Back then, this land was known as Pilkomañi, after my great-great-grandmother, who was a powerful and renowned *machi* [healer]." A stranger came to their home late one night, asking for a place to spend the night. Her great-great-grandmother kindly took him in and fed him dinner. The man stepped out to use the bathroom and returned with three other men with painted faces. The men, later identified as neighboring German and Chilean landowners, murdered both of Doris's great-great-grandparents with an ax, decapitating them. Her great-grandfather, then seven years old, witnessed the horrifying scene from behind the sacks of grain where he was hiding. He ran away and lived on the streets as a child, depending on the kindness of strangers. He did not return to Nüyü until many years later, compelled by his eldest son,

Manuel, who wanted to recover the land. Manuel returned with his wife to live on what was left of the Huaiquian family plot. Every morning, his wife would walk the perimeter of their land displaying a machete to let the settlers know that they were not to be messed with. "My grandmother, she was tough ... They say she barely spoke Spanish, but she defended what was theirs."

In her stories, Doris makes a distinction between the Chilean Spanish-speaking settlers and the German "gringos" who began arriving when her great-grandfather was a child: "The Chileans, the Spanish, they didn't cause as much destruction as the gringos. They took land, they killed our race, but at least they left some hills covered with native trees." She asserts that the German settlers and their descendants are largely responsible for the expansive timber plantations that threaten the biodiversity of the region:

> Those Germans took big, big *fundos* [estates], they filled everything with pine and eucalyptus. They cut down everything that is native. It makes it hard to recover *mapu*, [because] they took kilometers and kilometers.

Doris's account refers to the wave of German immigration to southern Chile during the late 1800s and early 1900s. One of the most influential Germans to be recruited by the Chilean government was the forester Federico Albert, who created the current monoculture forestry model of non-native pine and eucalyptus. His legacy lives on in the timber plantations that have now taken over nearly 21 percent of the region.

The timber industry grew exponentially following favorable neoliberal policies introduced during the military dictatorship of Augusto Pinochet (1973–1990). Over the course of his seventeen-year dictatorship, Pinochet initiated the first worldwide experiment with neoliberal state formation. Under the guidance of economists trained under Milton Friedman at the University of Chicago, he restructured the economy by privatizing public assets, opening up natural resources to private exploitation, and facilitating free trade and foreign investment. This economic shock treatment, often lauded as a "Chilean miracle," came at a great cost. It was methodically implemented through the repression, kidnapping, torture, disappearance, and homicide of tens of thousands of opponents. Pinochet gave ancestral Mapuche lands to private landowners and timber companies. He also subsidized timber companies, covering 70–80 percent of their operation costs. The Chilean model for incentivizing timber plantations has been deemed "economically successful" and has been replicated throughout Latin America.

Extensive monoculture plantations of exotic pine and eucalyptus are wreaking havoc on the ecosystem, provoking loss of biodiversity and altering hydrological processes, soil quality, land cover, and fire regimes. Mapuche communities near plantations are disproportionately affected by the environmental consequences and have little to no legal protection. Communities have witnessed the disappearance of species, medicinal plants, water, and ways of life. In *Race and the Chilean Miracle*, Patricia Richards (2013) echoes what many others have pointed out: the loss of biodiversity amounts to a cultural loss, for when species become endangered or extinct, so do the language and cultural practices tied to them.

Faced with few options and mounting police repression, many of these communities are becoming increasingly radicalized. Currently, parts of La Araucanía are hotspots of violent conflict between police and military acting on behalf of private landowners and the timber industry, and Mapuche communities defending and reclaiming their ancestral homelands.

Doris reflects on recent murders of people on both sides of the conflict:

> The violence is bad for my *piuke* [heart]. How someone could have it in their heart to kill . . . We all want to live . . . I respect the *newenes* [the life energy] of all . . . I don't think that it's okay to kill people . . . I think *Chaudios* gave everyone a life purpose, and we have to respect that. Whatever race, you have to respect them.

Doris is skilled at seeing situations from various perspectives, always mindful to return to her pacifist stance. She discusses the violent tactics employed by Mapuche activists:

> It's not so much the adults anymore, it's the *wechekeche* [young people]. I guess they think that without violence you can't recover anything . . . But I don't go with violence, I would rather talk to the state.

Yet she understands that dialoguing with the state and private landowners is no simple matter:

> What rich person will want to return their *fundos* [large estates]? If you talk to the rich people, they say, "those Indians," because they don't call us "Mapuche," they say, "The Indian is lazy, why do they want so much land?," but the land has always belonged to Mapuche. That's where the violence comes from, daughter, that's the *kewatun* [fight]."

In an effort to incorporate Indigenous communities into the timber industry and quell violence, the National Forest Corporation (CONAF) gives away exotic trees to Mapuche families throughout Wallmapu:

> CONAF comes along and gives away the pine and eucalyptus. They have come to my home many times, but I tell them "no thanks" because I live off the sea, I don't live off pine and eucalyptus . . . They're not even selling them, they're gifting them, pickup trucks loaded with pine and eucalyptus all around. I say, dumb people, . . . [planting] pine and eucalyptus when we don't have water left.

Doris becomes impassioned when she discusses the environmental impact of the plantations.

> Eucalyptus drinks a lot, a lot, of water! A lot of *ko* [water]! We are without *ko*, daughter! Imagine all that land full [of plantations] and now there are no *trayen* [estuaries]. When I was young, there were estuaries everywhere, with lots of *ko*, but now there are only little threads of water.

There is growing evidence that pine and eucalyptus plantations act synergistically with climate change, intensifying drought conditions and creating longer and more devastating wildfire seasons. These fast-growing non-native trees consume more water than native forests; the pine canopy intercepts rainfall and the needles retain rainwater, which then evaporates before hitting the soil. Pine also acidifies the soil, making it uninhabitable for the native shrubs and plants that would otherwise retain soil humidity and generating favorable conditions for other invasive species that increase fire fuel load. The effects of climate change in Chile, the rising temperatures and decreased rainfall, are made worse by the expansion of pine and eucalyptus plantations.

Climate Change and the Swelling Sea

In Lafkenmapu, Doris is faced with the paradox of water scarcity and a rising ocean that threatens to take what is left of her family's land. "The ocean is swollen," she says. "It will swallow people and homes." During my last visit in January of 2022, engineers from the government's transportation agency were in front of Doris's house, taking measurements for a new road. The government pays Doris to build the road through her land. They have already moved the road three times in the past ten years, each time closer up the moor to where her house sits.

Doris's house is a small cottage of approximately 40 square meters. The front room has an old iron wood stove and a large dining table that takes up the majority of the space. At the other end of the front room sits an old wooden hutch and shelves replete with food and supplies for Margarita's roadside food business. The second half of the cottage is divided into two small rooms of equal size: one for Doris, and one where Margarita and her sons stay during the summer months while she works at the stand. The walls and roof are made of uninsulated, unpainted plywood. The cold wind penetrates the walls even in the summer, and you can hear the slightest noise from the outside. The chickens and chicks gather by the front door, peeping loudly enough for us to hear them clearly from inside. Margarita jokes that they are angry because she cooked one of them for our lunch.

From the west-facing front room, we can see the road and the ocean. As of 2022, the ocean was about 500 meters from the house, but it used to be about thirty minutes away on horseback; her great-grandmother would ride her horse to the beach. The ocean is moving closer to her house at such a fast rate that she expects the remainder of her lands will be flooded in a couple of years. The rapid ocean rise is due to climate change, as well as shifts in the seafloor as a result of major earthquakes that have impacted the area, the largest of which occurred in 1960 and in 2010. Chile stretches along several fault lines, making the coastal region historically vulnerable to disasters caused by earthquakes and tsunamis. Climate change and rising sea levels intensify the vulnerability of this area. Doris is aware of this. She tells me that the ocean is increasingly "swollen" because of the melting "snow" (icebergs), and the tides are also increasingly erratic.

Doris is very familiar with disaster. She was born during a flood on a stormy August day, winter in the Southern Hemisphere. The midwife could not make it to her house because the road was under water, so her father delivered her. Perhaps, she muses, being born in a flood gave her a heightened awareness of impending disasters. She continues to have visions and dreams that something bad will soon happen. "It's beautiful here in Nüyü, *mi niña* [my girl], it can be calm and have all the *newen*, but then suddenly, like the day before yesterday, there's a huge tide that comes out of nowhere . . . I trust in *Chaudios*, he has been so helpful to me," she says, referring to her visions and dreams of impending disaster. "But there will be a moment when there is no peace. Something grave is coming, something very bad is coming," she says emphatically. "I have it in my memory, in my *kimün* [ancestral knowledge]."

She tells me the ancestral story of Treng Treng and Kai Kai Filu (snake). The story has many variations: some believe Kai Kai Filu and Treng Treng Filu were giant snakes made by the creator to ensure that people followed his original instructions. When people disobeyed, Kai Kai Filu would raise the waters and flood the land, killing and frightening people. The people sought refuge with Treng Treng Filu, who elevated the land and kept them safe. Doris's version does not take place in the past. In her version, Kai Kai Filu is "a deceiving hill." People who don't know better will dwell on Kai Kai Filu and then Kai Kai Filu will sink into the ocean and drown everything on it. "It's like a snake, it shrinks into the ocean then rises back up." In contrast, Treng Treng is a "good hill"; it gives life, everything grows on it, it doesn't flood and kill people. "Those without knowledge will climb Kai Kai Filu and die." Many cultures reference floods as fundamental events in their formation, and these stories are interpretations of natural phenomena according to their cosmologies. Doris's version of the story is a set of instructions for living on the earthquake-prone coast, where land can suddenly crumble into the ocean.

In 2010, she dreamed of a massive earthquake and tsunami four days before it happened. The catastrophic earthquake occurred off the coast of Chile in the Pacific Ocean, approximately 500 kilometers north of Nüyü. With a magnitude of 8.8, it was felt in three countries and triggered tsunami warnings throughout the world; entire coastal towns were wiped out by massive waves following the earthquake. Doris and her mom could not evacuate in time, but *Chaudios* protected her: the tsunami did not reach her house. Since the earthquake, she has noticed many changes in the landscape. "The earth lowered, and the ocean rose," she tells me, and she knew then it was time to leave.

Shortly after the 2010 earthquake, she began a legal process to request a plot of rural land, to which she is entitled as a member of an Indigenous group. Her plot will be an hour's drive inland from Nüyü. She reflects on the lengthy and complicated process of requesting land. "If we could . . . ," she begins. She pauses to rethink her words, then resumes:

> In the past, people grabbed their stuff and went to a safer place. Because before, the countryside wasn't measured [parceled out, with established boundaries] like it is now, there weren't people everywhere. [Mapuche] made a good *llellipun* [prayer], and they arrived at a new place and there they stayed . . . They would be owners, as the *wingka* [white people] say. But now you have to count on the authority of the state, otherwise there are no means for living.

The tradition of migration that Doris describes is not unique to Lafkenche. Mobility as a strategy of adaptation to abrupt changes in the environment is a prevalent theme throughout Indigenous philosophies and histories. Colonialism has constrained Indigenous mobility and adaptation. Immobility makes Indigenous people increasingly vulnerable to threats posed by climate change. Yet, despite the many constraints Doris faces, she continually expresses patience for the bureaucratic process and faith in *Chaudios* that things will work out to her benefit.

Mañum: Gratitude

This past year was very difficult for Doris, "I don't know if I drank dog piss this year, but it was a very bad year." She lost her mother to COVID, and her ex-husband died shortly thereafter. To make matters worse, the ocean has been growing increasingly angry. "It can't calm down anymore," she said. The ocean roars closer and louder than ever before; it won't let her sleep at night. "The other night it was thrashing like a volcano *y se me apretó el pecho* [and my chest tightened with fear]."

When I asked her why the ocean is angry, she tells me that it is because people don't acknowledge it properly anymore, they don't show gratitude. "They take from it, but they don't bless it . . . They're dismembering it . . . They want to take and take, like what the Chileans are doing now." Here she is referring to the industrial fisheries operating off the coast of Wallmapu. "They want free money . . . Before, if you wanted to fish, you had to give an offering, but now no one does it." She remarks on the loss of ancestral knowledge: "People say it's another era, but that doesn't mean our knowledge should be lost . . . The ocean is a living being, it also gets hungry."

Doris teaches me that the value of *mañum* (gratitude) should not be underestimated. While unique and place-specific, Indigenous knowledges across the Americas emphasize the interconnectedness of all life. Indigenous peoples have created diverse systems of governance that maintain human accountability to our nonhuman kin within a web of reciprocity. These systems of governance have been interrupted by colonialism in its various iterations. Climate change is a consequence of this "system change," to borrow the term from Donna Haraway (2015): an entanglement of genocide and ecocide, extractivist industries, ecosystem simplification, and burdens of toxins. The return of lands to Indigenous peoples and respect for ancestral knowledges are paramount to untangling our climate crisis and finding our way back into the web of reciprocity.

Fig. 5.4. *The view from Doris's house: the thinning row of pine trees, the encroaching ocean, and the roadside food stand with the Chilean and Mapuche flags.*

When talking about the move to her new home farther inland, she describes in detail the offerings of gratitude she will give. She dreamed that her mother's spirit took her to the new home and introduced her to the spirits that live there. They greeted her and told her they were awaiting her prayers. If she is to have a good life in the new place, she tells me, she needs to enter responsibly, with gratitude and respect for the land and the spirits.

She looks forward to creating a life in her new home, to building a traditional *ruka* (a Mapuche round house) where she can receive visitors. She will raise chickens and have a garden where she can cultivate organic produce and native strawberries. She used to have a garden beside her house in Nüyü. "I had such beautiful flowers, but then the rising tide came and took them all." She points to a place near the shore in front of her current home: "That's where I had my garden." "*Chaudios* washed away my flowers," she laments. "*Chaudios* didn't want me to have a garden here." She aspires to have many flowers in her new garden.

Doris has no regrets about leaving the land her family fought so hard to keep; resettlement will not interrupt her cultural grounding. The environmental philosophers Kyle Whyte, Jared Talley, and Julia Gibson (2019) indicate that Indigenous systems of responsibility and reciprocity are not based on static relationships with the environment; rather, these relationships are constantly changing and transforming. Indigenous migration and relocation, they say, does not preclude the possibility of cultural continuity. In her new home, Doris will build new relationships in accordance with the principles of gratitude, respect, and reciprocity. We are obligated to leave here," Doris says. "All we can do is ask *Chaudios* for *newen* . . . and give a prayer of gratitude when we get there."

Notes

1. The protagonist, Doris Huaiquian, requested that I use her real name.
2. The word "Nüyü," pronounced "nïjï" in Mapudungun, is often written as "nigue" in Spanish because, according to Doris, the Spanish "couldn't learn how to pronounce it properly." The name derives from the bromeliad plant *Greigia sphacelata*, which is endemic to the temperate climates in Chile. It produces a sweet fruit (*chupón* in Spanish) of many uses, and its leaves are used in basketry.

References

Baloy, Natalie J. K. 2011. "'We Can't Feel Our Language': Making Places in the City for Aboriginal Language Revitalization." *American Indian Quarterly* 35 (4): 515–548.

Haraway, Donna. 2015. "Anthropocene, Capitalocene, Plantationocene, Chthulucene: Making Kin." *Environmental Humanities* 6 (1): 159–165.

Instituto Nacional de Estadística (INE). 2018. *Síntesis de resultados Censo 2017*. https://www.ine.gob.cl/docs/default-source/censo-de-poblacion-y-vivienda/publicaciones-y-anuarios/2017/publicación-de-resultados/sintesis-de-resultados-censo2017.pdf?sfvrsn=1b2dfb06_6.

Lagos, Cristian, Felipe P. Arce, and Ver Figueroa. 2017. "The Revitalization of the Mapuche Language as a Space of Ideological Struggle: The Case of Pehuenche Communities in Chile." *Journal of Historical Archeology and Anthropological Sciences* 1 (5): 197–207.

Melín, Miguel, Pablo Mansilla, and Manuela Royo. 2017. "Mapu Chillkantukun zugu: Descolonizando el mapa del Wallmapu, construyendo cartografía cultural en territorio mapuche." Manuscript in the possession of the author.

Richards, Patricia. 2013. *Race and the Chilean Miracle: Neoliberalism, Democracy, and Indigenous Rights*. Pittsburgh, PA: University of Pittsburgh Press.

Vizenor, Gerald R. 1994. *Manifest Manners: Postindian Warriors of Survivance*. Middletown, CT: Wesleyan University Press.

Whyte, Kyle, Jared L. Talley, and Julia D. Gibson. 2019. "Indigenous Mobility Traditions, Colonialism, and the Anthropocene." *Mobilities* 14 (3): 319–335.

Zúñiga, Fernando, and Aldo Olate. 2017. "El estado de la lengua mapuche, diez años después." In *El pueblo mapuche en el siglo XXI*, ed. Isabel Aninat S., Verónica Figueroa H., and Ricardo González T., 345–374. Santiago, Chile: Andros.

Suggested Reading

On Mapuche Culture and History

Cayuqueo, Pedro. 2017. *Historia secreta mapuche 2*. Santiago, Chile: Editorial Catalonia.

Paillal, José M. 2006. "La sociedad mapuche prehispánica: Kimün, arqueología y etnohistoria." In ¡ . . . *Escucha, winka* . . . *! Cuatro ensayos de historia nacional mapuche y un epílogo sobre el futuro*, ed. José Millalén, Pablo Marimán, Sergio Caniuqueo, and Rodrigo Levil, 17–52. Santiago, Chile: LOM Ediciones.

Pairican, Fernando, and Marie Juliette Urrutia. 2021. "The Permanent Rebellion: An Interpretation of Mapuche Uprisings under Chilean Colonialism." *Radical Americas* 6 (1). https://uclpress.scienceopen.com/hosted-document?doi=10.14324/111.444.ra.2021.v6.1.012.

On the Impact of the Timber Industry in Chile

Klubock, Thomas Miller. 2014. *La Frontera: Forests and Ecological Conflict in Chile's Frontier Territory*. Durham, NC: Duke University Press.

Nahuelhual, Laura, Alejandra Carmona, Antonio Lara, Cristian Echeverría, and Mauro E. González. 2012. "Land-Cover Change to Forest Plantations: Proximate Causes and Implications for the Landscape in South-Central Chile." *Landscape and Urban Planning* 107 (1): 12–20.

On Traditional Ecological Knowledge and Indigenous Climate Change Studies

Hernandez, Jessica. 2022. *Fresh Banana Leaves: Healing Indigenous Landscapes through Indigenous Science*. Berkeley, CA: North Atlantic Books.

Johnson, Danielle Emma, Meg Parsons, and Karen Fisher. 2021. "Indigenous Climate Change Adaptation: New Directions for Emerging Scholarship." *Environment and Planning E: Nature and Space* 5 (3): 1541–1578.

Kimmerer, Robin. 2011. "Restoration and Reciprocity: The Contributions of Traditional Ecological Knowledge." In *Human Dimensions of Ecological Restoration*, ed. Dave Egan, Evan E. Hjerpe, and Jesse Abrams, 257–276. Washington, DC: Island Press.

Whyte, Kyle. 2017. "Indigenous Climate Change Studies: Indigenizing Futures, Decolonizing the Anthropocene." *English Language Notes* 55 (1–2): 153–162

CHAPTER 6

Aurelia
DISPLACEMENT, TOXICITY, AND THE STRUGGLE FOR HOME

Maricarmen Hernández

I first met Aurelia[1] in June of 2015. I spent that summer conducting research on environmental injustices in the city of Esmeraldas, Ecuador, where she was a longtime resident of one of the most contaminated neighborhoods in the city. Aurelia lives in the Cooperativa Río Teaone neighborhood, locally known as 50 Casas, and located only a few meters from the largest petrochemical complex in Ecuador. We were introduced by her friend Lety, who was the neighborhood president and who had agreed to meet with me to discuss the issues the community faced from living in a contaminated and marginalized area of the city, and to give me a tour of the area.

As we walked past Aurelia's house, we saw her sitting on her porch in a chair in front of two tubs filled with water. She interrupted her scrubbing, vigorously shook the excess water from her hands, and waved us over with a big smile on her face. As we walked over to Aurelia, she called for her grandson to bring out two plastic chairs for us. A small boy with a scowl on his face appeared in the doorway, struggling to push two stacked chairs through the frame. Lety introduced Aurelia as a longtime resident and original settler of the neighborhood. Aurelia is a small, plump woman in her early sixties. She has a round face and small, sparkling eyes that appear to smile as much as her lips. Aurelia has copper-brown skin with deep creases that etch complex patterns on her face and arms, as a result of her years of walking and working under the unforgiving Esmeraldas sun. She is both Indigenous and Afro-descendant, a common mix in the province of Esmeraldas, which has been recognized as Afro-descendant ancestral lands by the Ecuadorian government.

Aurelia was curious to know what we were up to, and added that doing laundry was always better with company and conversation. Aurelia's house is painted green with pink trim around the windows and door. It is constructed out of cement and cinder blocks that had been painted over, and it has tile floors in some rooms. Aurelia's porch has two levels: the first is higher, closer to the house, and has light-blue floor tiles, while the second level is on lower ground and closer to the street, a simple square of poured concrete facing the unpaved main road of the neighborhood and the bus stop. Both sections of the porch are covered with an extension of the sheet metal roof that covers the house. My first impression was that though Aurelia's house is not the largest in the neighborhood, it is well taken care of and more built up than other homes. It seemed as if Aurelia made an effort to keep a tidy and welcoming house, and, as I later found out, she took much pride in doing so.

I settled into one of the chairs that Aurelia's grandson had set out on the porch, while Lety excused herself, saying that she had to hurry back because her grandkids would be home from school soon. Lety asked Aurelia if she could make sure I boarded the last bus that would take me back to the city center before the routes stopped running, and Aurelia joked that she wouldn't stop me if I decided to stay in 50 Casas instead. She continued scrubbing the clothing floating in the soapy tub in front of her with impressive force. She rotated each piece of cloth consistently with one hand and used a plastic brush to scrub the rotating cloth with her other hand. She completed the task with such ease that weeks later, when confronted with the task of washing my own clothes, I was surprised at how hard it was on my unseasoned hands. I asked Aurelia about the process of doing laundry, and she explained that one tub had soapy water and the other had clean water for rinsing, and she told me that she provided laundry services for people in other neighborhoods and was nearly finished with work for the day. One of her sons had a motorcycle with a plastic crate secured behind the seat, and he would pick up and deliver laundry for Aurelia. This was one of many domestic and restaurant jobs that Aurelia had held throughout her life in Esmeraldas. Aurelia said that as she got older, she had a preference for laundry work, since she could do it at home. I asked if it was hard on her body, and she replied that she was used to it, and it gave her something to do while she sat on her porch "echando bochinche," or gossiping with neighbors.

Aurelia is a great storyteller. She has a flair for detail and a great sense of humor. Over the course of my fieldwork, I had numerous conversations with Aurelia sitting on her porch, and I also conducted four in-depth interviews and a life history interview with her between 2015 and 2021. At that first encounter, she began the first of many stories with laundry, telling me that it was much easier now that piped water had been installed in the neighborhood and the service was somewhat consistent. As in many informal neighborhoods in Latin American cities, running water is either unavailable or inconsistent. According to the United Nations, an estimated 25 percent of the world's urban population live in informal settlements like 50 Casas. These areas are characterized by a lack of tenure security, basic services, and city infrastructure, and the housing structures may not comply with planning and building regulations and are often located in geographically and environmentally compromised areas. As the scholars Brodwyn Fischer, Bryan McCann, and Javier Auyero (2014) describe them, informal neighborhoods are building blocks of Latin American urbanity and are deeply embedded in urban life rather than being unfortunate side effects of urbanization.

Before the arrival of running water in the neighborhood, Aurelia and her neighbors did laundry in the Teaone River, which borders the neighborhood to the northeast. Doing laundry in the river was more difficult and dangerous for a variety of reasons: first, because it meant hauling the clothing to and from the river, and second, because it involved sitting in the shallow river water for hours. Aurelia said that she didn't really mind either of those things when they had first arrived in the neighborhood, about twenty years prior to our conversation, but as the river became more and more contaminated, she began to worry about the dangers of soaking in the water for so long. This was the first time she mentioned the danger of toxicity from the refinery and chemical plant that stood right on the other side of the Teaone River from the neighborhood. She went on: "It has been about ten years since I stopped doing laundry directly in the river; if water didn't come on a day I had to do laundry, I'd send the kids to bring river water in buckets. I don't allow my grandchildren to swim in there either, but you know how kids are, they will do what they want, whether I let them or not."

I asked Aurelia how she found out that the river was contaminated, and she said that the first sign was that the fish started to die. When they first arrived, the river was filled with fish, and the neighbors fished there often, but now there were very few fish left, they were usually small, and everyone knew not to eat them. Then, she said, skin rashes and skin boils became a common problem for women who did laundry and those who swam in the river. She added that the scariest part for her was that urinary tract infections also became an issue, and though she was told at the local clinic that she needed to improve her hygiene, she thought that it really was because she sat in that river water for too long. Aurelia said, "So strange, right? That I did not have those infections before doing laundry in this dirty river, and then they went away when I stopped doing laundry there! Nothing else changed."

Aurelia and other residents I spoke to mentioned that over time, the river water turned brown and murky and that it smelled bad. They became suspicious that the petrochemical complex was dumping contaminated water directly into the river. Over the years, the local newspaper has documented dozens of incidents in which crude oil, gasoline, diesel, and other contaminants leaked directly into the water. These accidents have varied in scope, from minor leaks that occur often to a few major accidents and fires.

Aurelia and her neighbors are residents of a very contaminated area. I asked Aurelia if she believed physicians at the local health clinic when they blamed lack of hygiene and proper nutrition for the residents' health issues, and she was quick to dismiss their claims, saying that one must only spend some time in the neighborhood to know that the smells and sounds coming from the petrochemical complex across the river were not safe to live with. While she lacked the scientific and medical vocabulary to describe exactly how her own and her children's health was impacted by the exposure, she had come to this understanding in a more powerful way: through the embodied experience of dealing with her own and her family's health issues. So why do Aurelia and her neighbors stay there and continue making a home in such a contaminated place?

Aurelia's story is a familiar one in the milieu of the growing Latin American city. It is a story of precarity, hard work, inequality, solidarity, and toxicity. Most importantly, it is the story of a community that as a result of their marginalization, poverty, and racialization is disproportionately exposed to the externalities of an industry that it hardly benefits from. How did they come to inhabit such a toxic space? And why do they strive to continue improving their homes and neighborhood? The answer is etched into personal histories of displacement, surviving multiple disasters, and creating a familiar space that feels safe amid overwhelming risk.

Environmental injustices abound in our world today. Reports presented at the second UN Environmental Assembly indicated that environmental degradation and pollution have resulted in more than one quarter of child deaths under the age of five worldwide. Additionally, the World Health Organization reported that air pollution kills 7 million people across the world each year; 4.3 million of these cases are individuals who are exposed to pollution at home, particularly women and young children in "underdeveloped" countries often living in informal housing conditions. Clean, healthy, and safe living spaces are available to those who can afford to protect themselves and their families from toxicity by minimizing their exposure to contamination. Those who cannot afford a safe space, like Aurelia, her family, and her neighbors, build a home and a community wherever they can. This is their story.

Embodied Experiences of Toxicity

A couple of Aurelia's grandchildren spend most of their time with her, including Luis, who brought the chairs out for us, and who was five years old when we met. Luis was a very serious little boy. When I asked what his name was, he did not answer, but just stared directly at me with a scowl on his face. Aurelia laughed and introduced her grandson, who apparently did not like strangers. Luis was only wearing a pair of shorts, which was the custom for kids in the neighborhood. He was barefoot and was not wearing a shirt. He had sunbaked brown skin, and his legs were speckled with mud from jumping in puddles on the street. He also had a big, reddish bump on his left shin. I asked Aurelia what it was, and she said it was one of those *nacidos*, or boils, that kids in the neighborhood tend to have. She had taken him to the local clinic to see a doctor but was told that all the kids here have them, and that they were a consequence of poor hygiene at home. Aurelia added that she personally thought it had more to do with wading around along the riverbanks, since that water was contaminated, and then laughed, saying, "I suppose it is a lack of cleanliness then . . . cleanliness of the river!" Aurelia then showed me a similar but smaller red bump on her right foot. She explained that it was difficult to keep her grandson from playing in the river, since there were few recreational spaces in the neighborhood and the river was good for cooling off. In her own case, she sometimes had to use water from the river to do laundry, when running water was not available.

As the main caretaker of some of her grandchildren, Aurelia was intimately familiar with their health issues. I asked her what the most common illnesses in the household were. She replied that skin problems and trouble breathing were the most common ailments. She thought for a moment, and explained that sometimes it was trouble breathing and at other times it was cold-like symptoms that she called allergies, especially in her grandchildren. Luis was the most sickly of the family, and Aurelia attributed that to his restlessness and constant wandering off in the neighborhood and the river. This proved true as the years passed, and I saw Luis grow into an even more restless nine-year-old who played soccer every day, eventually developing asthma, and who ran away to swim in the river whenever his grandmother was not looking. Luis also developed splotchy discolorations on his dark brown skin, a very common ailment in young people in the neighborhood. Again, physicians at the local clinic attributed the discoloration to a lack of hygiene at home. Aurelia was also told that he had serious behavioral problems at school, starting fights and not concentrating on schoolwork.

Fig. 6.1. *Neighborhood kids fishing for shrimp in the river.* © 2015 by Donna De Cesare. Used with permission.

I interviewed a few teachers at the local elementary school who claimed that behavioral issues were a big problem among neighborhood children, which they attributed to bad parenting. I also heard from these same teachers that a few years prior to my visit to the neighborhood, a health brigade had visited the school to measure the children's blood lead levels. According to the teachers and school principal, the health workers did not return to the neighborhood to share the results after they took the samples.

The entire city of Esmeraldas is contaminated. It is a case of blatant environmental racism, since Esmeraldas City is the capital of the province of Esmeraldas, which has been formally recognized by the Ecuadorian government as Afro-Ecuadorian ancestral lands. According to the sociologist David Pellow (2007), environmental racism refers to racial minorities and other marginalized communities being disproportionately exposed to environmental contamination. The 2010 census established that the population of Ecuador was 14.4 million, and 7.4 percent of these Ecuadorians self-identified as Afro-descendants. Although there is an Afro-Ecuadorian presence in every province of the country, Esmeraldas is the province with the largest Afro-descendant population, with 44 percent of its population self-identifying as Black. The city of Esmeraldas has a population of approximately 180,000 people, and as of 2001, 40 percent of the population self-identified as Afro-descendant, although due to negative conceptions of Blackness and a complicated process that ties racial self-identification to class, that number is likely higher. In Ecuador, nearly 50 percent of Black families live in poverty, while the national poverty rate for Ecuadorian families is 38 percent. The Esmeraldeño intellectual Juan García (Walsh and García 2015) has described their experience as that of being the "ultimate other" in a previously colonized country that, for better or worse, highlights its Indigenous populations while maintaining political and economic power in the hands of the white and mestizo elite.

Within the localized context of the city, it is those living under informal conditions who are most at risk of toxic exposure because they lack the resources to protect themselves and their families. The case of 50 Casas illuminates an injustice that is often overlooked: the Latin American urban poor are more likely to live in contaminated places and lack the resources to take protective measures than their middle- and upper-middle-class counterparts. This environmental inequality cuts deeply into bodies and marks life chances even before birth. Those who are born and raised in a place like 50 Casas are at a disadvantage that reaches beyond their material dispossession, impacting childhood development and planting the seeds for health issues later in life.

I spent the summer of 2015 visiting several neighborhoods in the south of Esmeraldas, where the petrochemical complex is located, while conducting research on environmental injustices and toxic communities. I heard about 50 Casas from several people in the city who referred to it as the "barrio bajo," which translates to the "lower neighborhood." This descriptor was a reference to both the neighborhood's geographic location on lower ground, thus making it prone to floods, as well as the stigma of being of lower socioeconomic status and associated with criminal activities. What set 50 Casas apart from other neighborhoods around the refinery was that it was the closest in physical proximity to the industrial complex, one of the most informal in terms of the construction of homes and infrastructure, and also one of the poorest and most marginalized within the context of the city. Together, these factors resulted in residents' acute exposure to the heightened levels of toxicity found in the area.

Aurelia and many of her neighbors are the first settlers of the 50 Casas neighborhood. By 2022, the neighborhood had over 2,700 residents and access to some services such as public transportation and electricity, but as I heard numerous times from longtime residents, it was not always like that. This was a self-built informal settlement that had started out with only fifty homes—thus its moniker—and did not have access to services. "This was a jungle" was how Aurelia described it, but after many years of collective struggle, the neighbors had managed to make the place livable, an achievement they took much pride in. On the one hand, they were proud of their trajectory and struggle having led to small victories over time that essentially transformed the place; on the other, they were aware of and openly discussed the toxicity to which they are exposed and its impact on their health.

50 Casas

To get to the neighborhood, Lety instructed me to tell the taxi driver to turn into the first San Rafael entrance, by the María Auxiliadora church, drive all the way in, go down the slope where the road turns left, and drop me off in front of the Vidal Vivero school. I was relieved to find that the taxi driver knew exactly how to follow these vague directions. 50 Casas resembled other informal communities in the south of Esmeraldas, with its dirt roads lined with small, brightly painted homes built close together. Most homes that lined the winding dirt streets had a sheet metal roof and bars on the windows, although a few had been expanded with the addition of a second story. After one o'clock in the afternoon, when children finished their day at school, the neighborhood streets would burst with activity. On any given day, children walked along holding hands with their mothers or older siblings, older children played soccer in the streets, and a variety of street vendors sold items out of carts attached to tricycles. The hot sun usually made the humid air feel thick, and the distinctive smell of the refinery was overwhelming for me at first; I later got used to it. It smelled of exhaust fumes and smoke from a fire, mixed with the odor of sewage and garbage waiting to be collected. The neighborhood lacked a proper drainage system for the streets, which meant that light rains quickly formed puddles that would slowly evaporate. These puddles often lasted days, contributing to the variety of smells and droves of mosquitoes that were part of everyday life in 50 Casas.

The neighborhood main road was unpaved and lined with small stores that operated out of the front windows of homes. The more established storefronts had a variety of fruits and veggies in plastic crates arranged on the sidewalk. Regardless of what was in season, there were always green plantain bunches the size of large tree branches lying on the ground, and yellow banana bunches neatly hanging from the sheet metal roofs. Green plantains and rice are ubiquitous in the diet of any Esmeraldeña family, but they are an especially important staple for more impoverished residents of the city, such as the residents of 50 Casas. These foods are rich in carbohydrates and very cheap; although they are not very nutritious, they are certainly filling. On any typical afternoon, the main road was filled with teenagers speeding by on bikes and loudly greeting each other, children playing soccer or jump rope, and women sitting on their porches in front of water-filled tubs doing laundry or peeling shrimp.

Past the elementary school, the main road sharply curved right and continued on a stretch that cut across the neighborhood and led to a smoking industrial operation. The central point of the scene on the other side of the

Fig. 6.2. *50 Casas neighborhood main road.* © 2015 by Donna De Cesare. Used with permission.

road was a tall, cylindrical smokestack painted white with three red stripes near the top. It spewed a rising cloud of gray smoke. Next to the smokestack was a shorter and less protuberant gas flare, surrounded by a variety of metal structures and cylindrical containers. It looked as though the main road of the neighborhood led directly to the industrial complex, with homes on either side appearing smaller in the distance as they edged closer to the stacks. That stretch of the main road was even more lively than the entrance; it was the heart of the neighborhood. People usually gathered on the street carrying on conversations, and heavy-bass music blared from large box speakers set near windows of homes.

Aurelia's house was near the midsection of the main road, right across the street from the bus stop. From her house, the smokestacks could be seen ominously standing over the neighborhood. Like the neighborhood itself, Aurelia's house was also a work in progress. When we met in 2015, it looked nothing like her descriptions of the house she first moved into, almost twenty years before, when she had first arrived in the area after experiencing displacement and loss. The beginning of Aurelia's search for stable housing and a dignified life stretches back to her rural upbringing, far into the thick Esmeraldas jungle. Aurelia's experiences with housing and displacement after arriving in the city of Esmeraldas illuminate why she is quick to acknowledge that owning a home in 50 Casas is a source of both joy and worry, and why she continues to invest in improving her house despite her awareness of the toxicity in the area.

Building a Home in the City

Aurelia opened our first interview by declaring, "Yo soy Esmeraldeña, pero del campo! De un pueblo adentrísimo de la selva, Piedras Finas, Provincia Esmeraldas" (I am Esmeraldeña, but from the country! From a village all the way in the jungle, Piedras Finas, province of Esmeraldas). She went on to tell me that she had been a twenty-two-year-old mother of four when she moved to Esmeraldas City, the capital of the province of Esmeraldas. Aurelia and her husband were both from Piedras Finas, where they knew each other growing up and married when she was about sixteen, as was the custom in rural Esmeraldas. Aurelia and her then husband decided to migrate to the city because it offered more employment opportunities and a higher-quality education for her children, who were growing fast. "I wanted my children to have more than what I had access to in that small town where there was one teacher for all the kids in town, of all ages! Can you imagine? What are they going to be learning? I learned enough reading and writing to just get by, and I didn't want that for them," said Aurelia in our interview. She hoped that by moving to the city, her children would have the opportunity to at least finish high school, maybe even to go to college.

Aurelia and her family's migration to the capital of Esmeraldas was connected to, and in a way a consequence of, the arrival of the oil industry in the region. Petroleum exploration in Ecuador had begun in the late 1960s, and within a few years, the industry was taking off, and the country needed to build up its petroleum infrastructure. Esmeraldas City was chosen as the host of the country's only refinery, which began operating in 1976, only a few years before Aurelia's family moved to the city in 1979. The decision to build the refining complex in Esmeraldas was political from its inception: both state officials and Esmeraldeñas referred to it as a blessing that would advance the interests of the marginalized Esmeraldeña population, a position that few would take today. The idea was that it would bring jobs and economic prosperity by attracting other industries and putting Esmeraldas on the map as a center of (petro) power.

The refinery was originally built in a remote, uninhabited area in the south of the city, separated from the bustling city center by a large hill. However, in the late 1970s, the word began to spread in rural areas and neighboring provinces that the arrival of the oil industry would bring a huge economic boom and an abundance of jobs to the city. This prompted a migratory flow that lasted through the 1980s and drew thousands of people looking for a better life in Esmeraldas, including Aurelia and her family, who arrived in the city at the peak of the migratory boom. While still in Piedras Finas, Aurelia remembers hearing from friends and family members that a brighter future was coming to Esmeraldas and that they would finally become a place that was important nationally. "We didn't know if it was true or not, because our little town was so far away and small that I don't even remember hearing news or anything like that, it was just what the *comadres* heard and repeated. What we did know was that, little by little, people we knew started moving away to the capital, and that was when we got the idea of moving too, because who wants to be left behind?" said Aurelia. That was how she and her husband decided to make the move with their four children. Upon arrival, Aurelia and her family began their search, along with many other families arriving in the city, for both stable employment and housing, but both proved to be elusive. Aurelia found work in a restaurant kitchen preparing traditional Esmeraldeño dishes such as *encocao de pescado* and *bolones de verde*, a coconut fish stew and fried plantain balls. "At first I really liked the work because I was good at it and I felt useful, like I was getting paid to do the things I just did at home; I also did all sorts of other little jobs, like cleaning houses and providing laundry services," noted Aurelia.

While Aurelia liked working outside the home and utilizing her skills, the work was hard on her body, the hours were long, and the wages were low. Her husband found himself in a similar position: he found work in construction, building roads, and fishing for shrimp in the mangroves. The abundance of well-paid and stable jobs they thought they could find in the capital never fully materialized. They did not find the prosperity they sought working for what they expected to be a burgeoning petrochemical industry, because they did not have the technical skills required for stable, full-time employment in the refinery. Thus, a large sector of the refinery's full-time and well-paid positions went to elite Esmeraldeños who were able to leave the city to pursue training or were brought from larger Ecuadorian cities or abroad. The result was that most working-class Esmeraldeños who worked directly with the industry did so marginally in service positions, such as security guards and cleaning personnel, with even more Esmeraldeños, like Aurelia and her husband, working in the informal labor market created through the service and infrastructure necessities of a newly formed professional class in the city. It was mainly high-class Esmeraldeños who had the opportunity to compete for the better positions and truly benefit from the industry. This continues to be the case today.

Their search for stable housing was even more daunting than that for employment. The migratory flow had contributed to rapid growth in Esmeraldas. The city is wedged between the large Esmeraldas River on one side and the Pacific Ocean on the other, leaving very little room for growth in the two main areas of the city: the center and the beach areas. The new arrivals found an increasingly high cost of living and an overcrowded city center that proved unable to absorb them. Rents in the city began to rise in response to the increased demand for rental housing. Families who had long been established in the city and who owned property benefited from the rapidly growing population, while the new arrivals found themselves competing for small rooms at inflated prices.

Aurelia and her family first rented a single-room apartment in the city center. She recalled that the landlord was abusive and threatened to evict them without notice for being too loud, too dirty, and for having too many children living there. She said she remembered feeling unwanted by her landlord, who looked down on the family for being rural and not being familiar with the ways of the city yet. But more importantly, Aurelia recalled feeling as though she was throwing her money away every month and not really working toward anything that would eventually be her own. She said, "That was when I started thinking, thinking about how I could get a place that was my own, where I could have as many children as I wanted, and we could live in peace without some ugly man coming in here without notice, scolding the children, and demanding that I pay. I was worried that if I or my husband lost our jobs and we could not make ends meet, we would be thrown out; we wanted a place that was just going to be there for us." Aurelia and her husband started saving as much as they could every month and eventually bought the only parcel of land they could afford, high up on a steep hill. They legally bought this lot of land from a man who, prior to the rapid growth of the city, had used it for grazing animals. The land was not meant to be built on because it was steep and unstable, but the provincial authorities were unprepared to manage the burgeoning and haphazard growth, leading to numerous self-built informal communities proliferating on unsafe hills. In a city with limited physical space and an inflated cost of living, city life proved more challenging than many of these migrants had envisioned.

Aurelia and her husband first set up a tent type of shelter, with thick, heavy plastic as a roof, wrapped around wooden boards that served as walls. Eventually they built a wood-and-cane home with a sheet metal roof. The family had lived in that house for almost three years, during which Aurelia gave birth to two more children, when the situation at home began to rapidly deteriorate. Aurelia's husband began to drink frequently, spending a large part of his salary on alcohol, and mistreating his children and wife. When the situation turned violent, Aurelia decided to leave with her six children. First, they stayed with a friend of hers for a couple of weeks, until she found a small room for rent, and it was back to her initial housing situation: spending most of her salary on rent and not working toward anything that could be her own. Aurelia recalled the heartbreak she felt, thinking that she was moving backward, because after having lived in the city for almost four years, she was again stuck paying rent, living in a crowded space, and having few housing options.

The cycle of staying with friends and renting small rooms continued until one day she heard from a neighbor that there was a small plot of land for sale on top of a hill. At the time, she lived in an apartment right at the foot of that hill. She recalled looking up at the steep climb and thinking that it was far from ideal but a good opportunity to start working toward something that she could own by herself. The owner of the land asked for half of the money upfront and half later, which made the purchase even easier for Aurelia. This parcel of land was legally purchased but was not approved for construction. Aurelia remembered that at this point, construction on the hills had taken off, and it looked like a crowded neighborhood, with little houses everywhere.

Aurelia began the process all over again, starting with an *amarradito*, the tent-like structure made with plastic and boards, and cooked outside on a fire pit. She remembered that the land was steep and the ground soft, so she and her two older sons worked every day with picks and shovels to level the land and make it suitable for the construction of a home. While they were working on leveling the land, Aurelia met a priest who worked with an international aid organization, who agreed to secure a donated home for Aurelia and her family. Aurelia recalls her home with a big smile on her face, saying "¡Me quedó graaaaaande mi casita! ¡Bien amplia!" (My little house was quite large! Very spacious!).

Disaster and Displacement

One night in January of 1998, Doña Aurelia was walking home from work amid the heavy rains that characterize winters in Esmeraldas. She worked in a restaurant that was located about ten minutes away from the hill where her house was. She struggled through crashing water to reach her children waiting at home and arrived to find the house flooding. "I kept throwing out bucket after bucket of water that was coming into the house, so I told the children to get ready because we were going to spend the night at my friend's house at the bottom of the hill, right when we hear a loud crash. As I looked out the window, I saw our neighbor's home being torn from its roots," Aurelia said. She and her children spent the night at her friend's house, and at the crack of dawn, she went up to check on her house; she recalled the utter shock she felt when she found nothing left: "The entire hill had slid down in pieces; it looked as though the earth had been put in a blender. Everything was blended together in bits, and the larger parts of the house were completely buried." The years of work and sacrifice that Aurelia had devoted to having her own house were swept away with her house that night.

Aurelia and her children were evacuated into a series of temporary shelters: first one school building, then another, and then a church. "Those shelters for disaster victims are a disgrace; you've probably visited some of them, they're horrible! They put all these families together in classrooms, as if they know each other, and we had to separate our space by hanging up sheets to get some privacy. Of course, those sheets don't keep out the noise, and some people just have bad manners, and I had kids! I didn't want them exposed to the horrible things going on in there, the fights, the dirtiness of it all," said Aurelia. Aurelia and her children were bumped from one shelter to another for three months, until one day they were informed of the possibility of permanent relocation to a place in the south of the city where plots of land and donated homes had been designated for disaster victims who had lost their homes. Aurelia jumped at the idea because after losing everything and having to live in overcrowded and unsanitary shelters, the opportunity to have a home again was one she could not afford to waste.

She recalled visiting the area before accepting the offer and feeling unpleasantly surprised at how undeveloped and inadequate it was. Not only was it engulfed by thick vegetation and lacking basic services and infrastructure, but even more problematic, she thought, was its location in the south of Esmeraldas, in close proximity to the petrochemical complex. At the time, the south of the city was largely uninhabited, and land there was mainly used for agriculture and industrial operations. That was one of the reasons why the refinery had been sited there, away from the general population in the city center. However, increased migration, lack of adequately priced rental units, and lack of space for expansion in the city center prompted a move toward the south.

The south of Esmeraldas has since grown exponentially and is now home to nearly half of the city's population, and it hosts a variety of neighborhoods, from gated communities with mansion-like homes to more middle-class neighborhoods, and, of course, the poorest informal neighborhoods in the city like 50 Casas. The south is the newer part of the city, where there is more space to build. Many neighborhoods in the south were originally settled through land invasions, and their access to basic services and infrastructure varies widely from neighborhood to neighborhood. The south of Esmeraldas is a dynamic and class-diverse area, but within that microcosm, informality and heightened exposure to toxicity from the refinery are a class marker in the city.

The plot of donated land that Aurelia was offered was meters away from the refinery, and the only separation between the two was the Teaone River. She weighed her options and opted to claim her plot of land as a disaster victim. Her idea was to use it as a temporary solution to move out of the shelter and to buy herself some time while she looked for a safer place to raise her family. Aurelia could not have predicted that making the area habitable and building her house would consume much of her time, energy, and resources for years to come, leaving little room to pursue her initial plan of looking for a safer place to live. That was how she and her now adult children came to be founding residents of a very toxic neighborhood.

It is unclear whether the local government of Esmeraldas was unable, due to limited budgets, or unwilling, because of corrupt officials, to have carried out a more organized and efficient relocation process to a safer place. As many Esmeraldeñas have mentioned in conversations and interviews, it is most likely a mix of both.

Part of the deal was that each family would receive a donated palm-and-cane home after they had cleared their own plot of land. The heavy vegetation made the area difficult to access from the main road. From the beginning, the neighbors' experience in the area was plagued by a multiplicity of risks. They had to choose between continuing to live in an inadequate shelter under miserable conditions and accepting the relocation offer, albeit to a toxic place. Aurelia and her family decided on the latter option. The relocation program that Aurelia participated in included fifty donated cane-and-palm homes for fifty families. Every family had to clear their own plot of land to receive a donated cane home from the Ministry of Housing and their *derecho de posesión*, or the document granting them permission to live on the land. This document did not give families legal ownership of the land, but it allowed them to legally occupy it; it also included a path toward obtaining legal titles. Over time, this legalization process broke down and was ultimately unsuccessful—an issue that was still unresolved and continued to be a source of worry for neighborhood residents in 2022.

The ownership history of the land where 50 Casas was established and how it came to be designated for disaster victims is murky. The land that the initial fifty houses were built on was really an exchange between the local government and a private sports association, which had intended to build a soccer training facility there but had found the land to be too marshy and wet and exposed to too much air pollution from the refinery. The local government offered the private association a smaller piece of land, right on the main road, with access to water connections and public transportation and farther away from the refinery, where they later built the training facility. Why the space was deemed unfit for a sports facility but acceptable for displaced families to live on is yet another injustice.

The initial relocation was followed by a series of land invasions that began to settle other parts of the neighborhood. Most families who participated in these land invasions had also been displaced by the landslides and had heard about the relocation process while living in the shelters. They had not formally participated in the relocation program but had heard that there was space available in the area, so they organized and followed suit through land invasions.

Only the area where the initial fifty houses were built was part of the land exchange; the surrounding areas were owned by various large-scale landowners. One of these landowners was the infamous Luis Garrido, who owned most of the land that was settled through invasions following the relocation. The years-long conflict between Garrido and the neighbors over the land is currently locked in a legal battle that has stalled, leaving the neighbors in limbo with regard to the ownership of their homes.

During my fieldwork period, Aurelia was very active in the organizing to obtain legal ownership of the land where her house was built. I asked her why this was important to her, and she responded, "Because I'm an old woman, and what will happen to this house when I die? That paper that says this house is mine is as old as I am, and nobody takes it seriously. I have grandchildren who are growing up fast, and who have never lived anywhere but in this neighborhood; they will also need a place to raise their families. This is the only thing of value that I have to leave to them." Having children and

Fig. 6.3. *Streets in 50 Casas, Ecuador. © 2015 by Donna De Cesare. Used with permission.*

grandchildren inherit homes was the main reason neighbors worried about obtaining legal ownership over their plots of land, but others also mentioned being able to legally sell the houses if they chose to, as well as being able to use them as collateral to obtain bank loans.

"When we first arrived, we immediately got to work, cleaning, cleaning, cleaning, each family their own piece of land. There were at least three different layers of thick weeds to get through! We surely have had to work hard and get past so many barriers to turn the neighborhood into what it is today. We've come so far!" said Aurelia in an interview. The neighbors also carved out the roads in the neighborhood, leveled them, and kept them from becoming overrun by vegetation. They organized to elect a neighborhood president and board of representatives, through which they protested and demanded that the local government provide basic services, public lighting, and a public transportation route. Progress was slow, but eventually and after years of struggle, the neighborhood looked nothing like the jungle to which Aurelia had first moved with her children. One day, while I was complaining that the water supply had been gone for over a week, she asked why I had not stored enough water, noting that I had to learn the ways of the neighborhood, which included always having enough buckets of water for cooking and washing. Aurelia instructed me to keep them covered, or they would get "swimmers." She said that at least now, water was available often enough so that we could fill up our containers, and exclaimed, "You think it's hard now? This is paradise! We have come so far, people should come here on vacation!"

For a rural migrant like Aurelia, it was especially important to own a home, even if it was located in a squatter community with little access to services and infrastructure. She noted that since she didn't have family in the city, she lacked a safety net in the form of relatives she could rely on or ask for help; therefore the most important thing was to have a (physical) place to come back to. Aurelia said that after so much uncertainty and displacement, all she wanted was to pass her old age knowing she had a roof over her head, regardless of her employment situation or a landlord's goodwill. She explained the importance of owning her home: "No matter what happens out there, whether I find someone who will pay me to do their laundry or not, whether my kids can help out or not, and even if I have food in my belly or not, I know that this is my house and I am safe here. Nobody can kick me out, and I can rest my head in peace."

Oil and Environmental Injustices

Ecuador exports 415,000 of the 550,000 barrels of oil per day that it produces, and in 2019, oil revenues accounted for two-fifths of its gross domestic product (GDP). Oil is important for the Ecuadorian economy, and although it has funded massive infrastructure and public works projects, it has also had negative impacts on ecological and human health.

The petrochemical complex has proven to be both at risk of one-time, deadly accidents and the source of ongoing dispersion of toxicity that makes its neighbors sick. There are some reliable, but dated, studies measuring contaminants in Esmeraldas. The most complete of these studies was published by the European Union in 2006. This study found that air quality was very deteriorated in neighborhoods surrounding the refinery, with a concentration of 1,443.2 micrograms of particulate matter pollution over the standard permitted 150 micrograms (Jurado 2006). A medical study conducted in 2004 found a high presence of respiratory ailments, including a 25 percent prevalence of permanent asthma, in a sample of 1,554 students in public schools in neighborhoods surrounding the refinery (Harari 2004).

While official air-quality reports and medical studies measuring morbidity and mortality at the neighborhood level are either unavailable or inaccurate due to the neighborhood's informal status, the experiences of those who live there tell a poignant story of embodied manifestations of living with toxicity. In every interview, I asked children's main caretakers, usually mothers and grandmothers, about the most prevalent health issues in their homes. The most common answer included allergies that caused persistent cold-like symptoms in children, trouble breathing, and skin rashes from swimming in the contaminated river.

Children in the neighborhood spend a lot of time outside of their homes, but even while inside, they are still exposed to contamination. Most homes in 50 Casas are not sealed off from the outside; this is in part because the construction of homes is often a work in progress and because the traditional building method allows for ventilation. Pollution from the refinery easily enters homes, a problem that is intensified by the unpaved roads that produce clouds of dust that encapsulate the area. While living in the area, my own allergies worsened significantly, and I often swept what appeared to be a thin, black soot from the tile floor of my rental room. The neighbors' embodied experiences with illness are evidence of the negative impacts of contamination on their health, and they are especially important given the lack of available up-to-date environmental quality data.

This Is Home

Aurelia has six adult children and "too many grandchildren to count," as she told me, laughing. Four of her adult children live in the 50 Casas neighborhood with their own families, three in their own houses and one in Aurelia's house. Another daughter has been in and out of the neighborhood for a number of years due to her family circumstances. Her two eldest sons moved to Quito in search of work opportunities. As Aurelia replied when I asked about her family structure and housing arrangements, "Oh, these kids and their kids, you know, they come and go depending on what is going on in their lives. But I would say that unless they find work in another city, like my sons did, or they go join a husband, like my daughter, they can usually be found somewhere in the neighborhood, if not right here in my house." Many individuals who were born in the neighborhood or brought there as young children found partners who also grew up in the neighborhood. This means that in many cases, it is not only one part of the family that lives there, but both sides of the family, adding to the familial ties between households. This tendency to find spouses within the neighborhood produces tight community bonds, strengthening the feeling of safety and home, while at the same time decreasing the likelihood that residents raised in 50 Casas will demand or seek a safer location to raise their own families.

Aurelia, like her neighbors, is well aware of the dangers of the area, yet she continues to make improvements to her home and is actively organizing to formalize her ownership of the land. The challenging circumstances under which she and her family moved into the neighborhood after being displaced, followed by her struggle to build a community with her fellow neighbors and her longing for housing stability, have all contributed to her extended residential tenure in the area, even though she had considered the relocation to the area to be a temporary solution. Aurelia's story is not about finding a way to leave but is instead about trying to stay in place. It is also about the complex ways in which being poor, racialized, and displaced lead to disproportionate exposure to not only the stark threats of informal living but also the more diffuse and elusive threat of toxicity.

Aurelia has come to understand her life, her family, and her community as deeply rooted in this physical space. The neighborhood, and more specifically her own house, is the home she worked for many years to build and defend, and they both convey a sense of community and safety. Most importantly, Aurelia's house is her own; it has her history of struggle and survival inscribed in its very foundations.

Aurelia's experience is illustrative of what it means to live in a place like 50 Casas; her home represents the achievements of an ongoing and ever-present struggle. When she finished recounting her life history, Aurelia sat back on the couch and sighed, "Wow, I don't think I had told those stories like that, one after the other! I don't even think I had really spent much time remembering them. I was so busy with the work of just making it through the day, I hardly noticed so many years had gone by and so many things had happened! We really have had to work so hard to have our homes here. Being poor is a lot of work!" ended Aurelia, laughing.

Note

1. Names of people in this chapter are pseudonyms.

References

Ecuambiente S.A. 2001. "Auditoría ambiental integral a la Refinería Estatal de Esmeraldas." Quito: Petroecuador.

Fischer, Brodwyn, Bryan McCann, and Javier Auyero, eds. 2014. *Cities from Scratch: Poverty and Informality in Urban Latin America*. Durham, NC: Duke University Press.

Harari, Raúl. 2004. "Pobreza y otros factores de riesgo para el asma y las sibalancias entre niños afroecuatorianos." In *El ambiente y la salud*, ed. Raúl Harari, 37–53. Quito, Ecuador: FLACSO.

Jurado, Jorge. 2006. "El petróleo como fuente de conflicto ambiental urbano: Esmeraldas bajo la influencia de una refinería." In *Petróleo y desarrollo sostenible en Ecuador*, vol. 3: *Las ganancias y pérdidas*, ed. Guillaume Fontaine, 343–356. Quito: FLACSO Ecuador.

Pellow, David. 2007. *Resisting Global Toxics: Transnational Movements for Environmental Justice*. Cambridge, MA: MIT Press.

United Nations. 2016. Habitat III Issue Papers: Informal Settlements; United

Nations Conference on Housing and Sustainable Urban Development. Quito, Ecuador. https://habitat3.org/wp-content/uploads/Habitat-III-Issue-Paper-22_Informal-Settlements-2.0.pdf.

Walsh, Catherine, and Juan García Salazar. 2015. "Memoria colectiva, escritura y Estado: Prácticas pedagógicas de existencia afroecuatoriana." *Cuadernos de Literatura* 19 (38): 79–98. http://dx.doi.org/10.11144/Javeriana.cl19-38.mcee.

World Health Organization. 2018. "9 Out of 10 People Worldwide Breathe Polluted Air, but More Countries Are Taking Action." News Release. Geneva, Switzerland. https://www.who.int/news-room/detail/02-05-2018-9-out-of-10-people-worldwide-breathe-polluted-air-but-more-countries-are-taking-action.

Suggested Reading

Cepek, Michael L. 2018. *Life in Oil: Cofán Survival in the Petroleum Fields of Amazonia*. Austin: University of Texas Press.

Perry, Keisha-Khan Y. 2013. *Black Women against the Land Grab: The Fight for Racial Justice in Brazil*. Minneapolis: University of Minnesota Press.

Rob, Nixon. 2011. *Slow Violence and the Environmentalism of the Poor*. Cambridge, MA: Harvard University Press.

CHAPTER 7

Hamid

A LIFE DEFERRED IN BRAZIL

Katherine Jensen

On a leisurely Sunday, Hamid and I sit out on an apartment balcony in Rio de Janeiro.[1] There is a slight chill in the air, and it sprinkles lightly and intermittently. We smoke double-apple hookah—his favorite—between sips of coffee as he reflects on the trials and journeys of his life. It has been two years since Hamid obtained asylum in Brazil. "What, if anything," I ask him, "has changed about your life since you were recognized as a refugee?"

He folds one hand in the other, clears his throat, and answers, "Nothing changed . . . Refugee status did not do anything for me," he says. "What I have, I have for myself."

Hamid and I first met at the refugee center in Rio, where I was doing research. He has light-olive skin turned warmer by the Rio sun and thoughtful almond-shaped eyes beneath dark eyebrows. He keeps his hair short and tapered on the sides and a full beard groomed to a long stubble. Over the year, we become friends. We meet up for coffee, go for walks along the beach boardwalk, and snack on fried fish at the mall food court. He teaches me to make *maqluba*, a Palestinian dish of rice, meat, and vegetables cooked in a pot and flipped over. We speak in English, a language he learned in the refugee camp in Syria where he grew up. He shares with me his hopes and dreams for the future and his disappointment at what his life has become.

"In 2013, the war arrived in our city." When the conflict in Syria escalated, Hamid and his family decided he had to flee. He had already lost one brother to the war. "I remember the face of my father, the tears of my mother." Hamid used to believe in the revolution. Filled with hope when the democracy movement began in 2011, he became disillusioned as the uprising was violently repressed and full-scale war arose. Hamid tells me with love and loss in his voice of his brother, a paramedic killed in the struggle for a new

Syria. "He had been the real activist." Hamid feared that if he stayed, his only options were the army or death. His father begged him to leave. Hamid fled to Brazil.

At the age of twenty-six, Hamid became a refugee twice over. Hamid was born and raised in a Palestinian refugee camp in Syria, where his parents and younger sister stayed. Though Syria was the only home he had ever known, Hamid is not a citizen. "I am Palestinian," he affirms. "We are refugees there, too." Hamid was doubly displaced in Brazil.

Hamid came to Brazil because it was the only place he could legally go. He did not want to risk the treacherous uncertain journey over land or sea to Europe. While many countries denied access to Syrian refugees in what the UN Refugee Agency called "the biggest humanitarian emergency of our era," Brazil instituted an open-door policy in 2013, offering asylum to anyone from Syria who would come. Within the year, Syrians went from a nonexistent refugee community in Brazil to its largest.

Though most stories we hear are about refugees fleeing to North America or Europe, 83 percent of the world's refugees reside in the Global South. Colombia, for example, is the second-largest host in the world after Turkey. Brazil has become a major destination for forced migrants in Latin America and beyond. In 2018, Brazil was the sixth-largest recipient of asylum seekers globally.

Hamid's arrival in Brazil troubles the inevitability of restrictions seen in the United States and elsewhere, and points to how much more humane refugee policies look in Latin America. The region is a global vanguard in immigrant rights. Many countries recognize both migration as a human right and the human rights of migrants. As Luisa Feline Freier and Nicolas Parent (2019) write, its laws and policies make "Latin America truly distinctive." Brazil has been lauded as the best place in the world for refugees.

At the same time, Hamid's story pushes us to reconsider what refuge means in Latin America. It exposes the gaps between lofty legislation and the realities of poverty, informality, and inequality. While Brazil grants over 90 percent of refugee status claims overall, asylum comes with little support or opportunity.

We often assume refugees are grateful just to be alive, and that with asylum a new future becomes imaginable. While Hamid is thankful to Brazil for greeting him with open arms, that gratitude is tempered by loss and disappointment. This is not what he expected his life to look like.

For Hamid, the mobility of asylum has been downward. Before the war in Syria, he was attending university to become a dentist. In Rio, he sells food on the streets and lives in a church shelter. While he has carved out a meager but sustainable living, Hamid longs for the sense of purpose he had before he fled. Perpetually precarious and in disrepute as a refugee, Hamid dreams of becoming a citizen. A refugee twice over, citizenship is an experience he has never had.

Though his new life in Brazil has not put him on a path toward the future he hopes for, and he is continually presented with hurdles and roadblocks, Hamid is not resigned to his lot. In the face of aspirations stifled by bureaucracy and rampant inequality in Brazil and a global web of exclusions for refugees like him, in the indeterminate meantime, he navigates an irresolvable situation. He battles to chart a path forward. Maybe in Brazil. Maybe elsewhere.

Making Way in Rio

When Hamid went to the Brazilian consulate in Syria, he sought a tourist visa, not asylum. But the consulate gave him a humanitarian travel visa. Hamid provided his refugee travel document, and the officer told him to go the following month to the Brazilian consulate in Lebanon, two hours away by car. Hamid went to Beirut, got his visa, and a month later flew to Rio de Janeiro. He arrived in Brazil with $800.[2]

"To Brazil, I arrived with great ease." In 2013, Brazil's National Committee for Refugees (CONARE) passed Resolution 17 to facilitate travel from Syria for the purpose of seeking asylum. It removed the usual visa requirements, such as proof of a return ticket. Brazil was the first country in the Americas to offer Syrians humanitarian visas, and it never established a quota limit. By the following year, Syrian asylum claims in Brazil were 290 times those seen in 2011. Until then, Africans, particularly Congolese and Angolans, had predominated among refugees in Brazil. The government explained the policy as recognition of historical and ethnic ties between Brazil and Syria. In the early twentieth century, sizable numbers of Syrian-Lebanese immigrants came to Brazil, as elites sought to whiten that majority Black country. Today, Arabness is a celebrated contribution to the nation. Those from the Levant like Hamid are racialized as white, and Syrian refugees are seen as an economic opportunity rather than a burden.

Before fleeing Syria, Hamid was studying to become an odontologist and specialize in dentures. He has a warm, inviting smile characteristic of someone who has dedicated their life to teeth. Before flying to Brazil, Hamid contacted an odontology lab in Campos, a northern city in the state of Rio de Janeiro. When he arrived, he started working there. He called his family, and when they asked how he was, he said he was good. "But I wasn't good. I worked like a slave." Hamid had not yet applied for asylum, so he did not have the legal right to work, study, or receive other protections. Though he worked long hours, he was unable to save money. What he earned went to phone calls, internet, and rent. He felt isolated and depleted.

Hamid left much behind in Syria, a place where people knew, trusted, and respected him. "When I... decided to travel... I lost something because in my country I knew myself, who I was. Here I don't know who I am." While Hamid was working at the lab, he states: "I was lost, you know? I was lost." He was not organized in his mind, he tells me. Brazil has a different culture, and it made him tired. He tried to be patient and strong, speaking to himself in the mirror.

After a year at the lab, during the holy month of Ramadan, Hamid traveled 150 miles to the mosque in the city of Rio de Janeiro. He stayed in the mosque for ten days. He slept, prayed, and decided he could not to go back. "I decided... this is not good for me, I must study. How can I study, how can I get money?" Though he was working in his profession, the work was grueling and exploitative. It was a dead end. He didn't know what else was possible, but the lab was not the path back to a stable, fulfilling life.

At the mosque, Hamid met a Syrian who told him about the city's refugee center, which assists asylum seekers and refugees. "I was happy [when I heard this] because I just needed a little support, just a... bed to sleep in, not much at all." He went to the refugee center and told the social workers there about his situation. They contacted Father Benicio, a Catholic priest, who offers temporary shelter for refugees at his church. When I met Hamid two years later, he continued to call the church shelter home, living in a sparce but tidy room furnished with a simple twin bed and desk.

A Quick, Ambivalent Path

Now in Rio, Hamid applied for asylum, obtaining the legal rights and protections it afforded. In 1997, Brazil passed the first comprehensive national refugee law in South America, part of a broad trend of human rights–infused legislation following the end of the Brazilian military dictatorship (1964–1985).[3] Its Refugee Act is lauded as a pioneering model for the region and beyond. It provides both asylum seekers and refugees the right to reside, work, and move freely in Brazil, along with equal access to public health, education, and social services. Different from the United States, which gives migrants only one year to apply for asylum, Brazil does not set a time limit, which could have precluded Hamid's claim. And, unlike the United States, there is no policy of detaining or deporting migrants and asylum seekers.

To apply for asylum in Rio, the asylum seeker first goes to the refugee center, run by a civil society organization. At the center, they gave Hamid the application form that covered information about who he was and his history. Eduarda, a social worker there, invited him to eat lunch with her in her cubicle and gave him $130 without his asking. The kindness of a shared meal endeared her to him, and she became his favorite person at the center.

Hamid filed his application at the federal police office and got his asylum seeker protocol. The protocol provided him the right to legally live and work in Brazil while he awaited the decision on his case. At the federal police office, Hamid tells me, "They made everything easy for me." During that time, "I lived my life like a Brazilian."

Normally, an asylum seeker then waits to be called for an interview with an asylum official. In interviews, officials gather information to assess whether the applicant qualifies as a refugee. Cases from Syria, however, have been streamlined and expedited. Hamid's claim went straight for a decision.

Hamid was recognized as a refugee in just four months. Like most asylum seekers from Syria, Hamid had no contact with CONARE as he awaited the decision. His primary contact was the federal police office. Hamid went there whenever he had a change in his contact information, as is recommended. "I like to be legal." Hamid also went to the federal police office more than he had to. Every month or two, he would go to talk to one of the officers, Cecilia, whom he calls his friend. "I liked to talk with her about my life."

Hamid's affinity for the federal police is notable. He is not afraid of them; instead, he regularly seeks them out. He generally sees the treatment there as humane. Not everyone has that experience. When I met Hamid, I was conducting fieldwork to understand the asylum process in Brazil and how refugees experienced it. I worked with asylum seekers from dozens of countries as they navigated their claims. In contrast to Hamid, Black African refugees usually steered clear of the federal police office if they could. Frederic, a Congolese refugee, told me that going there entailed "moments of humiliation" and that the officials "try to make life difficult for refugees."

At the same time, not all of Hamid's visits to the federal police office are positive. After spending the day at the federal police office to renew his residency, Hamid messages me, depleted. "I passed all my life today waiting to get my documents." He sends me two emojis, a downturned face and another upset one. His new residency card would be valid until 2021. After that, an officer told him, he could apply for permanent residency. This was wrong. I inform Hamid that he can apply a year earlier. "It's so crazy. That seems so far in the future, 2020," he tells me, "like science fiction." When I explain that the federal police had misinformed him, Hamid is frustrated but unsure what he can do. "I believe everything is in the hands of God." He continues, "I won't worry now."

Frustrations with Brazil's shifting, arduous bureaucracies are shared by nationals and refugees alike. Its bureaucracies are infamously excessive—an acclaimed 1985 British satire film about an absurdist, Kafkaesque bureaucracy is aptly titled *Brazil*. As Adnan, a Syrian refugee I met at the refugee center, tells me, "their bureaucracy is . . . too much for any small thing, but it's not [just] applied to us because we are refugees, but to every Brazilian [as well] . . . It's general Brazilian culture." At the same time, refugees navigate a legal bureaucratic labyrinth that Brazilians do not.

I asked Hamid if he was ever nervous or worried as he awaited the decision in his asylum case. He was not. "With my protocol in hand, I was working." He didn't pay it much mind. "I just needed a document to give me residence in this country. Not this country, any place, so I can be legal and live my life." Eventually he sent an email to Eduarda at the refugee center, and only then discovered he had been recognized. Though the asylum application gathers contact information, and Hamid had dutifully updated the federal police, Brazil had no system for notifying those who were recognized.

When Hamid found out, he commented that "for me, it was . . . the same." He wasn't hanging on the decision because it changed little about his daily life. He knew when it came it would be positive, and he was already living and working legally in Brazil.

Hamid recognizes how different his experience was from that of other refugees he knows from the shelter. "For me, it was a short time. But for another person, it's a long, nervous time . . . It makes them tired. And I saw that my friends, they cry to get it—more than a year [they waited]." Because of allowances for those from Syria, for Hamid "everything about the *process* has been easy."

Yet, when I ask Hamid if he remembers any particularly positive moment, he does not know how to answer, as he does not think of asylum in such terms. His continued trials in pursuit of what he sees as a dignified life prevent him from characterizing his experience through a positive lens. "I don't remember my feelings," he says. "I don't know."

What is salient, for Hamid, is not asylum. His struggles have not been related to obtaining asylum but to restoring the secure, stable life he had before the war. In the process of becoming a refugee twice over in Brazil,

Hamid lost himself. What he has become does not make him proud. He has been unable to finish university, work in his profession, or secure independent housing. He is without prospects to see his family again or to start his own. While laws impact what is possible for refugees, so, too, does the broader world they navigate. In Brazil, formally inclusive policies combine with a lack of protection from economic precarity and social hierarchies in daily life. And Brazil is one of the most unequal countries in the world.

From Teeth to Falafel

Hamid has always been a refugee, but he did not live in poverty until Brazil. Like many other refugees at the shelter, Hamid learned to "cook a bit" and sell food on the streets to make money. "It was important for me because I needed to buy something for me. I missed many things. I needed more comfort, so I decided to do this work." With his refugee friends Mahmoud and Ahmed, Hamid sold Arab food like *esfiha*, a triangle of baked dough filled with chopped meat, on the sidewalk. Refugees from around the world sell such food because of its immense prevalence and familiarity. In Brazil, Habib, a national fast-food chain that sells Arab food, is second in popularity only to McDonald's.

While Hamid and his friends worked as street vendors without the proper licenses, which are difficult to obtain, "the people believed us because the priest . . . he told everybody, 'This is a refugee from Syria: buy from him, support him.'" With Father Benicio's support, they peddled their food products in the local neighborhood. But there was much competition. "Everyone was looking for a corner to sell on."

With the streets around the church saturated by refugee food vendors, Hamid moved his stand to the neighborhood of the refugee center. "I would bring a box of food that cost me $1.50, and I'd sell it for $3. I made money faster and I had more freedom." Hamid didn't enjoy selling food on the streets, but it provided him more autonomy than the odontology lab. He set his own schedule. Sometimes he went early, sometimes he didn't. When he didn't want to work, he didn't. When he sold, he stayed until he sold everything.

Yet now far from the church and Father Benicio's protection, the military police—a different branch from the federal agency that handles his legal documentation—gave him trouble and sometimes wouldn't allow him to sell. "I am a refugee, please help me," he told the police. "The license is difficult." At the time, Rio was trying to clear the streets of unlicensed vendors ahead of hosting the Summer Olympics. Hamid's friend Mahmoud also began to have problems with the police, and they confiscated Mahmoud's food. But it backfired when his customers quarreled with the police: "Let him work! He escaped from war!" A Brazilian woman who was watching this encounter recorded a video and posted it on social media. According to Hamid, the mayor saw it and got them a license. "They didn't want anyone on the street, they wanted to clean the streets, but they made an exception. I got my license, and I kept on with my work."

In Brazil, street vending is predominantly practiced by people on the poorest rungs of society, providing work for those with few other viable options. Labor informality is rampant in the country, with roughly half of workers informally employed. As the sociologist Jacinto Cuvi (2016, 398) has shown, street vendors in Brazil work in a gray zone where "legal norms are vague and erratically enforced." Whether a street vendor has a license is a crucial line that stratifies peddlers. While those with licenses "sell at fixed spots," in contrast, Cuvi writes, "unlicensed peddlers work 'on the run'—at lonely street corners or in crowded thoroughfares—constantly fleeing law enforcement to avoid the confiscation of their wares." Given the economic realities in Brazil, and despite run-ins with the notoriously repressive military police, for many, street vending feels like their only choice.

Like most refugee street vendors I met in Rio, Hamid had no prior experience preparing or selling food. To learn the recipes of his homeland, he called his mom, who taught him over the phone. Most vendors sold items like *esfiha* and *kibe*, deep-fried beef and bulgur wheat croquettes. Under his mother's tutelage, Hamid started to make falafel and other Arab foods no one else was selling. He cornered a market. Though cooking was a newly acquired skill, he was confident in what he made. "It's easy for me, and I earn." He started making more money and grew his operations. He and his friend Mahmoud rented a space in the city's suburbs to centralize and scale up production. They bought machines and brought in other refugees to work with them. Hamid made the dough. It was exhausting. "We would work all night and sell in the morning. We were selling and selling. It became much bigger than us; it was a company."

Hamid tried to legalize their business. He fretted that their unsanctioned operations could cause trouble with the city and become a "black point in my life here that would be bad for my citizenship." Fearing the growing business could bring problems from the state, Hamid split from Mahmoud. "I am a Palestinian without citizenship, without a passport. The most important thing for me is the passport." While Hamid tells me he left because he worried that any legal action would cost him his chance at citizenship, I wonder if this was the only reason. Regardless, the two stayed friends but went their separate ways. Hamid went back to selling small batches of food on the street, alone. It, too, was hard work. "I work every day. I fight the sun, I fight the rain, I fight the people."

Hamid returned to the refugee center and told the staff he needed money and a new partner. Instead, the journalist at the center posted about Hamid's Arab food on the center's Facebook page, and more customers sought him out. Business picked up, he made more money, and times were good. Hamid even appeared on local television. His work doubled.

Nonetheless, Hamid felt ambivalent about the attention. When he was on television, he didn't like it. Nor did he feel good about the Facebook post. "They used my picture and said, 'Refugee, refugee, refugee' . . . When they used my picture, I didn't like it. When they used my picture, I felt I lost myself."

The refugee center also set him up to sell his food at outdoor fairs throughout the city. At such fairs, foods are prepared by forced migrants from around the world—from Colombia and Venezuela to Syria, Nigeria, and the Congo—each with their own stall adorned with colorful striped overhangs. When the space allows, Hamid hangs a Palestinian flag behind him.

Hamid's specialty is sandwiches with falafel made and fried fresh to order, garnished with marinated red bell peppers, cucumbers, and greens like parsley and lettuce, wrapped in Arabic flatbread. He dresses the part, exuding a clean professionalism. He wears disposable gloves, and often sports a double-breasted white chef's coat with black buttons and a red half-apron tied around his waist.

I visit Hamid at one of these events in a middle-class neighborhood south of downtown, held at a cultural center in a grandly restored colonial mansion from the late eighteenth century. It is a picturesque white two-story building, with striking cobalt blue French doors and windows. Outside, there is a natural swimming pool, lush greenery, and string lights overhead. The space is stunning. Refugees and others sell food in the surrounding grounds.

As Hamid attends people at his booth, he is poised between a kind warmth and a trained focus. I know he doesn't love the work, but he hides it well. He is thoughtful about how he interacts with customers. "You don't treat the person buying as just someone handing you money, but like your mother." He generously feeds me, rejecting my attempts to pay him. Such offerings are one of the few joys that work affords him, along with providing jobs for others. Three refugees from Syria, Togo, and Gambia, respectively, labor alongside him—frying falafel, collecting food tickets, dispensing fruit juice. While Hamid finds little meaning in the work itself, it provides "lots of friends, lots of jokes."

As we chat by his booth, he shares that he had another event the day prior that had gone "so-so," but today's event was going better. On a day like today, he will make $600, he tells me with pride. At the time, the national minimum monthly wage was $250. Even with that day's success, he says, "for me this is temporary. I don't want to work with food, I want to go back to studying." Though these events sometimes bring in good money, they are sporadic. That event was one unusually successful day, and he continues to sell on the street. Sometimes the work is good, sometimes it isn't. It still is not his passion. "I don't believe in this work. I don't like this work, but I work." Working in food provides freedoms and possibilities that the lab did not. He decides what he makes and when he sells, and he earns enough to save for his goals. But it is an ambivalent experience; it makes him feel like the agent of his own life and reminds him how much he is not. He sells food, but he wants to be—should have already become—an odontologist.

On the streets, Hamid's woes continue, and his problems with the police, who are infamous for misconduct and corruption, return. The Rio military police have been called the most violent in the world.[4] They hassle him and ask for bribes, making it sometimes difficult for him to sell. And they are not the only ones. The shopping mall security guards also demand a weekly bribe. Street vendors operate largely at the behest of the variable whims of local authorities—self-restraint and benevolence, or abuse and profiteering. As with other peddlers, Hamid has to pay bribes if he wants to sell on the street. "I think everything is done with money here." Hamid bemoans this exploitation and his impotence in the face of it. We "don't know our rights [here]." He told a lawyer at the refugee center about the shakedowns, and "he took down my information I think, but I don't know." Nothing happened. Hamid didn't know what legal recourse he had, and the uncertainty made him worry about pressing the issue. "I don't know what will happen. Maybe if I make trouble, one day I will go to prison. And who will get me out of prison?"

Hamid is embarrassed by what he has become. "I am here in the street selling food—I studied, and now I am on the sidewalk." Selling falafel on the street "makes me shy because I am a doctor in my country." Though he had yet to become a dentist in Syria, that was the path he had charted for his life before displacement. Declaring himself to be what he has yet to become, Hamid reclaims in the present his future forestalled, seeking recognition that before he became nobody, he was someone who mattered. He doesn't tell his family or friends abroad what his life looks like, but he tries to tell himself that he is still happy. He finds solace in the fact that his work provides him more comforts than he knew at the lab, and that he feels it brings him closer to achieving his goals. Though his heart is not in food, Hamid talks about opening a small shop to sell Arab lunches to fund his studies. Since "nobody sells this food in Rio de Janeiro," instead selling snacks, business would be good. That work is important only to the extent it gets him back to university so he can be the dentist he planned to become. "I need to study." Rather than a passion for teeth, per se—he never talked about teeth—he longs to be someone with a profession.

With Father Benicio's encouragement, Hamid started using his earnings to pay for courses in Portuguese. Though the refugee center offers free lessons, when I ask Hamid if he takes them, he looks me in the eye and laughs. At the center, he says, "one day, you learn *ser* and *estar*, two verbs, right? But then a new person comes, and a new person comes, and another, and you spend four days learning the same thing." If you want to learn Portuguese, you have to pay.

Hamid had been studying Portuguese for three years, but he was far more comfortable in English. While we talk in English, he sprinkles in Portuguese words. When Hamid tells me, "I need to learn Portuguese like a Brazilian," it is not mastering Portuguese that matters. It is what that provides for: finishing his dentistry degree. "My problem is that I don't have documents, lots of documents . . . There's a lot of bureaucracy. If you don't have them, you have to take the *vestibular*." Over 90 percent of refugees have been unable to validate their diplomas and resume their studies in Brazil. To do so, they need documents most can't get. This also makes it difficult for refugees to work in their professions; 68 percent do not. To enroll, Hamid must pass the *vestibular*, a competitive college entrance exam—the same one Brazilians take—in Portuguese. Nor is higher education readily accessible for nationals. Only 18 percent of Brazilian adults have college degrees.[5] For refugees, their struggles to authenticate schooling they already have stifles them and sends them into downward socioeconomic mobility.

Unable to continue university, Hamid is uncertain about having left Syria. He frets over whether he should return, if he has lost his profession for good. He doesn't know who chose wisest: those who stayed or those who left. "I don't know if they are right or if I am right."

In some ways, Hamid is grateful to Brazil. "Brazil gives us peace." But rights came with little opportunity. While he appreciates what Brazil did for him, it is deeply unsatisfactory to the extent that it feels insignificant. "The government doesn't help," he says. "I depend on myself here in Brazil."

Though the government eased his path to Brazil and fast-tracked his asylum application, it is not all he needs to get his life back on its track. "I am fighting in life."

Hamid's perspective—that what he received has not changed his life enough to be seen as help at all—pushes us to consider what we believe refugees are entitled to, what they believe they deserve, and when and why they should be grateful. He needs more support to have the life he wants, and he believes such a world is possible. Living without fear of deportation is not enough to make a fulfilling life.

Many Syrian refugees I met thought things in Brazil would be different. They did not imagine the government would readily invite them to immigrate but then have no infrastructure to support them upon arrival. This disparity was disillusioning. Because of this, Hamid feels, whether he has asylum or not, "it's the same." The dearth of assistance coupled with bureaucratic labyrinths and social hierarchies—to resume university, find formal employment, start a business, obtain independent housing, learn Portuguese—means refugee status makes little difference to him.

Maybe Elsewhere

A conflict exists between the ease of Hamid's arrival and his struggles in Brazil. Hamid does not experience his legal status in isolation. His life is shaped by the broader realities in which his attempts to build a place in the world unfold. "There is a tension," noted Lucas, a lawyer at the refugee center, "between the policies for refugees and the realities of poverty in Rio." Despite its lauded policies, Brazil is far from an idyllic safe haven. Asylum did not get Hamid out of labor informality or into university and secure housing. That it did not—given the work precarity, social inequality, low education levels, informal housing, excessive bureaucracies, and poor public services seen in Brazil broadly—is not surprising. While life is hard for him, Hamid knows "it's hard for Brazilians also."

Hamid was disinclined to stay. Because he had none of what he aspires to in Brazil—a wife and children, a degree and career—"I didn't have anything to lose." Disenchanted, he planned other ways out of what his life had become.

After he obtained asylum, Hamid threw away his Syrian travel document. He hated what it stood for, and it offered him little. Though he tells people he misplaced it, the pain of all he lost drove him to cut that tie. "I don't need anything from the government of Assad." Hamid needs documents and yet wants to be free of them, as they both broaden and restrict his life chances. Throwing it away was a way to have a say in his own life. And, because it was a refugee travel document, not a national passport, it did not provide what he wanted: passage elsewhere.

Hamid hoped that by no longer having his Syrian travel document he could obtain a Brazilian passport. "I need a passport from Brazil so I can travel to another country." But refugees do not obtain a Brazilian passport. They instead apply for the yellow passport, a single-use international travel document. Many countries flatly deny entry to those who carry it. To obtain one, refugees request travel authorization from CONARE, detailing the destination and dates, reason for traveling, and contact information while "away from this home."

Hamid knew if he said he was going back to Syria, he would lose his refugee status. Voluntary return suggests a refugee no longer fears for their safety and ceases to need international protection.[6] So, Hamid said he was going to Lebanon for religious reasons. He paid the $85 yellow passport fee and got it. "When they gave me the passport, I thought that was my freedom."

He bought a ticket for Lebanon, but with a British airline so he would connect through Heathrow Airport in London, where his cousin Hassan lives. He made a plan: Upon arriving at Heathrow, he would throw away his yellow passport and wait until his plane departed. He'd then go to the police and say, "I'm from Syria." Hamid is pulled between the situations when having—and not having—documents might open up the world he seeks. But, to fly to Lebanon via London, he had to get a UK transit visa. The transit visa application "made me tired because I had to prepare more documents. I prepared more things, *just for transit*—and just for transit inside the airport, not outside." He paid roughly $650 for the transit visa, more than seven times what the yellow passport cost.

Hamid prepared his documents, paid the fee, and went to the British consulate for his interview. Though Brazil did not interview him to determine if he was a refugee, a British official interviewed him to decide if he could pass through a British airport. During the interview, "they took all the things about me. They took my fingerprints, scanned my eyes, photographed me. They took my everything, all the information about me." He began to worry that because of the information the consulate gathered, officials at Heathrow would know he had come from Brazil and not accept him as an asylum seeker. He called his cousin, and Hassan tried to calm him. "No problem," Hassan said. "When you get here, I'll get you a lawyer." "All my life then was up in the air, in this transit visa."

Two weeks after the interview, Hamid got an email. "You are denied."

He was devastated. "That time was hard for me. All my body was red. I was sick. I don't need anything from life. I just need to get to one place," he laments. "I need power. I need power for me."

I hate all airports in the world, because we are disrespected in airports. We can't travel where we need to go. When we travel anywhere, we don't see that place, if it's beautiful or not. Because you have more things on your mind, you don't see. You're not traveling for travel; you are traveling for your life. You are looking for something . . . and when you are looking for something, you miss everything around you.

Being denied freedom of movement has marked Hamid's life. Although he is Palestinian, he has never been there. Hamid and his family form part of one of the largest refugee communities in the world. Over seven million Palestinians are denied the right to return to their ancestral homelands, having been forcibly displaced by the founding and ongoing expansion of the state of Israel since 1947. Hamid has never been a member of a nation-state; instead, he belongs to a nation without a state. He yearns for a national passport because he wants citizenship and the rights that it affords.

"I did all of this. I got a passport, I did this and this and that, and it didn't happen." Hamid was confronted with the dark realization that a "passport equals freedom" and a "passport does not equal refugee." He continues: "The refugee does not have the right to a nationality." Hamid believes that only once he becomes a citizen will things start to change. Asylum in Brazil is an insecure steppingstone on the way to a stable future deferred.

His plan thwarted, Hamid imagined other possible futures. "I decided my life was not finished. I had to stay in Brazil and make money to try another way." Hamid threw himself back into his work and searched for a different hope somewhere else. He saw others going to the United States and Canada, and he started to plan with Mahmoud. "Every day we planned . . . I decided to forget my family, to forget Syria, to forget everything. I needed to think about my life, and we needed to figure out how to get to America." Mahmoud knew an immigrant, from Somalia or Serbia, Hamid doesn't remember, in São Paulo who would take them. "They told us, 'You need $3,000, the road is dangerous and depends on you. Maybe the police [will] catch you.'"

"They told me, 'You are a white person, it's harder for you. Because there're mafia in the streets. From Black people, they don't expect money. From you, they expect money.'" But Hamid was undeterred. "I didn't have anything to lose. This is my life, to be or not to be. So, I decided to go anyway."

He and Mahmoud continued preparing, working to save the funds to make the trip north.

Hamid's story of liminal limbo and displacement, struggling to decide whether to stay or chart a new path elsewhere, is shared by many in Latin America. Given precarity, violence, and displacement in the region, others likewise consider the risky journey. Over the last decade, migrants transiting through Latin America, with hopes of arriving in the United States, have come not only from Central America and Venezuela but also in growing numbers from Africa and Asia. Given their lenient visa policies, countries like Brazil and Ecuador have become an access point to the hemisphere in a long, treacherous path to the United States.

While many continue north, others like Hamid—confronted with the grave uncertainty of fluctuating visions of unknown futures—decide to remain indefinitely. Hamid changed his mind and resolved not to go. "Some other voice came to my mind and said to me, 'No, no, no.'" He considered going back to Syria. "I like how people live there." Beyond longing for his culture, he worries about his family, what will happen to Syria and to those who remained. He is anxious when the power goes out in his family's refugee camp, and he has no news from his mother. He feels alone, missing his loved ones in Syria. By the time I come to know Hamid, though, he is no longer seriously engaging the idea. "I believe everything is from God. Every day the sun is shining."

More often, Hamid charts a path that keeps him in Brazil, at least until he becomes a citizen. "Maybe now my goal is to continue here; I am good at Portuguese now, and I invest in myself," he tells me. "I like Brazil; I like Brazilians because they support us, they like us, they like Arab people more. And they said to us, 'Always welcome.' I think this supports us here. And I like these things." Despite his difficulties, frustrations, and unsettledness, if he stays and waits, Brazil offers him citizenship and a passport—rights he has found nowhere else. "Maybe I am here now," and after a few more years, "I can become a citizen. This is hard in another country. When I get citizenship, I can decide what to do." Maybe, once he becomes a citizen, he will use his Brazilian passport as his ticket to finally make it to Europe. He also daydreams of a future when, by that time, he'll no longer want to leave.

His mind never truly settles. Hamid is not sure he wants to stay in Brazil, as his life remains precarious. But he does not know where he could go. He has thus far failed in his attempts to find somewhere else to make a life for himself. Never finding a resolution that brings him peace, Hamid frequently changes his thoughts on his future. Often when I see him, he shares his latest concocted plan of how to make it to Europe or North America. He dreams of traveling to Germany, where his older brother and three-year-old niece live. He has never met her. Refugees have the right to family reunification, but under German law, siblings aren't eligible. Or maybe he will get a ticket to Canada and flush his identity documents on the plane. They would have to let me stay, he says, because they would not know who I am. Maybe he will travel north by foot to the United States. There are smugglers who would take him. As we smoke hookah one evening, Hamid discusses his latest plan: get a fake Brazilian passport and use his Portuguese to pass as Brazilian. Maybe he'll go to Argentina and then take "a plane from there to, I don't know, any country." Though he may seem erratic about the future, to see him as fickle would miss the immense weight of the global web of immigrant exclusions that encloses him. Refugees' struggle to seek "forward momentum in contexts of suspended temporality," as the anthropologist Georgina Ramsay (2017, 520) notes, must also be seen as "a political act."

Helping Others to Not Feel Helpless

Hamid wishes there were more help and that he didn't need it. As the political philosopher Hannah Arendt (2008, 114) wrote, based on her firsthand experience as a refugee: "If we are saved we feel humiliated, and if we are helped we feel degraded. We fight like madmen for private existences with individual destinies."

Hamid holds in his heart stories in which he and his people were the helpers, not the helped. At a World Refugee Day event, he speaks with pride as he recounts for the audience about when Syria took in refugees rather than produced them. In the twentieth century, Syria sheltered refugees from Europe, Kuwait, Palestine, Iraq, and beyond. He notes that Aleppo took in six thousand Armenians in 1943 alone. In the 1990s, "Lebanese stayed in my house." Hamid believes in humanity as a shared, familial community. "God made many cultures, many languages, many different types of people so they would know each other and help each other." Yet now this reception is rarely reciprocated. "It is not easy for Syrians to get to Europe."

Hamid dreams of giving back and paying it forward. From his earnings, he hopes to donate to refugees through the refugee center, "something for babies, clothes, anything. I hope I can support them in the future, that's important for me." When he becomes a professional, as he puts it, he also wants to give back to those who support refugees. If he has a house someday, he wants to have over for dinner those who have helped him, like Father Benicio, whom he sees as his best friend in Brazil, and Eduarda, the social worker at the center, so "I can give them what they gave me." He also wants a home of his own to serve as a refugee shelter "to help the rest." In the meantime, he supports as he can, employing other refugees, offering advice as they pursue their own asylum claims, and advocating on their behalf. He messages me about others' cases: "Do not forget them."

His plans recurrently forestalled and thwarted, Hamid finds strength as he can. Above all, he finds it in his Muslim faith. With his earnings as a street vendor, he pays for a gym membership, and invests significant time and energy in strengthening his body. He finds respite in the control and power that physical improvement and athletic prowess provide. And he loses himself in music to soften the stifling edges of his new life. He tells me he listens to one song a week on repeat, playing it while he sleeps. When he listens to music, he says, "I am flying." Music provides Hamid the escape and solace he has yet to find, and a stable constant in a world of uncertainty. It is not Brazilian music that he listens to. He listens to the songs of his homeland and becomes enamored with a song I introduce him to: "A Candle's Fire" by Beirut. *Just don't forget, a candle's fire is only just a flame.*

While the future Hamid dreams of remains out of reach because of forces outside his control, he labors to make it happen somewhere, anywhere. His aspirations for a different, more fulfilling life remain deferred but intact. "As long as I have legs, I will continue."

Notes

1. All persons' names are pseudonyms.
2. Monetary amounts have been converted from Brazilian currency to US dollars based on the contemporaneous exchange rate.
3. Its refugee definition is also more expansive than that seen internationally. While the 1997 Refugee Act includes the UN refugee definition based on a well-founded fear of individual persecution, it also, in the spirit of the regional 1984 Cartagena Declaration, recognizes as refugees those fleeing severe and generalized human rights violations.
4. For more on the violence of the Brazilian carceral state, see Alison Coffey's chapter in this volume.
5. This is lower than other countries in the region, like Argentina (36 percent) and Colombia (23 percent).
6. This is embedded in the cessation clauses of the UN 1951 Refugee Convention.

References

Arendt, Hannah. (1943) 2008. "We Refugees." In *The Jewish Writings*, ed. Jerome Kohn and Ron H. Feldman, 264–274. New York: Schocken Books.

Cuvi, Jacinto. 2016. "The Politics of Field Destruction and the Survival of São Paulo's Street Vendors." *Social Problems* 63 (3): 395–412.

Freier, Luisa Feline, and Nicolas Parent. 2019. "The Regional Response to the Venezuelan Exodus." *Current History* 18 (805): 56–61.

Karam, John Tofik. 2007. *Another Arabesque: Syrian-Lebanese Ethnicity in Neoliberal Brazil*. Philadelphia: Temple University Press.

OECD. 2019. "Education at a Glance: OECD Indicators—Brazil." https://www.oecd.org/education/education-at-a-glance/EAG2019_CN_BRA.pdf.

Ramsay, Georgina. 2017. "Incommensurable Futures and Displaced Lives: Sovereignty as Control over Time." *Public Culture* 29 (3): 515–538.

Suggested Reading

Acosta Arcarazo, Diego, and Luisa Feline Freier. 2018. "Turning the Immigration Policy Paradox Upside Down? Populist Liberalism and Discursive Gaps in South America." *International Migration Review* 49 (3): 659–696.

Fischer, Brodwyn. 2008. *A Poverty of Rights: Citizenship and Inequality in Twentieth-Century Rio de Janeiro*. Stanford, CA: Stanford University Press.

FitzGerald, David Scott, and David Cook-Martín. 2014. *Culling the Masses: The Democratic Origins of Racist Immigration Policy in the Americas*. Cambridge, MA: Harvard University Press.

Holston, James. 2009. *Insurgent Citizenship: Disjunctions of Democracy and Modernity in Brazil*. Princeton, NJ: Princeton University Press.

Jensen, Katherine. 2021. "Contexts of Reception Seen and Constituted from Below: The Production of Refugee Status Apathy." *Qualitative Sociology* 44 (3) :455–471.

Oliveira, Márcio de. 2019. "Perfil Socioeconômico dos Refugiados no Brasil." https://www.acnur.org/portugues/wp-content/uploads/2019/07/Pesquisa-Perfil-Socioecon%C3%B4mico-Refugiados-ACNUR.pdf.

Radio Ambulante. 2019. "Exodus." https://radioambulante.org/en/audio-en/exodus.

Yates, Caitlyn. 2019. "As More Migrants from Africa and Asia Arrive in Latin America, Governments Seek Orderly and Controlled Pathways." Migration Policy Institute. https://www.migrationpolicy.org/article/extracontinental-migrants-latin-america.

Zanforlin, Sofia Cavalcanti, and Denise Maria Cogo. 2019. "Mídia, mobilidade e cidadania no contexto do capitalismo global: Reflexões a partir da trajetória de um refugiado sírio." *Contemporanea|Revista de Comunicação e Cultura* 17 (1): 7–28.

CHAPTER 8

María

OBLIGATED BY CIRCUMSTANCES—FROM TEMPORARY TO PRECARIOUSLY PERMANENT IN THE UNITED STATES

Jennifer Scott

María[1] is a caregiver—in the fiercest sense of that word. Every time I visit her apartment, she ensures I (and often the upstairs neighbor and her daughter) have a meal, coffee, and cookies, regardless of whether I am hungry. The oldest of eighteen siblings and the mother of four—all now adults with their own families—María came to Louisiana from her home in Sinaloa, Mexico, to work seasonally in the crawfish industry. At slightly over five feet tall, María's presence couples a lightness with a protective energy that lets one know that those she counts as family she will defend with everything in her power. With naturally loosely curled hair and perfectly manicured fingernails, though a stocky rather than a fragile frame, María is often told that she "doesn't have the face of a worker."

Born quite literally during a flood in the late 1950s, María simultaneously was swept into and charted a course for her life that took her from a village of about one hundred people at the edge of a small town in Sinaloa, to Baton Rouge, Louisiana, where we met just over fifty years later. Although María was new to the seafood industry and the United States when she arrived, the region had long-established connections to both via trade routes begun generations prior to her birth. By 1915, nearby Los Mochis was annually exporting a high volume of food products to the United States, about 1 percent of which was shrimp from the port of Topolobampo.[2] Over the several years of our friendship, since first meeting over lunch with a mutual friend in Baton Rouge, I have learned how María has navigated family circumstances that demanded her life take a different course. Neither typical nor unique, María funneled obligation into desire, making the most of precarious jobs to build a different life for herself.

The White House

The day I met her, María had her belongings packed in preparation to move out of the Casa Blanca (White House). She had been living in the house, an unassuming structure located on a busy street north of Florida Boulevard and near downtown Baton Rouge, for most of the previous ten years. The first few years, María stayed several months before returning to Mexico. After the first seven seasons, however, she stopped returning. Owned by her employer, the Casa Blanca provided lodging for the immigrants like herself who worked next door at his seafood processing plant. Although seafood production is an integral part of the regional economy, the industries more frequently referenced—oil and petrochemical—are apparent miles before crossing the river from the west to reach the city. Refineries located in North Baton Rouge, visible from the Casa Blanca and downtown, mark the northern edge of a 100-mile area that public health scholars and community advocates refer to as "Cancer Alley."[3]

With a sentiment akin to nostalgia, María told me, "When I arrived at the house, I couldn't believe what house I had arrived at. From the entrance to the door—the house had been abandoned for like four months—spiders, rats, cockroaches—it smelled like you have no idea . . . This was the Casa Blanca . . . From the outside it looked pretty and everything. Inside, it was crazy."

María was the last worker to live in the Casa Blanca, her departure due to its being vacated permanently. It was only a few hours after we first met, however, that I first visited the house. I was picking her up for a community meeting at which I would serve as her interpreter. When we returned to the house, she invited me inside for a tour.

Walking into the front room, I was immediately struck by the dark, enclosed feeling of the space. María had piled her things on one of the room's several beds. Using our phones for flashlights (the electricity had been turned off days prior), we walked into the kitchen, where two stoves stood in close proximity. María told me that despite having two ranges, it was nearly impossible to cook regularly—their placement positioned two people cooking simultaneously literally shoulder-to-shoulder. The kitchen led to the back, where I saw a bathroom with an institution-style set of showers, and a series of four bedrooms filled with bunk beds. The first three held four bunks apiece (twenty-four beds), and the large room held six (twelve beds). In addition to the thirty-six beds in the back, the front held another twelve, six in the living room where I entered and another six in the former dining room. At the $50 per week her employer charged per bed, the house could bring in as much as $2,400 in weekly rent when all forty-eight beds were full.

Baton Rouge sits on the east bank of the Mississippi River, seventy miles north of where it meets the Gulf of Mexico at the port city of New Orleans. Transportation of goods and enslaved people on the river generated much of the region's early wealth before oil and petrochemicals.[4] Incorporated in 1817, the city became Louisiana's capital first in 1849, then continuously since 1882. Remnants of colonialism and the enslavement of people forced to labor in sugar, among other tasks, remain visible. Translated "red stick" in French, Baton Rouge is said to have been given the name around 1699 by early French explorers who noticed a reddened cypress pole now thought to mark hunting ground boundaries for the Houma and Bayougoula peoples, two of several First Nations in the area.[5] Many occupations and the city's neighborhoods are still largely segregated by skin color. Ask anyone to name an informal boundary, and they will name Florida Boulevard. A four- to six-lane street spanning the city's length west–east and connecting it to neighboring towns, it separates the predominantly Black northern half, home to the Casa Blanca, from its predominantly white southern half.

On her first night in the Casa Blanca, María recalled, "No one received us; we arrived at midnight to clean rooms, bathrooms, make beds, it was a disaster the house." On top of this, her friend Griselda who recruited her gave her bad advice. To this day, María can't figure out why she told her not to bring much on the trip. Despite Griselda's assurance that she would get everything she needed there, upon arrival, María discovered she didn't even have a sheet for sleeping on the bald couch. The poorly insulated house, she said, "felt like a refrigerator." Unfamiliar with everything, that first night María "put [her]self in a black garbage bag to sleep." The next morning, she borrowed a couple of dollars to spend at the secondhand store nearby. The shopkeeper allowed her to fill a bag with anything she needed for $2; she filled it with blankets. That first night was so miserable that María resolved to "never let anyone go through what I did."

The Precarity of Peeling Crawfish

"My gift has always been obedience, I've always been obedient in jobs," María explained when I asked how she had endured peeling crawfish for the same employer for more than a decade. "I'm obedient because I don't like when things go bad—when they complain, when they yell at me."

Fig. 8.1. *Peeling crawfish at the processing plant.*

After that first night, María said she was ready "to go ahead and go to work because the house grossed me out, but when I got there, it wasn't crab, it was crawfish." Before leaving Mexico, she enlisted a friend who worked in crab processing to "more or less give me an idea of what I would be doing." She learned the basics, despite her initial aversion and her refusal to quit doing her nails (I've never seen her without a proper manicure). Struggling with technique, it "gave her a headache" to think about how many *animalitos* (little animals) she would have to peel for 10 kilos of meat. When she arrived in Louisiana that April, she was unpleasantly surprised to learn she would not be peeling crab after all.

"I didn't know how to clean crawfish," she said, asking herself, "Why did I come here?" In fact, María admitted, she didn't know what a crawfish was before that first day. She struggled to learn, breaking shells awkwardly when extracting the meat. The only feedback offered was that she was doing it wrong. According to María, most of the workers, all immigrants, came from fishing communities with experience peeling shrimp. Although not quite the same, if you can peel shrimp effectively, you understand the basics of peeling crawfish. María herself grew up in a coastal fishing community that exported shrimp, but she was not skilled at peeling them.

Peeling crawfish efficiently is something in which those from South Louisiana take pride. A traditional food in Cajun and Creole culture, crawfish have transitioned culinarily from consumption primarily by poorer households to a food of choice. They are served at crawfish boils—outdoor parties where they are boiled live in a large pot with potatoes, corn, and

Cajun seasoning—throughout spring and early summer. Crawfish can also be found in staple dishes of fine dining restaurants offering Cajun cuisine in cities like Washington, DC, and abroad. To peel the small crustacean, professionals use two swift motions: first, twisting the head off in a downward motion to expose the meat; second, pressing the tail while pulling the meat from the shell in one piece. A quick swipe across the tail meat removes the central vein, rendering it ready to be eaten.

In processing plants like the one where María worked, the faster a worker completes these motions, the more pounds of meat they individually process, and the more money they earn. All live crawfish that arrived in the morning were processed before the end of the shift. After they are caught, live crawfish are first graded, meaning measured, by a metal machine—falling off a conveyor through slots according to size. Large crawfish are sold live. The smallest, the "peelers," are processed for tail meat. After they are boiled and loaded into large crates, the peelers are taken for processing. In the plant where María works, this takes place in a large interior room with no windows. The room's concrete floor and minimal stainless-steel furnishings make it clear that cleaning efficiently with a water hose is a priority.

I went with María to work once, donning a thin plastic apron, bonnet, and gloves to stand beside her as crawfish were poured onto the long metal tables. We worked alongside two women from Sinaloa and the son of one, who was on high school summer vacation. At the end of our table worked another two women, from San Luis and Vietnam. Behind us, two older women and a man, all from Vietnam, shared a table. To our right, working alone, was a woman from China whose incredibly fast technique produced over 100 pounds a day. María told me the woman replied, "I keep my family who are starving in my mind" when she asked her how she peeled so fast.

The older man dumped crawfish from the crates onto the tables in front of each group. Each worker peeled meat into their own metal dish until slightly overfull, 5 to 7 pounds of meat, before passing the bowl to workers in the adjoining room for weighing and packaging. Heads and shells accumulated until pushed into large garbage cans stationed underneath openings in the tables. The work flowed: once full, a garbage can was removed and replaced empty; once a pile diminished, crawfish were poured from a full crate in front of workers who continued peeling. The weighing and packaging team recorded the amount produced by each worker. Despite the constant activity, the space felt cavernous and underutilized. It was apparent that at the time of my visit the company was in decline.

María recalled her first season at the plant. The Casa Blanca was full, and its workers, primarily women, would walk next door to the plant early each morning. They peeled crawfish until afternoon, then often returned for a second, shorter shift in the early evening. María earned very little that first season, her checks totaling only around $50 a week after deducting the $50 bed charge. At $1.25 a pound, technique was everything. María's difficulties translated, by her estimates, to a production of only about 16 pounds a week and $3,000 for nine months of work—less than her combined earnings in Mexico. When I worked with María, together we produced 10 pounds in two hours without rushing, earning about $13 total. Admittedly, María was responsible for the majority of our production.

It wasn't until the second season when her boss, Mr. Tran, out of frustration, decided to teach her better technique. An older Vietnamese man, Mr. Tran had owned the plant for several decades. María remembers he began lessons after yelling, "Look at my money in the trash, now look!," watching her break a crawfish down the middle. After his initial "lesson," he appeared at her side every so often to demonstrate proper method. Eventually, she learned to mimic his technique—a fact that she believed contributed to his bizarre kindness toward her.

Once she learned, María began teaching new arrivals, eager to help them avoid the hardships she had experienced. Taking notice, Mr. Tran began to direct her to teach, not paying extra for this labor. If anything, taking time to teach others cost her, as it shifted her focus from producing pounds that earned her money. It became clear why no one taught her when she arrived: they had been unwilling to lose money for anyone, particularly a stranger. María saw things from a different perspective, telling me, "You don't lose time when you teach, Jen, you don't lose because it's something that stays with you in your heart. They always came up to me and asked me, 'How much do they pay you?,' and I would say, 'It's that not all of life is about money.'"

Temporary Labor Migration

Although Louisiana might not be the first state that comes to mind when thinking about Latinos living in the United States, Spanish-speaking and Latin American people have long been present. Colonized by Spain in the eighteenth century, Louisiana continued to attract Spanish-speaking emigrants after passing from Spanish control. Nineteenth-century steamship connections linked New Orleans to Western Hemisphere Spanish-speaking cities like Tampico and Veracruz in Mexico, facilitating sustained cultural and political connections.

Many longer-term Mexican emigrants of the early twentieth century hailed from the middle and upper classes of Veracruz (often fleeing the Mexican Revolution). This fueled what the historian Julie Weise describes in *Corazón de Dixie* (2015) as a more "conservative" expatriate culture of emigrants who cultivated a position in the white society of Jim Crow New Orleans. Lower-skilled workers were also recruited to work on sugar plantations. By the end of the 1930s, the class composition had flipped to a majority of lower-skilled workers. Recent decades have seen an influx of Mexican and Central American Latinos as demand for workers to help rebuild increased after consecutive natural disasters.

María came to Louisiana via a formal temporary work program—the H-2B nonimmigrant visa program—available to foreigners interested in doing nonagricultural work in the United States. In contrast to H-1 visas for workers of "distinguished merit," that is, with advanced degrees, professional expertise, or special talent, H-2B visas are available to workers whom policymakers categorize as having "low" or "less-specialized" skills. The H-2B visa permits workers to perform labor in the United States temporarily, so long as capable citizen workers are not available.

Formal programs facilitating temporary labor migration emerged during wartime to circumvent labor migration limits. The first, established in 1917 for a year, endured until 1922. The more widely known Bracero Program[6] was established in 1942 to address World War II labor shortages. This binational agreement with Mexico permitted US employers to temporarily contract Mexican men to perform agricultural and less specialized labor. More than 4.6 million workers participated in the Bracero Program before it was terminated in 1964, in part due to reports of human rights abuses. During periods of migration, workers established and strengthened social networks through which they shared knowledge of jobs and opportunities. As the sociologist Douglas Massey and coauthors demonstrated in *Beyond Smoke and Mirrors* (2002), this further entrenched a pattern of circular migration across the southern border.

H-2B program regulations, codified in 1952,[7] aim to protect both US citizen and immigrant workers. Employers must first obtain certification from the Department of Labor by demonstrating citizen workers are not available. Once workers are hired, employers are required to pay at minimum the adverse wage rate for the industry, provide workers' compensation insurance, guarantee work for three-quarters of the contract, and cover transport costs to and from the country of origin. In one major distinction, only employers of H-2A workers are required to provide housing. Both visas "tie" workers to the employer who petitioned, meaning they are only permitted to work for that employer. Should a worker lose their job, or if their employer no longer needs workers, they must return to their home country.

Louisiana has consistently been a top state for H-2B worker employment.[8] Although most employers want to treat their workers fairly, narrow profit margins pressure employers to maintain low costs, which may lead to cuts that negatively affect workers. In mild cases, employers with good intentions may short pay or facilitate poor working conditions. In the worst of cases, like María's, indifferent or abusive employers engage in exploitative practices exacerbated by these limitations.

Learning to Labor

María's venture into formal employment began later in life, at thirty-three years old—two decades before moving to Louisiana. She began working first in the informal sector by capitalizing on what she knew, cooking. She made and sold homemade *sopes* (a Sinaloan dish) and *tortas* (a Mexican sandwich) while also attending sewing school. She saved secretly to purchase a small one-bedroom house three doors down from her family's home.

María moved out of their home one day while her husband was at work. His drinking habit, she explained, had reached a point where she "was done." Irate, he took her to court, threatening to take her children unless she moved home. She said this only solidified her resolve to leave. Calling his bluff, she told him he could do what he thought right, but she was no longer willing to live with him. Although the children primarily slept in his larger house, they remained under her care.

When María set her mind to buy that home, she set a work schedule so punishing she became ill with a severe kidney infection. Her brother counseled, "You aren't going to have enough to pay for being sick. Look for a job where you have insurance, where you can get medical care, sister, even though you earn little." Following his advice, María searched for a job in the formal sector. Determined to work near her children's schools, she focused on an opportunity located at the end of the route of the bus she rode daily. Her persistence earned her a cleaning job at the transport dock at the Port of Topolobampo.

This first "real" job, one with steady pay and the medical benefits her brother suggested, resulted from a decision to stay on the bus. On her daily route to school, María noticed a woman routinely escorting a group of workers. Rather than exiting at her stop one afternoon, María stayed on the bus to learn their destination. When the woman disembarked at the end of the route, so did María. Not considering that she was dressed for school in heels and pressed clothes, María asked the woman for a job. Looking her up and down, the woman responded coldly, "Yo te aviso" (I'll let you know).

In response, María took the bus to the route's end daily, each time disembarking to ask the woman, whom she referred to as *la señora*, that same question. Each time she received the same reply. The señora's company worked at the Port of Topolobampo, where passenger and cargo ships docked to empty and reload. María's daily arrival eventually caught the dock manager's attention. He learned from the guard that on each visit María asked for a job, so he instructed the señora to offer her one. Thus began María's tenure at the port. She worked various roles in housekeeping there for twelve years, and by the end was simultaneously employed by two companies.

Her first day on the job, a cold day in mid-January, María arrived wearing brand-new shoes. The señora told her that if she wanted the job, she had to start immediately, beginning at 3:00 p.m. and staying until the final boat left, as late as 3:00 a.m. Desperate for a formal job, in her words "real work," María agreed. Her first task was to clean the kitchen. By the end of that first shift, her shoes were destroyed and she was soaking wet, so much so that she got sick from the cold. Despite this, she returned the next day and was put to work cleaning the men's bathroom.

What María perceived as the señora's determination to make her work life so miserable she would quit only increased her determination to stay. She gave up design school when the señora changed her hours to interfere with her classes, a decision María believed was intentional, given that it occurred immediately after she was asked for her class schedule. Her determination was partially motivated by her children attending school in the same part of town. Working at the port, she could be nearby if they needed anything. "That's why I was stubborn," she said.

Although the señora remained unimpressed, the dock manager took note of her persistence. After interrupting one particularly aggravating incident with a drunk man in the male bathroom she was cleaning, the manager changed her duties from bathrooms to the administrative offices and event room. After two years working for this company, another company next door contracted her to check trucks. As a result, she learned to drive—essential for moving the trucks—and obtained her passport—essential for boarding international boats. She worked for both companies simultaneously for over a decade before being offered the "opportunity" (said with a hint of sarcasm) to work in the United States.

Obligated by Circumstances

María told me she never desired to work in the United States. Whenever she was offered opportunities to go north, she'd reply, "I never am going to go, I have nothing to do with the gringos." Nevertheless, the "opportunity" that first brought her to Louisiana she felt compelled, if not almost coerced, to accept. A friend of hers, Griselda, had worked several seasons in a Louisiana seafood processing plant and was helping recruit workers for the upcoming season. María described their friendship as one of mutual support, both emotional and material. María would often care for Griselda's children, and, in semi-exchange, Griselda gave her clothes. Aware of María's financial struggles, one night Griselda mentioned, "If you had a passport, you could come work with me on the other side, because one of the women who was going to go is not going to go; there is an open space." María did not respond, neither denying nor confirming that she did, in fact, have a passport. It was María's sister who told Griselda about her passport and, according to María, ganged up with her brother to convince her that "it was the opportunity of her life."

"I can assure you that the happiest of the people you see here now didn't come here happy. One doesn't come here for pleasure," María once told me, "people" meaning immigrants to the United States. In her opinion, people like herself come to work for different reasons; however, no one wants to leave their home or family. They leave because there isn't enough work. In the van from Mexico on her second trip to Louisiana, María recalled sitting next to a young woman who smelled of newborn baby. The woman began to cry, telling María how she had to leave her baby to work so she could pay a lawyer to defend her husband, who had recently been arrested. María remembered the woman crying often, day and night, throughout her stay.

In her own case, as María put it, "My whole life I have done things, like I have told you, *obligada por las circunstancias* [obligated by circumstances]. I have struggled a lot." At the time of her first venture to Louisiana, María had a daughter in university, one son in an in-patient rehab clinic, and another son in another clinic. Although she worked long hours at two jobs, she was not making ends meet, given the costs of their care. Despite these pressures, upon arriving at the US border, María found herself praying that the border patrol officer would reject her visa so she could return home.

Staying Put to Move Forward

Although María felt obligated by circumstances beyond her control, as I got to know María I quickly realized that she does her best to bend them to fit her needs. Sometimes by sheer persistence, by just staying put, María is able to shape the course through which life takes her.

In Louisiana, buses were instrumental. María's life in Baton Rouge was initially more or less organized through her employer. Every Sunday, a van took workers from the Casa Blanca to Walmart for grocery shopping. The driver had little patience (though the workers paid his gas), constantly yelling "*¡Apúrate!* [Hurry up!]" and "*¡Rápido!* [Fast/Move quickly!]" One shopping expedition during her second season, María was at the end of a long line at the cashier when the driver approached yelling, "Look, everyone's over there, already done!" Embarrassed because, "even though people didn't understand, they realize [what is happening]," María told him he could wait or leave, but "he was not to come up and yell" at her. He left her behind.

Unsure how to return, María approached a police officer for help ordering a taxi. Instead, the officer drove María to the house himself. The next shopping trip, María refused the van. She chose instead to take a bus she'd seen stop near the house, despite not having previously ridden a bus in Baton Rouge. Once she finished shopping, however, María realized she still didn't know how to return. The police officer she approached this time took her to Customer Service and advised, for her safety, that she have them call her a taxi. The cost of the taxi—about $7, or 3 pounds of peeled crawfish—convinced María, "I have to learn [the buses]. I don't have any reason to depend on anyone here; no one here is going to humiliate me."

The next day, María got on a bus in front of the Casa Blanca and rode it to the central station on Florida Boulevard. That route ended there, so she boarded another, expecting it to eventually return to the station. "I was very content," she said, "looking at everything, and it took me very far, far, turned around, and then stopped." The driver got out, telling her something she realized later likely indicated it was the route's end. María had no idea what he said, or what to do, and was nearly in tears. Terrified and alone, she asked herself, "Where are they going to take me? . . . Where do I go?'" Not knowing what else to do, she stayed on the bus. She guessed it would return to the central station at some point, so she waited. Eventually the driver returned and drove María, alone, back to the station. It was dark when they finally arrived, and using the pay phone and a calling card (cell phones were less prominent in 2008), she called the phone at the Casa Blanca repeatedly until someone came to retrieve her.

Determined, María told herself, "Okay, fine, this is not going to stop me. I'm going to keep trying." She started taking random buses on the weekends, noting bus numbers and where she got on and off. Soon she found a bus to take her to church and one with a stop "right at the door to the Casa Blanca."

Trying to reduce costs, María noticed people riding multiple buses with a single ticket. She did her best to explain to a driver, who spoke no Spanish, that she wanted one ticket for all the buses. After much effort at communication, he gave her the magic word, "transfer." María soon discovered that a transfer ticket purchased on Friday lasted the entire weekend, and a monthly membership cost even less. She took full advantage, sometimes taking the bus to the Mall of Louisiana on the far south side of town just to eat. Although she often invited the women she worked and lived with on these adventures, they always declined. Instead of joining her, María said they would just tell her she was "crazy."

On one of these in-town adventures, María noticed a bus with a sign for New Orleans. Emboldened, she approached the driver and learned a ticket cost $7. She was surprised, as a ticket to New Orleans cost $40 from the central station. The driver explained it was a temporary bus line added after Hurricane Katrina hit New Orleans in 2005. Thousands of people displaced from New Orleans moved to Baton Rouge, so this line connected evacuees to jobs and family in the city.

Back at the Casa Blanca, María told the other women her plans to take that bus to New Orleans. She remembers them looking at her incredulously, asking, "Are you crazy? How?" She said she laughed, retorting, "Yes, I'm crazy, but sane crazy." María recounted her experience vividly: "Jen, my hands were sweaty. I remember that I arrived in New Orleans, and everyone got off the bus. New Orleans seemed to me so big, but so big that I thought we'd never arrive in the center. We arrived, and the person came to clean the bus. I said, 'I don't want to stay, I want to go back'; I was scared and everything. They took me to another bus to get the other ticket. They said they were going to clean this bus, but there was another, so I got on the other . . . It was right there, I just walked and got on it and returned."

María took this trip five separate times before she dared get off the bus in New Orleans. She thought the first time she would just learn the route; however, the bus stopped at a different place each of her first three trips. She later realized that each of those times, in true New Orleans fashion, a festival rerouted the bus from its usual stop. The fifth time, despite her fear, she told herself, "I'm going to get off. I'm going to risk it in the name of God." María walked a few blocks and happened upon a camera store. Delighted, as she wanted to buy a camera for her daughter who was studying photography, she called her to ensure she purchased the right model. Her daughter, shocked to learn María was in New Orleans, asked if she was scared. María said she lied, answering definitively, "No," telling her she had to learn to get around by herself; otherwise, she would be dependent upon the "whole world."

The Circumstances

The resoluteness María displayed in her determination to learn to navigate the transportation system—and her life in Louisiana—was evident in her approach to finding work and confronting the circumstances in Mexico that brought her to Louisiana. She was satisfied with her work at the port, where she earned enough to support herself and her children. Then, when her sons reached early adulthood, the family faced a crisis. Her oldest son had begun behaving strangely. "When I realized that my sons were not doing well, the first person to seek help was me. I went to Narcotics Anonymous," María told me.

Initially she experienced frustration. Her son had turned eighteen, and thus was considered an adult by the state. He had to seek treatment of his own accord unless he committed a crime. This presented a challenge, as he was convinced he didn't have a problem and was not interested in help. María tried many different places—clinics with support services, churches—but everywhere she was told the same thing: he had to take responsibility for his recovery.

María thought her son would finally be forced into treatment when police detained him. She still doesn't know why—the police only told her he didn't have his ID. They didn't charge him. Once at the station, María refused to pay the fine. Instead, she asked them to transfer him to the city of Los Mochis and require him to do community service. They told her no, as he had not committed a crime. Desperate because she could not get him into a clinic involuntarily, she suggested they invent something, "public urination, whatever," so she could have him committed. Pleading, she asked the officers, "How can parents help their children if the authorities don't cooperate?"

Acquiescing, they first required her to sign liability waivers. María rode in the front of the patrol car with the officer. Her son, "*de lo mal que andaba* [because of the poor state he was in]," bolted from the car while they were en route. The patrol car following braked quickly yet still hit him, though it did not gravely hurt him. "We arrived after only all of that," María said, "because he didn't want to go, because he didn't want to be with drunks and drug addicts."

The process was particularly difficult because her son hid his addiction well. He "fooled everyone, except me," said María, "even his dad." He struggled for several years, leaving the rehabilitation center, promising to stay sober, then returning after a relapse. He cycled through addiction and sobriety seven times before remaining sober for over a decade. María refused to waiver even though her extended family, neighbors, and daughter questioned her unconditional financial support of his clinic stays. From a perspective aligned with the fields of social work and public health, María saw addiction as an illness, explaining that she would send him "as many times as I had to" until he recovered.

Mainstream awareness of the trafficking of drugs like cocaine and marijuana over the Mexican border has increased in recent decades as international crime television and streaming series have proliferated. Typically, movement of drugs from Mexico to the United States is the focus, rather than traffic in the other direction. The drug to which María's sons became addicted, crystal meth, was first developed in the United States in the 1970s after the US government made most pharmaceutical uses of methamphetamine (first synthesized in the late 1800s) illegal. The distribution of it in this highly addictive crystallized form, as crystal meth, was first controlled predominantly by US gangs. When the United States began to regulate chemicals used to "cook" meth in the 1980s, however, an illicit market opened up that attracted Mexican cartels, and cross-border trade ensued.[9]

María's younger son fell into the same addiction not long after his older brother, yet via a different course. He began to use drugs on active duty in the Mexican marines, following in the footsteps of many US, Japanese, and German soldiers during World War II.[10] Years later in Baton Rouge, where he stayed after following a work opportunity and starting a second family, he told María everything. In the marines, he oversaw the night shift guarding contraband his unit intercepted. He was worried, as he was "always one who fell asleep too easily," so he accepted drugs from a colleague to help him stay awake. He later turned to other drugs, eventually leaving the marines as a "deserter" when the family decided to hospitalize him. At the time of his hospitalization, María's older son was in a different rehab clinic, and her daughter had begun university. Despite her disinterest in the United States, these financial pressures pushed María to accept the opportunity to work in Louisiana.

Bit on the Belly

Faced with these obligations, María tolerated conditions at the processing plant. She became acutely familiar with the characteristics of jobs that sociologists refer to as "precarious": long hours, low pay, stressful work environments, and schedules over which workers have little control. The first season, a crawfish punctured her glove, deeply cutting her finger. It hurt so badly María said it brought her to tears. Afterward she remembers Mr. Tran approached her yelling, "Stupid, you have to work!" When she said it was too painful, upon examining it, he told her a doctor would just "chop it off." Instead, he brought her a cream and warned that he would take her to the hospital if she was not better the next day. She never went to the doctor. The cream helped, she said, as she showed me her finger so that I could see how it still looked different.

Later that season, a blue crab did damage. María had learned the basics of quickly removing the shell, yet a crab slipped from her hand. Telling me the story she exclaimed, "¡Me picó la panza! [It bit my belly!]." The pincers had pierced the skin on her stomach. She still can't figure out how, especially given the heavy apron she wore over her shirt. This time, however, María kept working despite the pain. The next morning, she awoke with a giant blister on her stomach surrounded by red inflamed skin. She worried about Mr. Tran's reaction, given her experience with her finger. Noticing her absence at work, he came to the door "screaming." Embarrassed by her exposed stomach (covering it with her shirt was painful), María remembers his look of confusion when she opened the door: "No one, nor I, understood how it happened."

This time, a coworker took her to the hospital. Embarrassed and unable to explain the accident, María approached the hospital warily. Without hesitation, the doctors told her they would have to remove the infected skin. They warned her that she would need to take care that the exposed new skin didn't get reinfected—meaning she should not work. Although María managed to avoid handling seafood while she healed, she did work constructing packing boxes and organizing the office. She eventually resumed peeling crawfish for the season's duration, though never mastering the technique, before returning to Mexico.

Despite her injuries and a technique so terrible that María earned less than she would have at her jobs in Mexico, her friend called informing her that she was on the next season's visa list. Astonished, she asked herself, "Why does he want me if I am not useful to him at all? Why does he want me?" She refused until Mr. Tran himself called and asked, saying he needed someone "trustworthy" like her and promising to teach her better technique. María was happy to work despite being aware that it was exploitative and disliking Mr. Tran's treatment, which she described as "like a slave he had us." Going on to explain, she said, "He didn't want us to have visitors. I didn't know anyone, who would visit me? But for those who had been coming for thirteen, fifteen years—he would run off their visitors; they'd arrive, and he'd chase them off."

That second season, the workers organized to increase their pay. Several workers learned through family and friend networks that Mr. Tran paid the least. After trying, to no avail, to advocate for a raise through an interpreter (a friend of Mr. Tran), the workers eventually contacted the Mexican consulate and a local workers' rights organization. Consulting with the organizer, the workers decided to negotiate for a raise from $1.25 to $1.50 per pound. They coordinated a time to meet at the plant with the organizer, who would limit his participation to interpreting their request. However, when Mr. Tran saw them gathered, María said he "became like a crazy man," refusing to listen. When María tried to explain that they were only asking for a 25-cent-per-pound raise, it made him angrier. He called her "ungrateful" for defending the others, as he had "helped her the most." Instead of agreeing, Mr. Tran shut down the plant, firing them all; ordered a van to return them to Mexico; and cut the electricity and water to the house. It was another thirty-six hours before the van arrived.

María, irate at this treatment, suggested they go to the press. Although the organizer called the idea "'brilliant,'" María said the other workers responded "as though I had mentioned the devil." They thought it wasn't worth jeopardizing a future work visa. This fear was not ill-founded. Other workers have told me about what they referred to as the "black list," a list of workers considered insubordinate that is shared among processing employers. Whether this list is metaphorical or physical remains an open question. Although I have never seen such a list, and employers deny one exists, rehiring workers with whom they have had good experiences is common practice.

María later learned that Mr. Tran kept the plant open that season; however, he never called them back. He reemployed only the workers resident in Louisiana and hired a different company to bring additional workers from Mexico. It was those workers, María said, who ended up making things difficult. The eight workers complained to their labor agency, which, in turn, reported Mr. Tran. This, as María put it, "cost him a ton of money," much more than the wage increase would have cost. It also embroiled him in a legal battle still ongoing when she recounted the experience.

Improbable as it may seem, given her treatment and failed efforts for better pay, María would work for Mr. Tran again. She and several other women decided to forgo the transport to Mexico and chance staying the duration of the visa term. They lived in a trailer belonging to their mutual friend in Port Allen, a town on the west bank of the river, and walked to work in housekeeping at the cheap hotels in the area. María also sold homemade tortillas and tamales, perfecting a tamale recipe that would win a prize in a cooking contest at her church many years later. Two months later, Mr. Tran called asking her to return. She obliged, working another two months before returning to Mexico at the end of the visa term. During that period, María took on weighing and packing tasks, for which he paid her hourly—$6, then eventually $7—which supplemented her earnings from peeling. She began to average about $5,000 (after bed costs) for the nine-month seasons.

Becoming Undocumented

One night in December of 2020, shortly after Joe Biden won the US presidential election, I was at María's apartment when she showed me a video that she received via group text. In it, a lawyer detailed the citizenship pathways the Biden administration was expected to include in its immigration reform proposal. One proposed pathway offered current workers without official authorization and proof of living in the country before January 2021 a mechanism to regularize—a precise term for "legalize"—their immigration status. She asked if I thought this was true and would come to pass.

At the end of her first H-2B visa term, María returned to Mexico. The next season she returned to Louisiana on a new visa. After she was fired that second season, María sought advice at the free legal clinic offered by the Hispanic Apostolate, part of the Catholic Diocese that ministers to the Spanish-speaking population. She was told she could petition for a U-visa, available to crime victims willing to cooperate with authorities. Counseled to describe in detail her suffering from Mr. Tran's abuse and the working conditions, María refused. Although the advocates told her what she had suffered made her eligible, María said she was uncomfortable reporting Mr. Tran because she believed he "had not been abusive enough." Closing this door, María returned to Mexico at the end of that visa term. She returned seasonally on a temporary visa for the next seven years. The seventh season, Mr. Tran told the workers he was petitioning for a visa extension, instructing those interested to stay until it was granted. She stayed. The extension was not granted, however, and her visa lapsed when Mr. Tran didn't renew it.

María no longer had official documents granting her permission to work and reside in the United States, or any options for obtaining them. Despite this, María did not return to Mexico.

Although neither her work nor her daily routine changed, in that moment María joined the ranks of the estimated twelve million undocumented people living in the United States.[11] Lack of official permission, the "papers," authorizing a noncitizen to reside and work in the United States, renders a person subject to the constant threat of detention and deportation to one's country of origin. Once deported, an immigrant receives a ten-year ban on legally reentering the country. This "context of illegality," described by scholars like the anthropologist Nicholas De Genova (2002) and the sociologist Leisy Abrego (2011), is a precarity distinct from that experienced by temporary workers. Beholden to the employers to whom their visas are tied, temporary workers may face poor working conditions and abuse they are afraid to report. This power their employers wield over their continued employment situates them adjacent to, if not part of, what the sociologist Erin Hatton (2020) refers to as the "coerced workforce." Yet unlike undocumented residents, they are still entitled to many of the rights and privileges afforded citizens.

Those who are undocumented, however, are denied most of these rights and privileges, including permission to work in the formal sector and its associated benefits like social security, access to safety net programs, and health insurance. In many states, including Louisiana, this also includes a driver's license. Threat of detention looms particularly large in Louisiana, where immigrant detention facilities expanded in number from two to eight in 2018. Despite this insecurity, María refuses to live her life differently.

Although it did not solve her immigration problem, María's visit to the Hispanic Apostolate did bear a different fruit. While waiting to speak to the lawyer, the receptionist paused a phone call to ask those waiting if anyone was looking for work. Always open to opportunities and uncertain about her future with Mr. Tran, María volunteered herself and her friend. Once finished, they met a Colombian couple, an older man and his wife, Carmen, near the Apostolate. They needed someone to help with their business as food and novelty vendors at the festivals abundant throughout South Louisiana during the months when the weather is nice. The couple hired María, who, being the smaller of the two, they said would "fit better in the truck." Consistent with the loyalty María showed her employers, she worked for them not only during the period when she wasn't working for Mr. Tran but also on occasional weekends for several years, taking a day off from the plant when necessary. They developed a friendship that deepened after Carmen introduced María to the Baptist church they attend. Although raised

Catholic, "like everyone," María told me she believed God was the same, and that it always made sense to her that she could have a relationship with God not mediated by a priest.

When searching for work as the Casa Blanca was being vacated, a woman María knew from church told her of an opportunity cleaning a private family home. Unfazed by the woman's warnings about "very demanding" bosses who never retained a worker for more than a few months, María jumped at the opportunity. Her new employers, an architect and a cardiologist with three young sons, lived in a large home on the lakes near the campus of Louisiana State University where I work. Her duties included cleaning the entire house as well as providing occasional care for the children. As with her experience with Mr. Tran, María is convinced her lack of prior experience contributed to winning her new boss's trust. She simply did everything requested, exactly as instructed. Exhausted after her initial shifts, María quickly earned a regular position. Securing this steady work that paid more for fewer hours on fewer weekdays enabled María to leave peeling crawfish, and the Casa Blanca, behind.

Surviving the Storms

Despite being from a coastal city and working more than a decade at its port and another decade in the seafood industry, María never learned to swim. She told me that whenever she was invited to the river or ocean, she stayed on shore claiming she "forgot to bring her bikini" to avoid the water. At her current housekeeping job, María was terrified the first time her new boss asked her to watch the three boys in the pool, despite assurances that she need not worry. With a long-handled broom, she then demonstrated her plan to pull a kid to safety with a net if they had any trouble.

One afternoon we were walking along the lakes trail discussing the recent storm, during which lightning struck one of her employer's trees. She told me about the stress she still felt whenever she was watching the children, who were "little fish," in their pool. Laughing, María turned the conversation to the circumstances of her birth, saying she found her fear funny, given that she was literally "born in the water."

María was born in a small village near Topolobampo during a major rainstorm that flooded the river and town. Her mother was in active labor at her husband's parents' home as the waters rose. María's grandfather brought a boat to the house as her grandmother helped her mother give birth. In the moments immediately following María's arrival into this world, her grandmother wrapped her in the bottom layer of her three-layer skirt, climbed into the boat with her grandfather, and fled. Her father helped her mother escape to safety up the mountain. The rising waters separated the family on different sides of the mountain, neither group certain of the other's survival. Newborn María survived on goat's milk for several days until, after the floodwaters subsided, they all returned to the house and reunited.

María fell into her caretaking role early in life, the first (by a matter of months) of her father's twelve children and mother's six, and the only child of both. When her mother died, María and her five younger siblings moved in with their father's third family, joining four children and before the arrival of two more. This woman, she said, loved them all—even María's siblings from another man—as her own. It was soon after this move that María, still in high school, met her future husband on a city bus. They married and had the first of four children two years later. Even after she moved a few doors down, she was always responsible for her children's care.

The week I met her, María moved out of the Casa Blanca, where she had been living with forty other people, and into a one-bedroom apartment. It was the first time in her life she had truly lived alone. Though initially scared, she now enjoys it. "Hago lo que me da la gana [I do what I want]," she says. She cooks for herself, and others when she chooses, and maintains a large collection of plants.

Although her financial pressures have eased as her sons are in recovery and her daughter has graduated, and despite everything she has been through, María chooses to stay in Louisiana. As she explained, "I came because, as I told you, I was obligated by circumstances. Now I am happy, now I am here because here I am."

Notes

1. All names in the chapter (except my own) have been changed to protect the identities of the persons described. Quotes are verbatim from our conversations; all other details of María's life are presented as María told them to me. Prior to submission, I read the full chapter to María, who gave approval for its publication.
2. See the section "Mazatlan" (p. 9) by Consul William E. Alger in the August 9, 1916, *Supplement to Commerce Reports (No. 32a), Daily Consular and Trade Report,* issued by the Bureau of Foreign and Domestic Commerce, US Department of Commerce, Washington, DC.
3. Use of the moniker "Cancer Alley" to refer to this area dates back to at least 1988 when the *Advocate* reported on a Greenpeace banner depicting a check

addressed to the legislature from "Cancer Alley, USA"; see J. C. Canicosa, "The Term 'Cancer Alley' Has a Long History in Louisiana—and even a History before Louisiana," *Louisiana Illuminator*, February 5, 2021.
4. Many enslaved people were sold from declining tobacco plantations and shipped farther south down the Mississippi River during the period historians like Henry Louis Gates refer to as the "Second Middle Passage."
5. See the interpretive text in the electronic exhibition *From Red Stick to River Capital: Three Centuries of Baton Rouge History* of the physical collection curated by V. Faye Phillips, LSU Libraries, at https://www.lib.lsu.edu/sites/all/files/sc/exhibits/e-exhibits/redstick/cas1txt.html.
6. *Bracero* is the Spanish word used to mean "farmhand" in the southwestern United States.
7. By the Immigration and Nationality Act of 1952, the McCarran-Walter Act (Public Law 82-414; 8 USC ch. 12).
8. See the US Customs and Immigration Services (USCIS) table, *Approved H-2B Cap-Subject Beneficiaries by Petitioner's State, Fiscal Year 2017*, https://www.uscis.gov/sites/default/files/document/data/FY17-H2B-Cap-Subject-Characteristic-12.07.17.pdf; or data on program numbers from the Department of Labor, Office of Foreign Labor Certification.
9. This is a simplified explanation of the history of the drug methamphetamine hydrochloride's transition from legal pharmaceutical to cross-border trafficking of chemicals and production in clandestine meth labs, due, as Nicholas Parsons (2014, 5) argues, in large part to "drug policies enacted in a culture of fear perpetuated through the mass media." For a more comprehensive analysis of the history of crystal meth, see Parsons's *Meth Mania: A History of Methamphetamine*. For discussion of how the social construction of crystal meth shifted to focus on trafficking from Mexico, see pages 146–150.
10. See "Historical Context of Early Amphetamines, 1929–1960" in Parsons (2014, 56–59).
11. See reports by Jeffery S. Passel and colleagues at the Pew Research Center for regular estimates of the size and characteristics of the undocumented population in the United States.

References

Abrego, Leisy J. 2011. "Legal Consciousness of Undocumented Latinos: Fear and Stigma as Barriers to Claims-Making for First- and 1.5-Generation Immigrants." *Law and Society Review* 45 (2): 337–369.

De Genova, Nicholas P. 2002. "Migrant 'Illegality' and Deportability in Everyday Life." *Annual Review of Anthropology* 31 (1): 419–447.

Hatton, Erin. 2020. *Coerced: Work under Threat of Punishment*. Oakland: University of California Press.

Massey, Douglas S., Jorge Durand, and Nolan J. Malone. 2002. *Beyond Smoke and Mirrors: Mexican Immigration in an Era of Economic Integration*. New York: Russell Sage Foundation.

Parsons, Nicholas L. 2014. *Meth Mania: A History of Methamphetamine*. Boulder, CO: Lynne Rienner.

Weise, Julie M. 2015. *Corazón de Dixie: Mexicanos in the U.S. South since 1910*. Chapel Hill: University of North Carolina Press.

Suggested Reading

Immigration

Ngai, Mae M. 2014. *Impossible Subjects: Illegal Aliens and the Making of Modern America*. Princeton, NJ: Princeton University Press.

Precarious Work

Kalleberg, Arne L. 2011. *Good Jobs, Bad Jobs: The Rise of Polarized and Precarious Employment Systems in the United States, 1970s–2000s*. New York: Russell Sage Foundation.

Ribas, Vanesa. 2016. *On the Line: Slaughterhouse Lives and the Making of the New South*. Oakland: University of California Press.

The Intersection of Immigration and Precarious Work

Calavita, Kitty. 1992. *Inside the State: The Bracero Program, Immigration, and the I.N.S.* New Orleans: Quid Pro Quo Books.

Stuesse, Angela. 2016. *Scratching Out a Living: Latinos, Race, and Work in the Deep South*. Oakland: University of California Press.

CHAPTER 9

Ezequiel
A *LABURANTE* IN ARGENTINA'S RELEGATED NEIGHBORHOODS

Marcos Emilio Pérez

On a cold August afternoon, a small group of activists are getting ready to attend a rally. In recent years, a group of Wall Street vulture funds have sued to stop the restructuring of Argentina's debt and seize some of the country's assets. Today, various social movements are gathering in the most iconic indoor stadium in Buenos Aires to demand an end to what they see as colonialist aggression.

A rented school bus is supposed to pick everyone up from a vocational center run by a grassroots organization. To pass the time, most people gather in the building's kitchen and start a round of maté, a type of tea common in parts of South America. As I walk around, I find Ezequiel[1] alone in one of the classrooms, working on the models for a new project he hopes to start. In the three years since we met, this is the first time I have seen him attend a demonstration.

Ezequiel is a tall, middle-aged man who wears his long black hair in a ponytail and rarely goes outside without his sunglasses. He defines himself as an archetypical *laburante*, an Argentinean expression used to describe honest, hardworking people. His big hands and sturdy body contrast with the delicate labor he does as an electrician and plasterer. His first job was helping his father with construction work when he was twelve. Decades later, he has accumulated substantial practical experience and developed a perfectionist approach to his trade. He also raised a family and built a home, becoming the proud father of four children.

During his lifetime, Ezequiel has also seen his neighborhood, once a dynamic working-class community in Greater Buenos Aires, struggle with the consequences of Argentina's transformation from a country with generally low poverty and unemployment into one with far higher levels of marginality and exclusion. Neoliberal reforms since the 1970s caused a substantial increase in structural joblessness, inequality, and marginalization, which hit places like Ezequiel's community particularly hard. Faced with these challenges, residents engaged in various forms of collective action. Ezequiel is one of the countless people who did that by joining the unemployed workers' movement (also known as *piqueteros*, or "roadblockers"), one of the most influential experiences of grassroots mobilization in the country's recent history.

After a short wait, the bus arrives, and we start the trip downtown. Ezequiel sits down and rapidly falls asleep. When we reach our destination, he wakes up, grabs a big drum, and carries it to the stadium. The event, however, is not well organized, and a sea of people wait outside. Ezequiel and I become separated from those who came with us. When we finally enter, we find that inside things are even more chaotic: there are dozens of different groups, and the fellows from the bus are nowhere to be found. I see the banners representing Ezequiel's organization and try to get close, but people there are from other districts, and since no one recognizes us, an organizer tries to prevent us from joining this group. I manage to convince him: since I am holding a camera, he probably thinks I am a journalist. Ezequiel sneaks in with me.

The rally is lively. Between speeches by high-profile orators, people hit their drums and sing traditional chants. There are also video clips, music, and even excerpts from a children's show. Ezequiel, however, remains silent and barely uses the drum he carried from the bus. During my long conversations with him, he always shared his opinions, which overall align with today's event. Yet he appears to be uninterested.

To make things worse, a fight breaks out a few meters from us. Apparently, some group tried to hang its flags in a way that would block the flags of others. Within seconds, things escalate out of control, and about twenty young men trade blows. In the confusion, I end up alone. A few minutes later I catch a glimpse of Ezequiel: even though the national leader of his organization is speaking, he is heading for the exit.

Outside the stadium there are even more people and a much better climate overall. We find the other activists from the neighborhood; they left when the fight started. After half an hour, we decide to leave. The bus is parked a few blocks away, and we begin walking. Once again, Ezequiel is separated from the group. He sends text messages asking for directions, since he is lost. As we walk, an activist tells me that Ezequiel does not usually attend demonstrations, and with today's events, "he will not want to come anymore."

I met Ezequiel in 2011 at the same center where we gathered for the demonstration. He and a dozen other activists spent a whole Saturday morning preparing the registration for hundreds of students. After the meeting was over, he offered me a tour of the location. Situated in one of the poorest areas of the district, the place had over the years become a focal point for social and educational services. He highlighted the many improvements he and his fellows had made, sharing in detail his plans for building more classrooms.

During my fieldwork, I saw Ezequiel spend countless hours at the location, leading courses on electricity, organizing cooperatives, and working on anything that needed fixing. However, as I got to know him, I discovered that his enthusiasm for the group's daily tasks coexists with an apparent disregard for ideological debates and electoral campaigns. He comes from a family of activists, and his siblings joined the organization years before him. Yet, as one of his fellows says: "Ezequiel is not interested in politics. He is pure work. He does not go to any demonstration."

In other words, Ezequiel's story is one of resistance, albeit in a way frequently overlooked by observers. He is a smart, well-informed man who does not hesitate to express his personal views and is proud of his contributions to the movement. However, he is mostly interested in the mundane tasks and incremental improvements that allow the organization to serve the district's inhabitants. Through his everyday work, he materializes a particular sense of morality centered on the (increasingly uncommon) experience of blue-collar labor, a gendered breadwinner-homemaker family structure, and old-fashioned ideas of community life. For him and numerous others, *piquetero* organizations allow the persistence of an idealized proletarian lifestyle endangered by the undermining of the material conditions that made it possible.

The Life of a Breadwinner

Ezequiel was born in 1970 to parents who had migrated from Paraguay. His father worked in construction and specialized in plastering, while his mother was a homemaker. The varying fortunes of the family meant that he attended several different elementary schools. He describes his father as a well-meaning but uninformed person, who taught him a profession but did not appreciate the value of a formal education. At age twelve, Ezequiel began assisting him at work, gradually becoming a skilled plasterer himself:

> When there is no support from your elders, you do what you think is right or normal, like smoking, drinking, or ceasing your studies. In my case, my dad did not care whether you studied or not . . . in that sense he gave zero support because he never gave it any importance, because he was not raised with an education, he was raised working. So what did he do? He incorporated me and my siblings in his work, for many years.

It was also at this time that Ezequiel had his first experiences in politics, thanks to an uncle who participated in a far-left party. During lunch breaks, they would sit for an hour, reading and debating ideas. It was the mid-1980s, the country had just reestablished democracy, and civic engagement had rebounded from the tragic days of the 1976–1983 dictatorship. However, even though his siblings became increasingly involved in community organizing, Ezequiel remained distant. As the eldest son, he felt a responsibility to support the family, creating the opportunity for younger members to further their education and activism:

> My siblings were the ones who stayed involved. My dad had the idea of making a small plastering business; my uncle was involved in politics and sometimes was around and sometimes not. If I went with my siblings, who would remain? My dad alone. So those are like ties that I, as a brother, supported my siblings and my dad, covering for them and not leaving my dad alone.

As years passed and he accumulated experience, Ezequiel became an independent contractor. He also taught himself new skills that allowed him to do more complex projects. He frequently talks about the different sites where he worked and shows pictures of what he considers his greatest achievements. As his reputation helped him secure high-end jobs, seeing the contrast between the poverty of his community and the opulent wealth of some clients influenced him far more than any conversations with his uncle. Rich customers spent fortunes on unnecessary repairs and luxurious vacation residences, while it took him years to construct a dwelling for his family:

Through this work I see many social injustices that have to do with turbid [shady] things, because I was called by architects who work with people with a lot of money. We went to do the Patio Bullrich [one of the country's most exclusive malls], all the decorative plaster we did it with my old man. I learned a lot there, it was '87, '88. I was seventeen years old; I was doing that and I spent many years there. It is nice to earn money, but then I went to places where a few people had a lot of stuff, and what did these people do? You saw a tremendous house, and they destroyed it and did it again. Why so much expense, so much misuse of money, just for the sake of doing it, while for us it is so difficult to build our home? Our homes take forever, and there are people who do and undo just for pleasure.

In addition to developing his career, Ezequiel also built a family. In his early twenties, he got together with his common-law wife, eventually having four children, whose photographs (wearing the colors of his favorite soccer team) he shares happily. He claims to be a faithful husband and a strict-yet-understanding father, who, despite not being able to buy his kids the coolest toys or clothes, has always provided for them. Ezequiel takes pride in the fact that his efforts have allowed him to sustain the type of domestic structure that he associates with respectability, a man who leaves early in the morning for work and a woman who keeps a close eye on the children:

When we had the first child, I told my wife to dedicate all the necessary time to the baby, that she not worry about working [but about] his health and food, while I go outside to search for money. Due to our different occupations, I will make more money than her. She worked as a house cleaner, by the hour, and would not bring in the same money I bring. If we both work, we will neglect our baby, and I do not want that. So out of common accord, she stayed at home, and I tried to see that neither she nor the kids wanted for anything. The first kid grew up, and my wife wanted to work, so I gave her the opportunity to go work. She went but realized that she would not be paid [much]; they will pay whatever they pay per hour. So we agreed—she agreed with me later—I told her when the kids began school, it is important to be careful, that means taking them and bringing them; I prefer that to the school bus, where you give the responsibility to someone else. It is our child, we have to take care of that.

At first sight, Ezequiel's embracing of traditional masculinity seems at odds with much of the agenda of his organization, which, among other things, has been active in the expansion of reproductive rights, the promotion of gender equality, and the provision of safe spaces for LGBT individuals. An unsympathetic observer would use this apparent contradiction as evidence of political immaturity or nefarious manipulation. However, discrepancies between individual ideologies and organizational platforms are normal reflections of the complexity of political participation. The lack of complete agreement with an agenda is rarely an obstacle to personal commitment, because individuals find different aspects of collective action meaningful in their own particular ways (Wolford 2010; Viterna 2013). For Ezequiel, the validation of his public identity as a responsible worker and old-school family man is a major appeal of his involvement in a social movement. For people like him, *piquetero* organizations offer an oasis from what they perceive as the collapse of the conditions that made respectable life possible. In recent decades, structural transformations in Argentina's society caused an expansion of inequality, poverty, and interpersonal violence, which have affected working-class communities particularly hard. In this context, not only supporting yourself and your loved ones but also doing so in morally sanctioned ways becomes a significant challenge. In Ezequiel's neighborhood, as in countless similar places throughout the nation, the practices that used to confer honor and status to men and women are increasingly difficult to sustain. Thus, it is not surprising that for someone like him, the remaining opportunities to engage in such routines are highly valued.

Socioeconomic Decline and Its Consequences

Between the 1940s and 1970s, Argentina developed one of the most extensive welfare states in Latin America and experienced relatively low rates of unemployment and inequality. The demand for workers generated by import-substitution industrialization promoted the settling of internal and foreign migrants in cities, sustaining a large urban proletariat. Despite intense political conflicts, recurrent military interventions, and repeated crises in the balance of payments, the combination of strong unions, a substantial light manufacturing sector oriented to the internal market, and widespread government intervention kept poverty at bay.

Starting in the 1970s, however, the country entered a period of sweeping neoliberal reforms that drastically affected its productive structure. First implemented by authoritarian governments, these profound changes were either ineffectively resisted or actively promoted by subsequent democratic administrations. Times of economic expansion were followed by increasingly severe crises, which reached their peak between 1998 and 2002, when the nation experienced the deepest recession in its history. As a result, in the roughly three decades after the mid-1970s, Argentina's GDP per capita remained stagnant, and disparities in wealth and income became entrenched.

Since 2003, these numbers have improved, aided by economic recovery and changes in public policy. The governments of Néstor Kirchner (2003–2007) and Cristina Fernández de Kirchner (2007–2015) took advantage of high prices of commodity exports to implement generous social policies and expand the role of the state in strategic industries. However, several years of impressive growth were followed by a period of stagflation, especially after 2011. The victory of Mauricio Macri in the presidential elections of 2015 led to a restoration of neoliberal policies, which failed to revitalize the economy and reduce inflation. Complicating things further, the COVID-19 pandemic slashed all hopes of a fast recovery under Macri's successor, Alberto Fernández.

These transformations had drastic effects on Argentina's working classes, as individuals with lower levels of formal education were among the hardest hit by a shifting economy. Stable occupations became more difficult to attain, and the quality of available jobs declined. The percentage of the labor force in the manufacturing industry more than halved, while employment in areas requiring more credentials doubled (Alvaredo, Cruces, and Gasparini 2018). Long-term joblessness, underemployment, and informality skyrocketed (Groisman 2013).

In sum, over the past forty years, Argentinean society has entered a new normal in which a large portion of the population faces remarkable barriers to upward mobility. In 2018, less than half of the economically active population had access to a job with full benefits, and workers in low-socioeconomic-status households were 13.5 times more likely to be employed in the informal sector than their upper-middle-class counterparts (Donza 2019).

These processes directly affected Ezequiel's neighborhood. The area was first settled in the 1910s. Over the decades, its proximity to a key transportation hub, coupled with its low elevation (which kept land affordable), attracted internal and foreign migrants seeking a place to live. Enticed by job opportunities in the import-substituting industries that grew up around Buenos Aires starting in the 1930s, these workers and their families created a growing community. Cheap prices allowed people to purchase lots and build their own homes, generating a strong identity with the location. Such was the experience of Ezequiel's parents, who moved to the area in 1965. To this day, it is easy to tell residents from outsiders because of the particular way the former pronounce the name of the district.

However, in recent decades, the neighborhood has experienced a sustained process of decay. The closing of factories and the collapse of the businesses that relied on them severely undermined the material conditions that gave residents a decent standard of living, a sense of stability, and a source of social status. Manufacturing jobs with union-provided benefits have become uncommon, and the educational opportunities necessary to access well-paying service sector occupations remain hard to obtain. These deficits express themselves in two ways. On the one hand, young people have difficulty accessing their first job, especially if they have not finished high school. Lacking extensive formal education and unable to accumulate practical experience, boys and girls are locked in a vicious cycle of unemployability that will only worsen with time. On the other hand, laid-off residents above the age of forty face substantial barriers to reinsertion in the labor market due to the elimination of jobs for which they have practical skills and the absence of training opportunities for the occupations that are in demand. Too old to begin a new career yet too young to retire, these workers can only access the most menial, unreliable, and precarious jobs available.

In other words, steady occupations with a living wage are out of reach for a large portion of the neighborhood. Confronted with this situation, families rely on a combination of informal labor, government-funded cash transfer programs, and direct food assistance. As many activists say, even in the midst of widespread joblessness, most residents find ways to survive. Some set up small off-the-books shops or sell goods in the streets. Others search trash for cardboard and recyclables to sell. Even those at the very bottom can rely to some degree on soup kitchens and donations. Yet few people have long-term, sustainable ways to access resources.

The lack of opportunities has also contributed to a substantial increase in different forms of interpersonal violence. Moreover, decades of underinvestment and neglect by the authorities, coupled with rapid population growth, have caused a severe deficit in public infrastructure (everything from parks and recreation to paving and sanitation). The result has been a marked deterioration in communal life, as residents spend less time outside their homes, disengage from shared activities, and trust each other less.

In short, economic transformations in the last four decades severely affected this community. Even so, residents have not remained idle when confronted with these challenges. Instead, like many others in the country and region, they have reacted to exclusionary processes by developing new forms of collective action. The *piquetero* movement has been among the most visible instances of this dynamic (see Svampa and Pereyra 2003; Pereyra, Pérez, and Schuster 2008; Rossi 2017). During the second half of the 1990s, community organizers began to establish groups of unemployed workers and their families in different Argentinean cities, demanding access to jobs and relief programs. Although these groups had origins in diverse branches of the political left, they rapidly developed a similar combination of repertoire and organizational structure that helped them recruit members and gain influence. Most organizations function as clusters of local groups that stage roadblocks and pickets to demand the distribution of social relief, usually in the form of foodstuffs and positions in workfare programs. If successful, they distribute part of these resources among participants and use the rest to develop a broad array of social services. The prospect of obtaining assistance draws people into these groups, which in turn helps them continue demonstrating.

Over the years, *piquetero* organizations have remained a major actor in national politics despite changes in Argentina's socioeconomic conditions, thanks to a combination of effective repertoires of protest, flexible internal structures, and pragmatic decision-making. These organizations have also benefited from their resonance with established local traditions and exhibited from the beginning a marked tolerance toward different perspectives among participants. Few cases illustrate this as clearly as Ezequiel's group.

Becoming a *Piquetero*

As Ezequiel was busy living his life, raising children, and developing a career, his siblings got involved in an organization that offered educational services to the community. Despite its large size, the neighborhood had no high schools. Hence, in the late 1980s, a group of residents occupied an empty lot belonging to the state-owned railroad company, built a few precarious rooms, and successfully demanded that the authorities offer classes there. As the 1990s progressed and living conditions in the area deteriorated sharply, a group of left-wing organizers took control of the place and gradually expanded its work. What started as an extension of public schools began to manage soup kitchens, distribute foodstuffs, and administer emergency subsidies for an increasing number of unemployed families. This work inevitably put the group in contact with networks of *piquetero* activists, and by the turn of the century, the place was already affiliated with an organization in the movement. During the worst periods of the 1998–2002 economic recession, this location was essential for the survival of countless families.

As the economy began to recover in late 2002, the situation in the neighborhood slowly improved, and activists were able to switch their attention to matters less urgent than food safety. Through an uneasy alliance with the national government, the organization gradually received more resources, which allowed it to focus again on education. As Mario, the group's leader, reflected ten years after the crisis:

> Compared to the end of 2001, this feels like Europe. Let me tell you, I am talking to you now and I am figuring out how I can buy more computers [for a classroom]. Back then, I used to go house by house asking for rice, in solidarity, because if we gathered 10 kilos of rice and made a big stew for all, the big pot fed more than if everyone ate rice separately, at their homes.

Like what happens throughout the *piquetero* movement, the relation between this particular organization and the authorities has been complicated. Nevertheless, as the years passed, grassroots groups across the country increasingly began to be recognized as efficient managers of social assistance. Despite occasional disagreements, activists and public officials typically maintain a symbiotic relationship. By funding grassroots initiatives, cash-strapped authorities have a convenient way to delegate part of their responsibilities onto other actors, while organizers receive funds to support their work. In the case of Ezequiel's center, the local government finances teachers' salaries and many of the operating costs, thus offering high-quality job training and remedial classes to thousands of people at a low cost. In addition, through a constant process of negotiation, the group regularly obtains resources to expand their work. Not only does the municipality frequently donate construction materials (which are much cheaper than actually operating a state-run vocational center), but different public agencies offer second-hand assets. For instance, through a deal with the local school district, activists received forty broken desks and chairs, which served as a training exercise for a welding workshop, and once repaired, became furniture for other classrooms. Something similar happened with a handful of old streetlights, which Ezequiel and his students fixed and reinstalled outside the building.

Yet perhaps the most crucial way in which *piquetero* organizations have strengthened is through the consolidation of internal networks of committed participants. Although the size of the movement as a whole has varied over the years, organizations within it have been able to solidify an inner core of reliable and experienced members. Ezequiel's life history exemplifies

Fig. 9.1. *The vocational center.*

this dynamic. Despite the group's growth, he remained on the margins for many years. He was happy to help when asked and even took advantage of the soup kitchen occasionally. However, his family responsibilities (especially at a time of crisis and with four small children) prevented him from getting more involved.

A further obstacle was his perceived lack of knowledge about politics, especially compared to other participants who attended college and had more time to read: "For you to fully commit to activism, doing is not enough; you need to instruct yourself politically. Your tool will be the word. I cannot incorporate into that part, because I have a family, I got together [with my wife], I have children, I have to prioritize other things, find money each day."

Ezequiel only got involved in the daily operation of the place when he had a chance to apply his skills. As the economic crisis gradually abated, the organization started to offer short courses to help residents get better jobs. However, the lack of skilled teachers was a major hindrance. It was in this context, between 2006 and 2007, that Ezequiel's siblings invited him to teach a course on electricity. He first worked as a substitute in another district, and eventually began leading his own course in his own neighborhood. It became a deeply enjoyable activity, to the point that when a temporary alliance with a powerful local politician opened the possibility for him to be permanently hired in another location, he declined because it would involve working away from his community: "My goal is not to go there, my goal is to work in my neighborhood."

The low wage of an instructor forces Ezequiel to continue working outside of the group. However, the course was always more than an addition to his income. Participating every day in a community-based training center allows him to teach others the skills essential to what, from his viewpoint, is a wholesome life. By learning a trade, people can increase their chances of getting a job at a time when employment is becoming more precarious. Ezequiel's contributions to the community thus validate his identity as a worker: "My passion is to be able to generate things for people—businesses, genuine jobs—because we have the tools, the only thing missing is the will of people. I would love that, that is what I want the most, work to give more life to this place, in different trades: electricity, masonry, welding, printing, textiles, cooking."

In sum, over the years, Ezequiel has become increasingly involved in his organization, from being largely an observer as the group developed, to contributing occasionally, to teaching in another district, to finally working daily in his neighborhood. But his personal investment in the mission of providing services to the community has not been accompanied by a growing interest in broader ideological or strategic matters. As he insists: "My strength is not politics, it is to accompany a group of fellows who are doing good politics, but in the area that I dominate and know about."

Working Politics

On a sunny Saturday morning at the vocational center, I join Ezequiel and half a dozen activists for a volunteer activity. Our goal is to improve the patio connecting all the classrooms: we need to add a smooth layer of concrete over the rough surface. Alan, a young instructor, tells me, "It is a disaster, mothers come with strollers and cannot pass."

Mario, the director of the center, is present, but he is not that involved in the event. He leaves for a bit to buy chickens to cook, then has a meeting with a representative of an allied group, and finally spends time doing paperwork. The clear boss of today's activities is Ezequiel, who seems to be in his element. He has been talking for a while about "giving a special touch to the place": "Here we need to have a good patio, what I want to do in the future, like landscaping, is a fountain with a waterfall with plants and things like that." He recently suffered a knee injury, but today he plays loud classic rock and dances to some of the tunes as he oversees everyone's work. He also scolds those who make mistakes: almost everyone is younger than he is, and many are professors and students who are not as familiar with

Fig. 9.2. *Celebrating Children's Day.*

construction work. Some of us prepare the mix of cement, lime, sand, and water. We gather heavy bags, fill buckets with the right proportion, blend it all together, and take it in a wheelbarrow to where it needs to be poured. It is tough work, but people are in great spirits, making jokes and drinking *fernet* and Coke (Argentina's most popular cocktail) from a shared jug.

Throughout the event, Ezequiel teaches me how to do each task. He shows the proper technique for lifting heavy stuff and using a spade without hurting your back and legs. He also checks that the proportions used in the mix remain consistent; otherwise the floor we are building will not last. At one point he asks me to help dig a ditch for a water pipe. He assists with the work constantly, but his role is more of a supervisor. Every time people need any tool or material, they ask him first.

The hours go by, and we start getting hungry. There are two fellows cooking the chickens, the smell is alluring, and people begin to suggest stopping for lunch. Nevertheless, Ezequiel says no break until the work is complete: "It depends on you guys," he adds with a smile. It is an effective incentive, but the task is complex, and it takes us until four in the afternoon to finish it. Eventually we sit down, joking that the chickens are undercooked despite taking so long.

The big test for the new patio comes two weeks later, when the organization celebrates Children's Day with a festival. As I arrive mid-morning on that day, I find Ezequiel loudly complaining that none of the people who had signed up to organize the event had arrived yet. There are lots of things to prepare, and as he tells me, "if people do not start doing what they said they would do, all their ideas for today are going to stay up in the air." However, minutes later, other activists show up and the mood improves. Everyone begins to collaborate. From that moment until he leaves hours later, Ezequiel never stops setting up things for children to play. First, he places barriers on the street to block traffic, then arranges a space for sack races, a tennis net, and a rented inflatable castle.

However, the main task for today is preparing a portable stage so performers (clowns, a master of ceremonies, even a series of rap battles) can entertain the audience. As soon as we begin working, a problem emerges: the bolts needed to put everything together are missing. Ezequiel rants about the carelessness of people ("Those bolts are worth four hundred pesos") while he figures out a solution. He takes wire and begins tying together the loose pieces. The idea works: we climb on the stage and see it is sound.

The event turns out to be a success. It is an unseasonably warm day, and many children from the community show up. At any given moment, at least thirty kids are playing together, along with a similar number of adults. The clowns make everyone laugh, there is a funny game of musical chairs, and teenagers enjoy the music. Just like the volunteer event two weeks ago, we eat roasted chicken. As I depart around five, I look for Ezequiel. Others tell me he left a bit ago because he had something to do.

Moral Boundaries

It is noon and instructors share lunch with students at the vocational center's kitchen. As we finish eating, we talk about different topics: a new TV show about the famous drug lord Pablo Escobar, which brand of maté is the best, and the relative benefits of a vegetarian diet over a meat-centered one. At one point, Ezequiel begins talking about parenting. "Becoming a dad is easy," he says to a few teenagers present, "but filling the role of a dad, that is difficult." Luis adds, "When you are a dad, you learn every day."

Along with Ezequiel, Luis was a frequent presence at the location. A short man in his forties, he had almost three decades of experience working as an informal vendor in public transportation: "I sold sewing machines on the buses, I sold hair clippers, I sold all sorts of things, whatever you can think of. I even sold Bibles." He began participating when he took Ezequiel's course on electricity. After that, he enrolled in a remedial high school program offered by the organization, receiving a small subsidy in exchange for doing community improvement work (which usually entailed cleaning piles of trash accumulating on street corners) and attending a short course at a local university.

Luis was open about his hopes to get a diploma, enroll in higher education, and become a teacher like others in the organization. He made progress toward his high school degree, and frequently talked about the contents of the college course he was taking. He also described his fears as an aging street vendor without any retirement plans: "I do not want to sell on the buses anymore. I do not want to end up like many people I know, many fellows who died, they were old, I was young, I was beginning to sell, they were grown men, who ended dying with nothing. Not being able to talk, barely able to get on the bus."

Luis's fellows were supportive, but privately many expressed doubts about the feasibility of his plans, focusing on his family troubles and struggles with alcohol abuse. Some referred to him as a "loose cannon" (*tiro al aire*): "He hits the bottle . . . you will see, as soon as he gets paid, he vanishes." Other participants described him as a well-intentioned guy who had made many mistakes in his life and did not pay enough attention to his children.

Ezequiel shared many of these views. He was sympathetic, but also deeply skeptical, about Luis's efforts. From his perspective, the problem was that Luis never ceased to behave like a reckless youth, in contrast to people like himself, who eventually matured and settled: "Luis is only now studying. I knew him young; he was a street sweeper. A drunkard and womanizer, which are things that are fine in their moment. I liked to party, I went out on Saturdays and Sundays, I shared beers with my friends, things that are fine, but to dedicate [oneself] completely to that for years, that is a different thing." For Ezequiel, Luis's troubles were the result of his incapacity to plan for the future: "Drinking with your friends, two or three hours drinking, that is an investment of time. Being with a girl, two hours here, three hours there, losing time and money. Luis found ways, street vending, and with that he survived. He invested twenty-five, thirty years in that, and the moment came when his body responded differently, and besides he had tons of kids."

Luis was painfully aware of other people's criticism and frequently unloaded on me about the ways in which selling on buses had given him valuable knowledge, and how the very people who berated him had announced projects that ended in nothing. From his perspective, he was taken advantage of because of his willingness to work before getting paid, whereas others like Ezequiel "would not grab a shovel even if a judge ordered them to." His past was not the real issue, he maintained.

The conflict extended for months until eventually Luis left the organization. He obtained his high school diploma but could not obtain the better job he was hoping for. People in the group said he had returned to street vending, and after a few weeks, I was able to meet with him during a lunch break. He complained bitterly that others had exploited him, recalling the times when he was told to wait for job opportunities that never materialized.

Ezequiel had a different take on the situation. According to him, Luis lacked "the essence of work," the personal drive to improve oneself: "He did not worry about learning. I have all these things, but that is because for many years I bothered, I worked, I prepared." Luis had done too little, too late: "He thought that with a small course he did at the university he was going to progress, but it is not like that, you have to make a bigger effort."

The situation with Luis was not an isolated instance. In fact, even though Ezequiel is a friendly fellow, always willing to chat, share a meal, and help with work, he is also very strict and defensive about the organization's resources. This frequently put him on a collision course with other activists. Referring to some who left around the same time as Luis, he grumbled: "They came here, sat down, and drank maté They did not even clean, take care of the place. They liked to earn money each month, doing nothing."

Ezequiel also clashed with neighbors who approached the organization seeking help. When the group received funds to administer workfare cooperatives, beneficiaries complained about him. This situation, however, only confirmed his perceptions. While other places may distribute assistance without requiring much effort in return, his organization was different: "We made them work: we built the perimeter, the foundations, the floor, all that. And they learned, they did not know how to do anything, and here they learned to raise walls. What did those who were in other cooperatives learn? To sweep the streets."

By comparing himself to individuals of whose behavior he disapproves—establishing what Michèle Lamont (2000) calls "moral boundaries"—Ezequiel is able to construct a sense of personal worthiness. He juxtaposes people like him, who accumulate and share valuable skills, with others who waste their time doing little more than cleaning curbs: "They disappoint me because they prefer to sweep a street, which is not bad, but if you are an electrician, a painter, a plumber, what are you doing sweeping the street? You have no initiative. You studied under me, you are a professional electrician, what are you doing sweeping the street?" Ezequiel's identity is rooted in traditional notions of working-class masculinity, which place high value on public displays of hard work and delayed gratification. Therefore, his contributions to the community help him claim membership in categories associated with higher moral status not just by association with respectable activities but also through the separation (both in his eyes and those of others) from stigmatized behaviors.

Materializing Ideas

As I arrive at the organization's building at noon on a Wednesday, I am surprised to find the door closed. I knock for a while, but no one answers. I call Constanza, the unofficial daily manager of the place. She tells me that if the door is not locked, it means Ezequiel is around. I open and enter, but the place looks deserted. I eventually find two young activists cleaning the textile workshop.

About ten minutes later, Ezequiel shows up: he had left to buy supplies. He happily tells me that he and the two fellows will "play around" with the machines, and proceeds to show me the many videos he downloaded from the internet, explaining how to use paint and household items to print images onto cloth. He shares the design of a shirt he made for his son. The product did not turn out very well, but he is enthusiastic about learning a new trade and, more importantly, getting others interested in it. His goal, he says, is to make T-shirts for the students in his electricity class.

Over the course of many days, Ezequiel continues working on this project. The workshop has been inactive for a while after the person who used it left the organization, and Ezequiel seems bent on making the whole thing productive again: "People do not take advantage of this place, we have this workshop, we have the machines there, we have everything. You will see, I will begin to fill this place with people." A few weeks after I first saw him try his luck with the project, he proudly gives me one of his course T-shirts: the quality is much better than the first attempts.

In the three and a half years I did research on his organization, I almost never saw Ezequiel idle. The group's building, with its many rooms filled with machines, tools, and computers accumulated over the years, is an ideal place for someone like him who is constantly seeking ways to keep busy. This role is particularly important because, as a small independent contractor, Ezequiel is affected by the ups and downs of the construction industry. Life has taught him that plentiful employment never lasts long, so to make a living, he must take every gig available when opportunities arise: "I teach a course here, and then all the other jobs are off the books. Mowing grass? I go and mow grass. They need to fix plumbing? I go and fix the plumbing. Those are small jobs that add up; since I am multifunctional, they call me from all places, I know how to fix plumbing, gas, construction, painting."

Occupational instability is far from the only expression of Ezequiel's professional vulnerability. As one of the weakest links in a business characterized by few protections and frequent abuse, he is also exposed to fraud and wage theft: "The contractor that succeeds . . . it is because he's screwing his people, his workers; he hires people and does not pay them." He recalls with bitterness the time when he was swindled out of half his pay for the renovation of a whole house. Three contractors and an architect "washed their hands," passing the buck to one another and leaving Ezequiel, as an unregistered worker, without legal recourse.

In other words, having many skills and a reputation for dependability has allowed Ezequiel to sustain his family but has never shielded him from lean times and unscrupulous employers. Contracts are not always enforced, and periods of intense employment and tight deadlines follow intervals with little to no work. The organization thus acts as a refuge from a frequently unreliable job market, not only providing a small yet regular salary but also allowing him to fill unwanted empty time with productive things to do. This opportunity reinforces the perception he has of his role in the group. Ezequiel sees himself as a doer, a person who produces what others can only conceive of. While other activists use their formal education to envision elaborate plans for the group, without his extensive practical experience and work capacity, those plans would not be possible: "The ideals that the fellows say to me captivated me, but you have to work on them because otherwise it all ends up in words. Of all the words that the fellows say, I try, from the role I fulfill, to make it real. Materialize the ideas of the fellows." Therefore, Ezequiel's limited participation in debates and rallies is not a sign of weak commitment. From his perspective, a higher investment in such activities would in fact undermine his contribution to the organization, because it would divert him from the things he can do best: teaching, building, and producing.

The Things That Strengthen You

The men's soccer World Cup is reaching its climax, and Argentina's team has just won a crucial match. For the first time since 1990, it will play in the tournament's final. The next day, an exultant Ezequiel tells me: "Yesterday was a day of joy for our people. Everyone was celebrating. We returned to a place where we had not been for a long time."

Ezequiel's comment indicates more than his passion for soccer. It also reflects a common interpretation among Argentineans of their nation's history as a long fall from grace. Members of different social classes are confronted with the consequences of the country's economic decline. For higher-income citizens, this situation is experienced as shame over the nation's unfulfilled potential and a sense of growing isolation from the world. For people like Ezequiel, the decline takes on a more immediate expression, as a profound deterioration of living conditions. Born in the early 1970s, he has seen firsthand the consequences of rising unemployment and violence in his community. Life in the neighborhood was never easy, but during his lifetime, the present has become more chaotic and the future less certain. Structural transformations have drastically affected working-class families, undermining the institutions that shaped daily life and reducing opportunities for upward mobility.

Faced with these challenges and taking advantage of the consolidation of democratic rule, countless groups in Argentina have organized in the past few decades to demand access to what they see as their rights. The fact that protests in public spaces are far more common than sports celebrations contradicts the frequent self-deprecating comment that Argentineans only care about their country during the World Cup.

Given their important role in recent history, it is not surprising that social movements like the *piqueteros* have received substantial attention from observers, journalists, and scholars. However, the great diversity of experiences among rank-and-file members has sometimes been drowned out by stigmatizing and idealizing narratives, which downplay the stories of people like Ezequiel if they fail to fit preconceived notions of what political participation should look like.

For Ezequiel, activism offers a way to voice grievances, support his community, and most importantly, get involved in what he considers wholesome activities. He sees himself as a hardworking man in a community where good jobs are gone. His capacity to toil for long hours, do high-quality labor, and learn new skills has allowed him to weather the worst consequences of neoliberal reforms. However, others in his neighborhood have not been so fortunate. By teaching vocational courses, improving his organization's vocational center, and generating job opportunities, Ezequiel has devoted the past few years to incorporating at least some people into a cherished yet threatened lifestyle. As he says with pride: "We need to keep this place working, because even if we made it with a lot of sacrifice, with many defects, most people who came here looking for work learned something. Those are the things that strengthen you."

Note

1. Names have been replaced by pseudonyms.

References

Alvaredo, Facundo, Guillermo Cruces, and Leonardo Gasparini. 2018. "A Short Episodic History of Income Distribution in Argentina." *Latin American Economic Review* 27 (7): 2–45.
Donza, Eduardo. 2019. *Heterogeneidad y fragmentación del mercado de trabajo (2010–2018)*. Buenos Aires: Observatorio de la Deuda Social Argentina and EDUCA.
Groisman, Fernando. 2013. "Gran Buenos Aires: Polarización de ingresos, clase media e informalidad laboral, 1974–2010." *Revista CEPAL* 109: 85–105.
Lamont, Michèle. 2000. *The Dignity of Working Men: Morality and the Boundaries of Race, Class, and Immigration*. Cambridge, MA: Harvard University Press.
Viterna, Jocelyn. 2013. *Women in War: The Micro-processes of Mobilization in El Salvador*. New York: Oxford University Press.
Wolford, Wendy. 2010. *This Land Is Ours Now: Social Mobilization and the Meanings of Land in Brazil*. Durham, NC: Duke University Press.

Suggested Reading

Pereyra, Sebastián, Germán J. Pérez, and Federico Schuster, eds. 2008. *La huella piquetera: Avatares de las organizaciones de desocupados después de 2001*. La Plata, Argentina: Ediciones Al Margen.
Rossi, Federico M. 2017. *The Poor's Struggle for Political Incorporation: The Piquetero Movement in Argentina*. New York: Cambridge University Press.
Svampa, Maristella, and Sebastián Pereyra. 2003. *Entre la ruta y el barrio: La experiencia de las organizaciones piqueteras*. Buenos Aires: Biblos.

CHAPTER 10

Nelson and Celia
FEELING POTHOLES AND DEBT IN THE BONES

Jorge Derpic

Only months before the major political crisis that hit Bolivia in late 2019, Nelson and Celia,[1] residents of La Paz—the government seat—in their early forties, debated selling the family's car. For the last three years, serious medical difficulties had largely affected Nelson and, recently, Celia. Growing debts for long-term healthcare expenses, a car loan, and Nelson's limited ability to continue working as an independent taxi driver pushed the couple to consider selling the vehicle to ease their economic burdens. On the one hand, such a decision would have implied losing the family's main source of income and jeopardizing their two teenage kids' educational future. On the other hand, however, they would have gotten free of debt and potentially started over.

In the end, Nelson and Celia held on to the car. Despite the overwhelming economic pressures they faced, it soon proved to be the right decision. A few months later, the car became more essential than ever for the family to weather two major crises. First, between October and November of 2019, the country was paralyzed due to widespread mobilizations that forced Evo Morales, the first Indigenous president in the history of the country, to resign. In a highly contentious scenario, the opposition accused Morales of having committed electoral fraud. His supporters, in turn, claimed that he was the victim of a coup.

And, second, while preparing redo elections to elect a new president, the caretaker government, led by former opposition senator Jeanine Áñez, introduced tough stay-in-place orders to contain the COVID-19 pandemic. These measures worsened the situation for those who, like Nelson and Celia, lived off the informal markets and were attempting to recover from the impact of the preceding political crisis. Throughout both crises, a convalescent Nelson partially returned to work and managed to at least cover the family's most

Fig. 10.1. *A view of La Paz from a Teleférico cabin in 2019.*

basic needs, though still far from what he had made prior to getting sick, in less difficult times.

I met Nelson in 2011 through a mutual friend from the US expat community who lived in La Paz at the time. For foreigners who move into the city, having the contact information of a trustworthy taxi driver is as crucial as drinking bottled water. I myself, being Bolivian but then a graduate student at the University of Texas at Austin, relied on Nelson on several occasions for my trips between La Paz and El Alto, either for research or trips to the airport. As they did with me, I shared Nelson's contact information with acquaintances and friends, who continue to rely on him when they need his services.

The country's stability at the beginning of the 2010s contrasted with the uncertainty that most Bolivians faced between 2019 and 2020. By the end of the decade, the overall economic well-being and optimism in the country were practically gone. On top of struggling with Nelson's medical expenses, the family confronted a volatile political scenario that significantly cut their income due to their total dependence on Nelson's trade. By August of 2020, when we resumed talking over the phone after almost a year, Nelson and Celia explained how close they felt to reaching a full collapse: "One thing came after another. The pandemic finished us off," Nelson told me. Sheltered and isolated for months due to the stay-in-place orders, and with almost no income, they struggled to cover expenses.

How did Nelson and Celia cope with unexpected family and national crises after experiencing palpable economic improvements for a decade? The couple's struggles since 2016 offer a glimpse into the reality of other Bolivian citizens who, like them, came up with all kinds of resources to make ends meet. Fiercely competitive and uncertain labor markets, nonexistent social benefits, growing debt, and overreliance on a single trade brought their vulnerability to the fore.

Informal Work in Stable and Critical Times

Over the last two decades, Nelson and Celia have enjoyed high levels of economic stability but have also encountered periods of uncertainty. Since 2016, their everyday struggles highlight some shortcomings of Bolivia's social and macro-economic success under the administration of Evo Morales (2006–2019). While in power, Morales and his party, the Movement toward Socialism (Movimiento al Socialismo; MAS), pursued a strong anti-imperialist rhetoric and distanced itself from the preceding so-called neoliberal governments. From the mid-1980s until the early 2000s, these governments privileged free market policies over social spending, strictly following the dictates of the World Bank and the International Monetary Fund. In contrast, since 2006, the MAS adopted a nominally socialist and decolonial agenda that, in practice, emphasized national development, strengthened the state apparatus, and aimed to include historically disadvantaged populations symbolically, politically, and economically.

Morales's first term (2006–2010) stands as one of the most successful Pink Tide administrations of the 2000s across the region. Besides increasing the state's participation in the economy, the MAS government negotiated better natural gas prices with transnational companies and led the constituent assembly that transformed Bolivia into the first Latin American plurinational state. The boom in global commodity prices that benefited the region brought with it sustained economic growth and reduced poverty and inequality. This promising international context also allowed the government to maintain and expand conditional cash transfer (CCT) programs, recommended and disseminated by the World Bank throughout Latin America a decade earlier.

Nelson and Celia also enjoyed economic well-being during these years. Nelson's stable income as a taxi driver and Celia's multiple jobs allowed the couple to pay off some debts and improve their overall living situation. However, the combined effects of declining international commodity prices and an unforeseen illness dramatically changed their fate. The instability inherent in informal work coalesced with the legacy of neoliberal reforms introduced in the mid-1980s, pushing Nelson and Celia into a vulnerable situation.

Indeed, fully dismantling neoliberalism proved difficult for the MAS. Especially regarding labor and income stability, the economic improvements were not sustainable over time. By 2012, seven out of ten inhabitants of Bolivian cities relied on intermittent and precarious jobs to make a living. Five out of ten inhabitants of La Paz, and more than six out of ten in the neighboring and Aymara Indigenous-majority city of El Alto, worked in the informal economy. The 2020 pandemic worsened the situation. By the end of that year, the National Institute of Statistics (INE) reported that more than eight out of ten Bolivian working-age individuals lived hand to mouth, that is, getting by with the earnings they made each day.

To cope with uncertainty and get some control over their lives, informal workers in Bolivia and elsewhere develop all kinds of strategies. When problems beyond their reach affect their daily income—such as the subsequent crises of 2019 and 2020—solidarity and patronage networks complement the meager support, if any, that these workers receive individually from the state. As Larissa Lomnitz (1977) has argued for the inhabitants of a Mexican shantytown in the 1970s, marginalized citizens tend to rely on real or fictive kinship networks to survive. Nelson and Celia's case, however, demonstrates that these relationships can also allow citizens to significantly improve their living conditions or, like some Aymara entrepreneurs, even to accumulate profit.

Living in the Hills

Nelson and Celia's children regularly contribute to the household income, although they often reassess their priorities. For example, before the COVID-19 pandemic, the couple's daughter and son, a college and high school student, respectively, helped Celia sell clothes in El Alto on some weekends. They were able to do this because Nelson was slowly returning to work. Had the family sold the taxi car in mid-2019, the siblings would probably have entered the labor force as full-time workers and dropped their studies. And Nelson would have lost his two-decades of experience as a driver and the flexibility he still needs to treat his ongoing symptoms and heal.

As a taxi driver, Nelson can choose his own schedule, which is why he offers to pick me up for our first interview one morning in June of 2019. "It will be easier than giving you my address," he tells me over the phone and asks me to wait for him across from La Paz's General Cemetery. On that morning, I take one of the public transportation minivans, locally known as *minibuses*, from the house I rent in the middle- to upper-class neighborhood of Sopocachi and head toward the cemetery. The area is buzzing with the occasional cemetery visitors, regular street vendors, stores selling everything from wholesale groceries to veterinary services, and dozens of public and semiprivate transportation vehicles that pick up and drop off passengers wherever they can, sometimes in the middle of the street. This is a historically working-class area of La Paz, adjacent to the Uyustus, the largest street market of the city. I stand across from the 20-foot-tall arch of the cemetery's entrance while listening to the sounds of music playing on speakers, beeping cars, and engines that accompany the voices of flower vendors who sell prayers to those mourning their deceased relatives. Behind me, small stands almost completely cover the walls of the block-size neighborhood food market.

Nelson arrives in his blue sedan soon after our scheduled time. I follow the car as it slows down and jump into it as soon as Nelson finds where to park. At 12,000 feet above sea level, we are both layered up, but still freeze in the shade despite the shining sun. He looks healthier than he did a year and a half earlier, when I visited my family in La Paz for Christmas and last saw him. He is not as pale or skinny, and his eyes do not look sunken. He has lost some hair and is still not back to his weight prior to his surgery in 2016 but remains as friendly and kind as ever. We try but fail to give each other a hug while sitting in the car before he starts the engine and drives us away from the cemetery. Along the way, I realize that he was right about his home address, I would have gotten lost trying to find it on my own going uphill through meandering and paved but deteriorated streets. Later, I will learn how much pain potholes bring to someone experiencing Nelson's health issues and why he is swerving to avoid driving over them that morning.

Nelson and Celia live on the second floor of a brick building that she and her two sisters inherited from their parents. The unpainted façade matches the look of most buildings in the area. At the entrance, a lightbulb hanging from the ceiling scantly illuminates a narrow and poorly illuminated cement walkway. On the right, piled-up wooden poles and stones give me the impression of a place under construction. Farther along, on the left, cement stairs with neither handrails nor sunlight lead to the second floor. The apartment interior seems to belong elsewhere. It is a modest but well-furnished home with kitchen space, two bedrooms, a bathroom, and basic amenities like a fridge, a television set, a dining table for six people, and a sound system. The large living room window offers a magnificent view of the northern part of La Paz and the surrounding mountain range. Warm sunrays come through the same window and fill the room with plenty of light. Upon a closer look, one can see the city's bowl shape from here.

Nelson and Celia's living standard might qualify as middle class. They lived comfortably and managed to improve their assets for almost a decade. However, structural constraints and unexpected emergencies limited the efficacy of their inventiveness. An uncertain labor market, prevailing neoliberal policies, and insufficient support from the state when facing physical illnesses forced the family to seek help beyond the support networks traditionally available to families of their socioeconomic status. Besides Celia's sisters who live in the same building—and sometimes cooked or offered the family free internet access—loans from their extended family and quick cash from an unusual group of Nelson's friends, foreigners whom he met through his job as a taxi driver, were also key in providing emotional, economic, and other kinds of material support. These friends—myself included among them—allowed the family to cover the most expensive healthcare costs for Nelson's treatments; preserve some of their key assets, like the car; and in the worst moments, have something to eat.

From the Mountains to the City

By mid-2019, I had not yet met Celia. Nelson had mentioned her and their two kids in previous conversations, but I only got to meet her when I visited their second-floor apartment for the interview for this chapter. Because Celia had broken her left wrist when shopping for groceries in El Alto, she wore a cast that she held up with her right hand in our first encounter. I sat on the sofa below the large living room window, across from Nelson and Celia, who sat on the orange loveseat she herself had upholstered. This image of the couple sitting next to each other, and the fact that they answered the questions that I initially planned only for Nelson, made me realize that doing things together was natural for them. From then on, in our face-to-face encounters or over the phone, I learned about their mutual admiration and that they do not think about themselves, or their future, as separate from each other. They form a single unit.

Nelson and Celia have shared a life for over two decades and have many things in common. However, they come from slightly different backgrounds.

They were born in the late 1970s—Celia is seven months older—and grew up in lower-working-class families. Celia was born and raised in La Paz as the daughter of a construction worker and a stay-at-home mother. By 2019, her seventy-nine-year-old father was her only parent still living. Following the pattern of informal housing developments across Latin America, Celia's parents built the first-floor apartment above which we met for our interviews and lived there with their three daughters for many years. As the family grew, they expanded the premises. "My oldest sister lives on the fourth floor; the one in the middle lives on the third one," Celia explained, describing her family's living arrangements in our first meeting.

Nelson's trajectory, in turn, illustrates the struggles of rural migrants of Indigenous background who have moved in waves to the main Bolivian cities since the 1950s. Nelson was born in the rural community of Chisi, now Villa Rosario, located two hours away from La Paz by car. His parents migrated to El Alto in the early 1980s with Nelson and his two younger siblings—a third one died at birth. A few years later, the family moved to La Paz.

These were tumultuous times for the country. Soon after the return of democracy in 1982, Bolivia faced political instability and one of the highest hyperinflations in the world in the twentieth century. In 1985, President Víctor Paz Estenssoro—reelected after two decades out of power—introduced aggressive economic reforms that consisted of cutting governmental spending in public services and shutting down state-owned companies. Among those who took the hardest hit, around thirty thousand workers of state-owned mines were laid off between 1985 and 1986. Additionally, Paz Estenssoro removed protections and undermined job stability while privileging private business owners and foreign investors. Together, these measures paved the way for the exponential growth of the informal sector.

Once settled in El Alto, Nelson's father found his first job as a driver at the town hall in La Paz, to which he commuted every day. He stayed in the position for two years until he got into an accident while driving an official vehicle and was fired. Next, he took a job as the custodian of a building in Sopocachi, also in La Paz, where he moved with his family. After three years in that job, he joined a public transportation drivers' guild, and his wife took on the custodian job. Nelson's mother stayed in the position for thirty-two years and grudgingly retired in 2018, when the building owners' association acquired surveillance equipment and told her that they no longer needed her services.

Unlike Celia, who is a native Spanish speaker, Nelson grew up speaking the Aymara language. Due to his accent, he suffered discrimination at schools in El Alto and La Paz. "I spoke more *cholito* [with an Indigenous accent]; I struggled with Spanish," Nelson tells me. His classmates in both cities bullied him for his accent, but the situation was worse in La Paz. "I was bullied all the time. It was hard to study in middle school. Even the teachers asked me, 'Why do you write like this?' It was really hard for me to study there. Speaking and writing were tough." He attended day school until eighth grade, when he started working to support his family economically and switched to night school, which he enjoyed more. "I found more understanding at night. There were more kids like me who also had jobs during the day." He also met Celia at night school. They were friends for three years and dated for four before forming a family without getting married.

In our interviews, Celia did not mention suffering discrimination when growing up. However, like Nelson, she started working from a very young age, something still largely common for younger populations in Bolivia. By 2016, one in four children and teenagers in the country were engaged in some form of paid or unpaid labor. Throughout her life, Celia has held all kinds of temporary and long-term jobs, such as house cleaner, street vendor, nanny, and hairdresser. Nelson, as the oldest son, was the only child in his family who combined work with school time. "I had to work to help my parents, especially my dad, from a very young age. I gave them all my income," he tells me. Celia believes that Nelson's younger brother and sister "had it much easier in life because their older brother took greater responsibilities for the good of the family." These tough early-life experiences taught Nelson and Celia how to avoid getting sucked into extreme poverty and seize the good times to improve their lives. In the late 1990s, when Celia was nineteen and pregnant with their first daughter, they paused school and moved in together. They did not have much. "My only belonging was a jacket when I moved into Celia's house," Nelson recalls.

Living off Informal Jobs

Nelson began working as a public transportation driver in the late 1990s, when his daughter was born. He learned the trade from his father and soon joined a public transportation guild to drive a *minibús* in La Paz. He and a friend used to show up at the guild headquarters to wait for other drivers or vehicle owners to let them drive their cars. Since the two friends were good and careful drivers, they quickly earned the trust of car owners. "We got plenty of rides because we were very responsible," Nelson recalls. One time, the owner of a *minibús* told Nelson that his wife saw him working and recommended that he "give Nelson the car always. He takes care of it as if he owned it."

The labor deregulation policies of the mid-1980s allowed public transportation drivers to participate in a system that combined private ownership of vehicles with guilds providing public transportation service. In theory, municipal governments determine the price of fares and routes. However, authorities usually make such decisions only after reaching consensus with ever-more-powerful guild organizations, often after highly contentious negotiations.

Under this business model, the public transportation service in and around La Paz and El Alto is fragmented and highly competitive—slightly more so since 2014, when the national and municipal governments of both cities introduced their own public transportation services and the Morales government introduced a state-of-the-art cable-car system, the Teleférico, which connects La Paz and El Alto by air. These services struggle with different degrees of budget deficit, but users widely praise the Teleférico and the Puma Katari bus from La Paz. In contrast, El Alto's Wayna Bus suffered from several shortcomings related to the limited number of vehicles offering the service. Met with resistance by the guilds and private taxi company owners, who feared losing their profits, the Teleférico and the municipal bus services now coexist with the semiprivatized forms of public service that preceded them, although tensions resurface from time to time.

The slightly higher cost of state-owned services and their limited geographical coverage have, in fact, allowed guilds and private companies to continue to dominate the streets of both cities. Public transportation guilds that grew or emerged after 1985 offer three types of service: *minibuses* (minivans), *micros* (buses the size of a school bus), and fixed-route taxis commonly known by the composite word *trufi*. Additionally, private taxi drivers and taxicab companies, similar to guilds in that individual drivers participate by paying a daily fee in exchange for using their brand and radio frequency, offer public transportation services via phone calls or by picking up passengers on the streets.

Due to its advantages—basically more income for effort equal to that of other forms of public transportation—Nelson and Celia sought to buy a *minibús* when they moved in together. However, young workers like them did not have easy access to credit. So, lacking experience and advice, they took a high-interest $5,000 dollar loan from a woman who made a living offering predatory loans. This amount was still insufficient for the couple to buy a *minibús*, even after Celia added her small savings to the pot. Consequently,

Fig. 10.2. *Religious ornaments inside Nelson's car.*

they opted for buying a second-hand sedan, which became Nelson's vehicle for joining a private taxicab company.

Soon after starting in the new job, Nelson and Celia felt the weight of the high-interest loan and saw themselves forced to look for alternatives. "The interest [payments] for the car loan were so high . . . Every month we paid US$250 only for interest. Regardless, we ran the risk and bought it." To cover the interest rates, Nelson also started working as a phone dispatcher, answering phone calls and assigning drivers to pick up customers in the same taxicab company. This position offered him a stable income. As time went by, they hired a driver, who drove the vehicle, kept a portion of the daily income, and gave the rest to the couple. Nelson, in turn, extended his working hours at the desk and used the hired driver's money to cover the daily fee for using the taxi company's radio frequency as well as some of their living expenses.

The arrangement worked well until an unexpected event pushed Nelson and Celia into their first serious legal and economic setback as a couple. One night in the early 2000s, the driver they hired hit and killed a pedestrian while driving their car. He fled the scene and was never seen again, but

Nelson became liable for the victim's death since he was the vehicle's registered owner. The police seized the car, suspended Nelson's driver's license, and told him that he needed to pay the victim's family a monetary compensation to recover the vehicle. The accident and the ensuing legal process pushed Nelson temporarily out of the taxi company, and Celia turned into the family's sole income earner. During this time, she worked as a house cleaner at a diplomatic mission, a position she kept for several years. While she got paid in US dollars, the money she made was insufficient to hire a lawyer, much less to compensate the victim's family to recover their car.

Four years after the accident, by the mid-2000s, Nelson had renewed his driver's license and was working as a substitute driver in the same company. Celia had kept her cleaning job at the diplomatic mission and simultaneously studied to become a hairdresser at a local institute. There, one of her instructors, also a lawyer, offered the couple free legal advice to recover their car. Six months of multiple searches through different midsize towns near La Paz finally paid off when the couple located it. They paid pending fees at the police and immediately sold the car to pay off the last portion of the predatory loan. Crucial in this process was Celia's job at the diplomatic mission. "The lady paid me my Christmas salary in advance. It almost fell from heaven. I was able to allocate the money to retrieve the car and sell it," Celia recalls. Once they paid back all their debts, the couple were left with US$1,500, which they used to apply for their first bank loan and buy another second-hand vehicle for close to US$6,500. They also renovated their apartment with the remaining amount.

The couple's experience with the second car was significantly better than with the first one. They paid off the bank loan within six years and benefited from a bit of good luck. Nelson serendipitously found a market niche that added even more stability to his until then irregular income and was later crucial in overcoming his illness. A US expat and tenant in the building where Nelson's mother worked as a custodian lost his regular ride and asked her if she knew someone who could help him. Nelson's mother recommended her son, and from that moment on, the expat not only hired Nelson regularly but also befriended him and recommended him to a broader network of foreign customers who mainly, though not exclusively, hired Nelson to go to or from the El Alto airport.

Nelson and Celia also benefited from a government ban on second-hand car imports, intended to control their negative safety impacts and capture tax revenues that spilled over to municipal governments. These vehicles get into Bolivia primarily via contraband through the border with Chile and have generated significant wealth for informal workers elites dedicated to the trade. However, second-hand vehicles also present important challenges. Due to less than thorough inspections, they are a gamble in terms of safety, and they have flooded street traffic in large and midsize cities, negatively affecting the revenues of public transportation drivers. The impact of the ban on both issues remains uncertain, but for Nelson and Celia it meant they could resell the car at a higher price.

Indeed, when the couple put the car on the market, they quickly obtained as much as half their investment from a decade earlier, an unthinkable price without the ban. Then they added money from a new—and much better—bank loan, which they easily obtained due to their good credit record. With this money, they bought their third and current second-hand vehicle and were on their way to paying it back when Nelson's illness and the family's difficulties in covering his healthcare expenses changed things again.

Informal Drivers in the Public Transportation System

Despite the growth of the Bolivian economy—or perhaps because of it—competition among and between self-employed and guild drivers intensified within the first two decades of the twenty-first century. In 2018, the number of vehicles in the department of La Paz (the equivalent of a state in the United States) increased threefold in relation to 2003. Back then, La Paz registered 130,000 cars, but by 2018, this was the number of public transportation vehicles alone, while the total number of vehicles jumped to 450,000. Simultaneously, minibuses in the department multiplied by more than seven times, doubling their share of the total vehicle population from 7 to almost 15 percent. The 9,000 minibuses in 2003 turned into 67,000 in 2018.

The extraordinary growth in the number of vehicles turned driving on the streets of highly populated cities like La Paz and El Alto into an experience to be dreaded. But the rides to El Alto airport transformed into a gold mine, especially for taxi drivers like Nelson who mostly worked in La Paz. Indeed, the rides to the airport pay several times as much as regular in-town trips, thus allowing drivers to boost profitability. For instance, if by 2019 the longest ride from La Paz's downtown to its wealthier neighborhoods in the south ranged from 35 to 40 bolivianos (around US$5 to $6), a ride from any of these neighborhoods to the airport doubled or tripled that amount, often going above 100 bolivianos (around US$12.5).

These profits explain, in part, why Nelson avoids hustling for passengers across La Paz and prefers airport rides. In our three interviews and the informal conversations we've held over the years since 2019, he labeled these rides as "a second form of labor." They are "different and much easier than to hustle around [the city] for passengers, which was already hard back then [when they got their first car], and even harder today," he told me. The group of expats that hired Nelson for relatively frequent rides to the airport allowed him to earn extra income on top of his regular earnings and granted him more flexible working hours. For instance, with only two roundtrips to the airport, Nelson made the same amount of money he would make by driving around the streets of La Paz, searching for passengers, for an entire day. In addition to granting him more control over his daily schedule, airport rides meant Nelson had to spend less on gas and lessened his daily physical and mental effort. In healthier times, when he was able to work for longer hours, he also valued having more time to take care of household chores and to spend with his family.

Things changed when Nelson got sick. The rides to the airport became essential to maintaining his family as well as literally surviving by working for fewer hours. Traffic jams or endlessly hustling for passengers on the streets of La Paz endangered his life. For example, after his first surgery, when he drove while carrying a colostomy bag, becoming caught in heavy traffic could have prevented him from getting access to a public bathroom or to miss his scheduled medications at the times he was supposed to take them. Still, due to debt pressures and family needs, he was compelled to go out on the streets for at least two or three hours per day if no airport rides were available.

Life and Debt Decisions: Nelson's First Health Crisis

Nelson first noticed that something was wrong with his body in September of 2016. A doctor diagnosed him with kidney stones and recommended surgery. Within three years, his kidney disease rapidly evolved into multiple problems with other bodily organs and several surgeries. "I already had health issues but had no money at the time. They told me, 'The surgery is going to cost 5,000 or 6,000 bolivianos [from US$700 to US$850]. You need to check in and get them [the stones] removed,'" Nelson recalls. As an informal worker, Nelson did not have health insurance nor did he consider going to a public hospital. While public hospitals offer health insurance at a relatively low cost, their service is widely known to be deficient and often discriminatory against individuals of Indigenous background. They also lack sufficient resources, personnel, specialists, or even basic items, such as enough beds for patients. And there is always the risk of ending up at a private hospital either way. Many doctors who work in public healthcare privilege the private practices where they work or that they own.

With no health insurance and the pressure of the new car loan, Nelson could not afford surgery on his own, so he asked his mother for a loan of 3,000 bolivianos (around US$400), half of the expected costs for the medical procedure. But his mother said she did not have the money and that she was also sick—she recently had undergone laparoscopic surgery. Celia believes that had she known Nelson was short of money or had they asked for a loan earlier, they could have prevented his health crisis and the overwhelming expenses that came along with it. "His mom had a stable job and could have loaned him 3,000 bolivianos, because the laparoscopic surgery only costs between 3,500 to 4,000 bolivianos, whereas our surgery was between 5,000 and 6,000 bolivianos. But she said no, and he let it pass. I was preoccupied with our bank loan [for their third car], and he told me about asking his mother for a loan only when he was already very sick. I asked him, 'Why didn't you tell me? I would have tried to get a loan from wherever I possibly could,'" Celia said, recalling the moment.

Nelson opted for postponing his surgery until early 2017. "I felt fine, except for some heartburn," Nelson tells me, "and January is almost empty [of passengers], there is no movement." At the time, he thought, "I will get my surgery then and will get the money, no matter how." The holiday season was indeed coming, and the increased demand for taxi rides could potentially allow him to accumulate enough money to cover the bill for his surgery. However, his body did not wait. In mid-December of 2016, only days before his thirty-seventh birthday, he entered the emergency room for the first time.

Nelson's health condition had turned serious. His kidney stone situation turned into a pancreatic problem. "He was all yellow," Celia tells me when describing her partner's look when the doctors at a private clinic in El Alto saw him. A few years earlier, Celia had had successful gallbladder surgery at the same clinic and got back home from the procedure within two days. With this experience in mind, she hoped that Nelson would also return home quickly. However, things did not go as planned. The doctors first recommended taking him to the public hospital that specialized in gastroenterology, the Gastro, in La Paz, but Celia found there were no available beds. So, Nelson stayed at the private clinic in El Alto, despite the significantly higher medical bills. Three MRIs and three days in the intensive care unit later, Nelson's health condition worsened. He became unconscious, and according to

Celia, the doctors were ready to give up. They explained to her that Nelson's pancreas had "lost its head and the body. Only the tail was left." There was no hope. He was going to die.

In these dramatic moments, the medical bill at the private clinic quickly mounted to nearly US$10,000. Yet this was not Celia's main concern. The doctors gave Nelson only a few days to live. Facing such a devastating prognosis and hopeless, Nelson's sister, probably thinking about the additional expenses for a terminal case, asked Celia to decide whether to take Nelson to a different clinic in La Paz or to disconnect him from life support. Sobbing, Celia remembered the moment when she told her in-laws: "He wants to live. He does not want to die." Nelson's sister replied to Celia, "You will have to deal with all the expenses if you decide to take him to La Paz."

Celia took Nelson to the emergency room of a private clinic in La Paz. Dr. Rojas, a gastroenterologist in his thirties who had successfully operated on Nelson's father two years earlier, offered a glimpse of hope after looking at Nelson's tests. The doctor wanted to try a new procedure to save him, but offered no reassurance that Nelson would make it. Celia agreed to the procedure despite the additional medical expenses. With no financial support from her in-laws, she reached out to Nelson's foreign friends for the first time. They were Celia's last hope to cover Nelson's medicines and hospitalization bills. Fortunately, they responded fast. Within two days, Celia gathered enough money to pay for the surgery.

Nelson went into the operating room on his birthday, but all he could think of was the medical bill. "The intensive care unit charged us 6,000 bolivianos per day, so the only wish I had for my birthday, while being almost unconscious and during the surgery, was to end up in a regular hospital bed as soon as possible," he tells me. His body responded satisfactorily—he moved into a regular room on the day after his surgery—but Nelson attributes his speedy recovery mostly to Dr. Rojas. "I was his miracle. I am alive," Nelson warmly recalls. Celia agrees: "Not many people do this kind of surgery, but the doctor now does it because Nelson survived. Usually, people die."

According to the couple, Dr. Rojas is also proud of Nelson. During recovery, he received Nelson with a hug at every checkup and told him once that he expected to see him riding a donkey to Copacabana—the Catholic pilgrimage town near his birthplace. Nelson jokingly replied that he planned to get a bike with squared wheels and join a *tinkuy* squad, referring to an Indigenous Quechua ritual adopted as a physically demanding national folkloric dance.

While the first surgery turned out well, the couple felt sorely their lack of health insurance. An affordable plan or better access and lower costs for

Nelson's procedure in the public healthcare system would have allowed them to keep some savings while paying off the car loan. However, at the time, such forms of state support were still unavailable for people facing similar health challenges, despite the government's efforts to reduce healthcare costs for target populations. Until 2019, the government offered support to uninsured pregnant women, women of reproductive age, children under five, elderly people over sixty, and the disabled for procedures ranging from preventative care to hospitalization. In early 2019, the government expanded partial healthcare coverage to the entire uninsured population of the country through the Universal Health Care program, or SUS (its acronym in Spanish). However, medical doctors mobilized against the program, calling it an electoral stratagem for Morales's third reelection bid that did not take into account that the public healthcare system had already collapsed. In response, the government accused the doctors of seeking to protect their profits in the private system, and later, once Morales had resigned in November of 2019, of participating in the plot to oust him in a coup.

Feeling Potholes in the Bones

When Nelson first got sick, Celia lost her support for taking care of their household together and had to reassess her own priorities. She suddenly found herself in the same situation as a large portion of women informal workers across and beyond the region. As noted by Arlie Hochschild and Anne Machung in *The Second Shift* (2012), besides dealing with income instability, Celia simultaneously had to sustain the family economically and double her shifts at home. To balance these pressures, she quit her hairdresser job at the salon where she was working twelve-hour shifts. "I quit my job when he [Nelson] got sick. I took care of him; there was no one to buy his medications," she recalls. Then, she looked for jobs that offered her a flexible schedule in order to take care of the family.

Both parents considered it a priority that their daughter and son keep studying, and they protected them from entering the labor force. "We resumed night school when our daughter was four to give them [their kids] an example," both Nelson and Celia tell me, bringing back the memories of the time when they put school on hold for a few years, after which they returned to finish it. They valued their kids' formal education above everything else.

Between 2017 and 2019, after leaving the hair salon, Celia worked in several informal jobs. For a few months, she worked as the nanny for one of

Nelson's doctors. At the same time, she intermittently cleaned houses and offices on demand and sold clothes at her sister's stand in the largest weekly street market in El Alto. "I traveled to Desaguadero [a town on the border between Peru and Bolivia] to figure out how to sell clothes," Celia tells me and explains how she also tried to sell jewelry on consignment and cushion covers of Andean designs that she herself sewed in El Alto. The number and variety of jobs that Celia held to keep the family afloat led Nelson to acknowledge that "she is marvelous. She never gives up."

The family did find some relief for a few months after Nelson's first surgery. He even attempted to drive the taxi but found that he could not do it for as long as he used to. After some time, he started noticing that his body still had issues. He felt weak, tired, and his back and shoulder were in pain. He was far from being his old self. In fact, between mid-2017 and early 2018 he ended up in an emergency room twice. The second time at the hospital, Nelson learned that the issue with his pancreas had degenerated into diabetes. Another expense was added to the family's monthly budget: Nelson is now obliged to take medication for life to keep his diabetes under control. "I need 450 bolivianos (around US$65) to cover my monthly prescriptions," he explains to me.

Besides developing diabetes, Nelson underwent two additional pancreas-related surgeries in August of 2018 and January of 2019. The second surgery took place at the Gastro. He was lucky to find a bed in the public healthcare system this time around. Nelson's back and shoulder pain had become unbearable by the end of July 2018, almost a year after he started feeling it. He underwent surgery a few weeks later. The team of doctors at the Gastro performed a cleansing in which they removed liquid and blood surrounding Nelson's pancreas and stomach. They told him that a faulty procedure from the first surgery had caused this. Nelson then tried to return to work, but he felt abdominal pain, especially when driving on poorly maintained roads. As he put it, "I felt the potholes in my bones."

The second surgery did not solve his health problems, and by January of 2019, his condition was, once again, critical. The doctors at the Gastro recommended a new cleansing, but Nelson and Celia had already lost faith in them for two reasons. First, one of the doctors switched his first diagnosis that pointed to a problem with Nelson's spleen and joined his colleagues in recommending a new cleansing. And second, Nelson and Celia felt that the new cleansing was a cover-up for the doctors' misdiagnosis of a faulty previous procedure prior to the second surgery.

Fearing malpractice at the Gastro, Nelson went back to Dr. Rojas. After a few tests, the doctor alerted Nelson that his spleen had indeed enlarged to a life-threatening size and could explode at the slightest impact. That January, Nelson went back to Dr. Rojas and underwent his third surgery in three years. After the procedure, the doctor came out of the operating room holding a bodily organ the size of a football in his hands. "A normal spleen should be the size of a mango," Celia explains to me.

Each visit to the operating room and subsequent recovery processes entailed new medical bills and increasing economic uncertainty for the family. Due to Nelson's inability to return to work full-time and Celia's limited and unstable income, they heavily depended on the urgent support of the network of foreign friends who chipped in to cover Nelson's medical expenses several times. By 2019 and later throughout the pandemic, these friends established a system by which those in regular contact with Nelson collected the money from those living in Bolivia or abroad and then either wired or deposited the collected amount in Nelson's bank account in La Paz.

Taking Turns Getting Sick

Nelson's health significantly improved after the third surgery, but then it was Celia's turn to become ill. One morning in early June of 2019, weeks before our first interview, Celia tripped and fell on her left arm, fracturing her wrist. She had been making biweekly trips to El Alto to take advantage of that city's lower grocery prices as compared to the market close to her home in La Paz. After breaking her wrist, Celia reflected on how the family could have benefited from the SUS, had the program been available earlier. However, she was also doubtful of its potential, because she ran into several obstacles when she attempted to get healthcare for her wrist through the program. Precarious health facilities and long lines of patients waiting to receive medical attention, some of them sitting on the floor, prevented her from getting a doctor's appointment. This seemingly isolated experience does indeed raise questions about the feasibility of implementing the SUS and highlights the overall precariousness of the public healthcare system. These pressures became even more evident during the pandemic, when ICUs and ICU specialists were overwhelmed by the number of patients, many of whom they could not even attend to.

After her surgery to reset delicate bones, Celia put work and other activities on hold for six weeks. She also dropped out of the computer classes that she had started taking when Nelson's health showed signs of improvement. Nelson took the opportunity to return the care he had received from Celia for three years, as he went back to being the family's sole income earner. In mid-2019, he worked with the taxi in the mornings and took a temporary part-time job as the private driver of a upper-middle-class family in the outskirts of La Paz. Although he struggled with daily hour-long commutes as a *minibús* passenger, this job gave him a more stable source of income. He was making around 1,800 bolivianos, or US$250, per month, the amount the family needed to cover their most basic expenses, including Nelson's medications. For the first time in years, things looked more promising, but then the political crisis hit the country in October, and a few months later, the COVID-19 pandemic put everybody's life on hold.

Never Giving Up

Dealing with the shortcomings imposed by the political crisis and the pandemic after three years of sustained health issues was not easy. As in the case of the slum dwellers in Argentina analyzed by Ariel Wilkis (2015), Nelson and Celia had to go into debt to compensate for the lack of support from the state. Additionally, they relied on some of the most common strategies that informal workers use when confronted with obstacles: a great deal of creativity and reliance on friends as well as fictive and real kinship networks. However, the context in which Nelson and Celia carry on with their daily lives exhibits the "poverty of resources" that Mercedes González de la Rocha (2001) identified when analyzing the effects of structural adjustment reforms from the 1980s and 1990s. Inequality, precarious labor, and, in Nelson and Celia's case, the insufficient transformative power of social policies during the booming economy of the late 2000s has put in jeopardy their chances of finding sustainable economic well-being. Nelson and Celia's plight dramatically illustrates one of González de la Rocha's metaphors: with fewer job opportunities to work as anything but a taxi driver, his family had fewer "ingredients to make the soup."

Still, as when Celia gave birth to their first daughter and throughout their life as a couple, she and Nelson have had it engrained in their daily practice to never give up. During the political crisis of 2019, Nelson found ways to take passengers to the airport. His deep knowledge of the city's routes and shortcuts turned him into an invaluable asset for those seeking to avoid blockades or potential violence. During the pandemic, Celia started selling masks on the streets and supported Nelson's work by sewing a plastic screen that protected him from his taxi passengers—he kept working despite his vulnerability and the high risk that COVID-19 entails for someone with diabetes. These efforts will most likely allow the couple's daughter to finish her graphic design degree and their son to enter college to study psychology. Besides their initiative and inventiveness, which prepared them to face all sorts of—mainly economic—difficulties, they have learned to adjust their goals depending on the demands of the moment while always aspiring to a better future. They have learned to keep going, to never give up, or, as Celia clearly puts it while touching the cast over her broken wrist in one of our face-to-face encounters: "We have overcome so many things that I do not even feel the pain."

Note

1. Names have been changed to pseudonyms to preserve the anonymity of the subjects.

References

González de la Rocha, Mercedes. 2001. "From the Resources of Poverty to the Poverty of Resources? The Erosion of a Survival Model." *Latin American Perspectives* 28 (4): 72–100.

Hochschild, Arlie, and Anne Machung. 2012. *The Second Shift: Working Families and the Revolution at Home*. New York: Penguin.

Lomnitz, Larissa A. 1977. *Networks and Marginality: Life in a Mexican Shantytown*. New York: Academic Press.

Wilkis, Ariel. 2015. "The Moral Performativity of Credit and Debt in the Slums of Buenos Aires." *Cultural Studies* 29 (5–6): 760–780. doi:10.1080/09502386.2015.1017143.

Suggested Reading

On Urban Dynamics in Bolivia

Albó, Xavier, Tomás Greaves, and Godofredo Sandoval. 1981. *Chukiyawu: La cara aymara de La Paz: I. El paso a la ciudad*. Cuaderno de Investigación CIPCA, no. 20.

Barragán, Rossana. 1990. *Espacio urbano y dinámica étnica: La Paz en el siglo XIX*. La Paz: Hisbol.

Bessire, Lucas. 2014. "The Rise of Indigenous Hypermarginality: Native Culture as a Neoliberal Politics of Life." *Current Anthropology* 55 (3): 276–295.

On Debt in Bolivia

Ellison, Susan H. 2018. *Domesticating Democracy: The Politics of Conflict Resolution in Bolivia*. Durham, NC: Duke University Press.

On the Plurinational State in Bolivia

Postero, Nancy. 2017. *The Indigenous State: Race, Politics, and Performance in Plurinational Bolivia*. Oakland: University of California Press.

CHAPTER 11

Big Love
A POLITICAL BROKER AT WORK

Javier Auyero and Sofía Servián

Introduction

March 31, 2021, marks the twenty-first anniversary of La Matera, an informal settlement located in the southern suburbs of Buenos Aires. Pancho, the neighborhood's main political broker, wants to organize a massive celebration, but the COVID-19 pandemic thwarts big social gatherings. Instead, he is hanging commemorative banners and painting murals around the neighborhood. Twenty-one years have passed since he joined other Peronist Party militants and activists from unemployed workers organizations (known as *piqueteros*[1]) and Catholic church groups in the planned squatting of this roughly 2.4-square-kilometer suburban plot. Like thousands of the Latin American poor before them, in March of 2000, residents and organizers were squatting as a way of accessing land on which they would later build their own homes.

Back then, La Matera was all "mud . . . an empty field," many of the original squatters remember. Today, La Matera has an elementary school, a kindergarten, a central square with a playset, a community center building, and more than a few paved streets. Infrastructural needs still abound (floods are a recurrent issue, streetlights are scarce, garbage collection is intermittent at best), but most of the longtime residents and original squatters agree that "huge progress has been made." Many credit Pancho for the barrio's improvements.

Amalia, Pancho's current wife, takes pictures while he paints a mural that reads: "Happy Anniversary La Matera. March 31, 2000. March 31, 2021." Despite the heat, he is wearing a shirt and long jean pants. Under them, an electronic ankle bracelet monitors his movements. Accused of illicit drug trafficking, Pancho was arrested in March 2018 and spent two years in a jail in Greater Buenos Aires. In December 2020, he was released and is currently under the supervision of the prison system. At the time of this writing, he is still awaiting "su juicio"—his trial was first scheduled for May 2021, but due to the COVID-19 pandemic, it was postponed until May 2022.

When he is done with the mural, Pancho takes to social media. He posts on his Facebook page: "Hola, compañeros. Today is La Matera's birthday. Twenty-one years of much sacrifice. With happiness and with sadness we got where we are today. Due to the pandemic, we cannot celebrate, but, God willing, we will next year. Take good care of yourselves, stay at home, a big hug . . . The organizing committee is always at the same place in case you have any questions. We will continue to work for our neighborhood." Dozens of comments express the support of his neighbors with hug and love emojis.

In La Matera, Pancho is loved by many and criticized by others. For many residents, he is a man who "gets things done." He is a man with loyal followers and fierce detractors; a man who some believe is a drug dealer, others a tireless grassroots activist; a man who professes endless love for La Matera and who complains that, sometimes, his love is not reciprocated. A father of six children, he has many unrecognized offspring in the area, some say, and more than one lover.

Most people in Buenos Aires would have trouble pointing to the location of La Matera (and most other marginalized neighborhoods) on a map, but they would be quick to pass judgment on the work of political brokers like Pancho, who are said to manipulate poor people and to buy their votes. For La Matera's residents, on the contrary, who Pancho is, what he does, and how he does it are far from settled issues. Delving into the pragmatic possibilities of everyday poor people's politics in contemporary Buenos Aires, we take a close look at Pancho's actions and at what he says about himself and the neighborhood. We also dive into what his loyal followers and his opponents think and feel about him.

The fieldwork on which this chapter is based was mostly carried out by Sofía. She is a student of anthropology at the Universidad Nacional de Buenos Aires. She grew up and still lives in a squatter settlement, La Paz, established in 1981 and now a consolidated low-income neighborhood adjacent to La Matera. Some of the interviewees we cite here are her relatives and friends who live in La Matera; many others know and trust her as a *vecina* (neighbor). Four years ago, we began a joint research project on poor people's survival strategies. During these years, Javier visited both La Paz and La Matera a few times and had informal conversations with Sofía's relatives and acquaintances. A few months into our fieldwork, we began to hear about

Pancho—the things he did and still does in La Matera, and the oftentimes ambivalent opinions about him. Before immersing ourselves in all things Pancho, let us briefly describe the history and present-day reality of the squatter settlement.

La Matera

Most of the settlement's five thousand residents (roughly 1,140 households) are poor. More than half of the households have no titles to their homes or the land on which they live. Living conditions are extremely precarious: a third of the households have no running water, a third are overcrowded (more than three people per room), and most have neither sewage nor gas connection.

In the mid-1990s, the government of the province of Buenos Aires began planning a public housing complex in this flood-prone area. Toward the end of 1999, construction stopped, and rumors abounded about the illegal appropriation of the funds destined for its completion. In March 2000, residents of neighboring areas, together with future beneficiaries of the half-finished houses, occupied the land assigned to the housing complex along with the adjacent area. Future settlers found out about the imminent land invasion through word of mouth among friends and relatives. Pancho was among the main organizers of the *asentamiento*, as an informal settlement is known in Buenos Aires. The testimonies of those who participated, either as occupants or as leaders, speak to their extensive organizing experience: several participants or their relatives had been part of other land occupations on both private and public lands. Pancho himself grew up in a nearby squatter settlement his own mother helped organize.

"My husband organized residents block by block. He had a lot of squatting experience," María (who is fifty-four) told us. Squatters knew how to set the boundaries for each individual plot and how to open up the streets and dig trenches so that water could flow. They knew how to demarcate and reserve plots for public spaces (the main square, the future school, and the health center), how to evade a police siege so that they could bring in building materials, and how to confront the police who wanted to evict them. And they knew how to negotiate with government authorities.

Those present at the land invasion remember that "all this was like an empty field . . . It was all mud." They also recalled the "pigs, sheep, horses, cows" and that "you could fish" in the creek. "There was fauna, there were hares," several neighbors told us, immediately adding, as if to prevent any misunderstanding, that this proximity to nature was far from idyllic. "The mud was up to your knees"; "The bridges to enter the neighborhood over the stream were made of wood or used tires—bridges of terror [we called them]—you were afraid to go across"; "We brought the water with a hose, [but] you couldn't drink it." Although they remember a time of much "union between neighbors," they also emphasized that "you had to take care of your home, because if you left it alone, someone would steal your plot." Lucía (fifty-eight) best summarized the beginnings of La Matera: "It was hard to level this plot [so it didn't flood]. Truckloads and truckloads of rubble, dirt, a lot. But, hey, it was a struggle . . . We had no water. We had to go and find it on the other side [across the creek], and when it rained, the mud covered our boots. It was tough. We cleaned *el barrio*, we cut reeds, the tall grasses, with a machete. We did so many things . . ."

"Two years after we took over, you didn't recognize the neighborhood. It improved a lot," Julio told us. And every resident we spoke with agreed: "It was huge progress" [adelantó muchísimo]. This shared view of progress refers mainly to public infrastructure and facilities: the elementary school, the community and health centers, the plaza, some paved streets, the sidewalks, and the concrete bridges over the creeks that came to replace the "bridges of terror."

Fast-forward to 2019. "Now it is easier to live here. You have a school, paved streets, a health center . . . There's running water, street lighting," Antonio, an original squatter, tells us. Although there is a certain consensus regarding collective improvement, neighbors—old and new—insist that the recurring floods continue to be a threat, an exception in that shared history of neighborhood progress. In various conversations, the neighbors told us how far the water had reached in the last big storm: depending on the area of the neighborhood, up to the front door or even more than a meter of water inside their bedrooms or kitchens. The absence of garbage collection, the lack of adequate lighting in all the streets of the neighborhood, and the presence of street-level drug dealers (and the sporadic violence associated with their presence) are the three other issues that residents mention as recurrent problems.

Many recall that those "improvements" to their neighborhood were a result of their own "struggles." Others remark on the actions of Pancho, who "got resources for the neighborhood." For Pancho himself, it was all about "sacrifice," his own sacrifice in what he calls a "long struggle" on behalf of "the barrio I love . . . my barrio."

All Things Pancho

It was a cold day in August 2019. Over maté and cookies, Teresa, a neighbor who coordinates one of the several soup kitchens in La Matera, gave Sofía details about what she called Pancho's "tireless" political work on behalf of the barrio. She spoke about the workfare programs and welfare subsidies that he used to distribute among the neighbors, about his many followers, and about the rumors that circulated as to whether or not he was, in fact, a drug dealer—what residents would call a "transa."

"We are just good friends," Teresa said somewhat mischievously. A little later, her cell rang. Sofía glanced at the caller ID as it flashed on the screen; it read "Gordo Amor." This was Pancho, calling from jail. "He gets bored there," Teresa smilingly told Sofía, "and he calls me to see how things are in the neighborhood." This was the first time Pancho talked to Sofía over WhatsApp. An hour and a half later, they hung up. Pancho promised Sofía they would talk again after Teresa vouched for her. Teresa told Pancho that Sofía was "a girl from the neighborhood and is writing a paper for the university about La Matera."

Soon after Pancho's release from prison, in December 2020, Sofía met with him for a three-hour-long interview. In the months that followed, they would meet a few more times. She twice joined him in his makeshift office, in the front of his house, while he was busy at work: listening to neighbors' complaints, registering them with a workfare program, and informing them about when and where they could obtain food.

During dozens of interviews and informal conversations with residents, Pancho often comes up as a topic of debate, the subject of neighbors' critique and praise. For example, in February 2021, soon after his release from prison, Sofía had this dialogue with her friends and neighbors Noelia and Romi. They told her about the "things" Pancho requested in exchange for his favors.

> NOELIA: Romi, Sofía is doing research about La Matera, and I gave her a summary of who Pancho actually is. He is a womanizer. *Re-gato.* "I offer you this thing or a better position, but in exchange you . . ." Why do you think I won't even come close to him? I don't want anything to do with him. Okay, Sofi, get your recorder ready [laughs]. Romi also knows him. Everybody at some point has depended on him, because in economic terms that is useful. You go to him and you ask him for a "plan" [a welfare subsidy, or access to a workfare program].

ROMINA: I once went to see him. I was renting and needed a house. He wanted me to be his woman if he was going to give me a house.

SOFÍA: How did he say it? Do you remember?

ROMINA: He told me, "You need to give me some other thing [vos me tenés que dar otra cosa]." And he checked me out [*me miró de arriba abajo*] . . . I told him thanks but no thanks . . .

NOELIA: He did that with many girls. They say that he does that to everybody. . . . Financially, it is useful. The guy will give you a job, or a place in a workfare program . . . but it's "come into my room first [*pasá para el cuarto primero*]." It's like that. Many people ask him for stuff. But I will never go. I know how he is. [My husband] Dani and Pancho talk all the time. Dani would follow him because he was always promising stuff, but then he wouldn't deliver. But Dani would still follow him like an idiot. He didn't have a job back then, so it was useful for him to follow Pancho. He attended so many rallies. Pancho wanted to have his soldiers, he always played with people, with the money, with their feelings. He was always promising things. That's why nobody likes him. And then there's the issue of all the women. You will find many that will say the same thing. He is a little Pandora's box . . .

We are not sure if Pancho engaged in the sale of illicit drugs, as the criminal accusation says (or if these drugs were planted by the law enforcement officers themselves, a fairly widespread practice among the Buenos Aires police).[2] What we do know is that through well-oiled connections with municipal and state officials, Pancho obtains material resources for neighbors in need (food, access to workfare programs, and welfare subsidies). With a combination of personalized negotiation with officials (what he calls "gestión") and organization of street mobilizations (rallies and road blockades), he also puts pressure on the government to provide public works in the neighborhood. His time in prison might have affected his reputation but not his brokering capacities.

Many say that he demands a cash kickback from the state subsidies he procures for them. A few of the residents we talked to have personally experienced his predatory behavior. Many others believe that he keeps part of what he purportedly obtains for others for personal gain and to finance his own political career. Despite believing that Pancho profits from their misery, despite being aware of his (presumed) illegal actions, many residents support his work because, as we heard dozens of times, brokers "steal, but they give away." For some, his is grassroots work based on love and sacrifice. For others, his is grassroots work driven by his own monetary interests. Not a few have uncertain, ambivalent opinions about him and about the love he professes for his neighborhood.

Pancho According to Pancho

A robust man, with long black hair tied in a ponytail, a goatee, and a prominent belly, Pancho was born in 1973. The son of a construction worker and a community organizer, he grew up in precarious conditions. "I constantly lived flooded. The water came and took down the shacks. Ever since I can remember, my mother would carry me out of the house when it flooded . . . the water was always up to her chest. Every time it rained, the water took everything away; that's why I fight so hard so that people don't get flooded, because since I can remember I have lived with flooding . . . Forty-six years have passed, and it is still the same problem . . ."

Pancho began to work at thirteen as a street vendor: "I started with charcoal . . . but I also sold bread." He would later become a stevedore in the Buenos Aires Central Market, and then partnered with a friend to sell candy in bulk. "I always wanted to have my own job . . . one that didn't depend on the state."

Throughout his extensive political career, Pancho has worked with many municipal, provincial, and national officials. He self-identifies as a Peronist—a member of the political movement founded in the mid-1940s by Juan Perón. Pancho has his favorites within the movement: his Facebook page is filled with posts praising past and present figures of *peronismo*, as well as pictures of him posing with former president Néstor Kirchner and a few of his ministers. Yet, as he told us, he does not love politicians: "They all lied to my mother . . . She was an organizer and she dealt with a lot [of] politicians."

"Working with" a politician, for Pancho, means the possibility of accessing material resources for the neighborhood and, by extension (although he doesn't say it), for himself. When he began his activism, alongside a man who would later become an important minister in the federal administration, he received about thirty "Barrios Bonaerenses" workfare plans with which he put his people to work digging and cleaning ditches. A few years ago, at the height of his power in the neighborhood, he managed to arrange workfare programs for about three hundred beneficiaries. Today, recently released from prison, he compiles a list of applicants for state workfare programs he then sends to the mayor's office. Such is the nature of his personal connections with powerful politicians.

Pancho has a prodigious memory when it comes to the history and material needs of La Matera. He knows exactly how many families participated in the initial land invasion, what day of the week they did it, the weather on that day and the days that followed, the number of people who joined later. He also remembers each and every one of the claims that he, along with his neighbors, made at the different levels of government: from the earliest efforts (such as opening the streets and bringing in state surveyors), to the most recent ones (paving the roadways; canalizing the stream; and constructing the health center, elementary school, and community center). He can accurately describe the day on which he managed to draw the attention of the Argentine president at a rally. He painted a flag with a misspelled demand for a school and paved roads ("En La Matera, nesecitamos [sic] escuela y asfalto"). "To La Matera," he recalled the president saying in public, "first we are going to give the school so that they can make a correction to that flag." He can provide details of the neighborhood's many public work projects (start dates, costs, etc.); when and why they were suspended; and the names of the first-, second-, and third-line state officials involved in those projects (both those completed and still unfinished).

"When we started, it was a slum [*era una villa*], 2,300 families, on embankments, everywhere . . . We were moving people, moving houses . . . relocating families. We brought surveyors from the province to measure block by block. It was a ton of work . . . because we did not want to be a slum," Pancho told us. He thus restated the desire of many squatters to reside in a "barrio" instead of a "villa"—that urban form in which spatial stigma and social fears converge. In Argentina, being a "villa" and being a "villero" is where you don't want to live and who you don't want to be.[3]

Pancho presents a larger-than-life image of himself and his actions in the neighborhood. Until he was arrested, he said he was the district commissioner; the firefighter; the nurse; the funeral home director; and the supplier of DirectTV, roof shingles, and food. Like so many other political brokers, he places himself in the center of the scene: "If I'm not there, nobody does anything . . . I built the houses, I laid the asphalt, I built the school." And he complains somewhat bitterly about the ingratitude of his neighbors: "People forget the things you do."

"I did that asphalt."

"Did you see the school? I got it."

"I'm fighting so that they build the bridge the right way."

"Good morning, Antonio, come over, I'll sign you up [for a workfare program]."

BIG LOVE

Pancho not only remembers each public work that "he" achieved, but also the "struggle" that each one entailed, the long and contentious march through state institutions to obtain resources for those at the bottom: "Because things don't come along on their own . . . Before making a mess [*antes de hacer quilombo*], you have to negotiate. You have to go [to the state office], come back, go again, wait to be attended to . . . and all that takes time."

After the land occupation of 2000, the neighbors, led by Pancho, began to demand a healthcare center. A short time later, they organized to demand an elementary school: "We presented notes, and then it was the pressure of the people. When we presented the application for the school at the local council, we mobilized with the people, and that's how we got things done." To achieve the canalization of the stream and the construction of houses, they manned traffic blockades in key streets, stopping traffic for hours, "and thus we managed to start the works."

Pancho has an awareness and appreciation for the many tools the poor have at their disposal to make effective claims (going to an event with a visible flag, interrupting traffic on a busy avenue, waiting hours in a public office, making a ruckus with a small but loud and determined group of neighbors). He also has a kind of intuitive sociology about who can express these demands and who "takes advantage" of the generalized situation of misery: "The one who really needs is the one who demands the least, because that is the one who has to cope with need every day, to get the children out of the water when it floods . . . Those who are in real need are the ones who demand the least . . . Those who receive resources are *the sly ones* [*unos vivos*], they sell the stuff they get—the food, the shingles, the steel beams" (our emphasis).

Pancho According to His Neighbors

Outside of neighborhoods like La Matera, state assistance to the poor is criticized for creating a supposed dependency and for discouraging "the culture of work." In the dominant discourse, welfare programs not only degrade the poor but also make them easy objects of political manipulation that can determine their electoral behavior. According to this narrative (which incorporates and amplifies some arguments from the so-called culture of poverty), welfare programs and food assistance turn the poor into what some in Argentina call "choriplaneros" for presumably living off a combination of *choris* (meat sausage sandwiches given away at political rallies) and *planes* (welfare programs). This damning, moralizing, and stigmatizing discourse is hardly unique to Argentina. In the United States, government programs are also criticized by conservatives for presumably producing lassitude and moral deviation—the "choriplaneros" of Argentina are, analogically speaking, the "welfare queens" or "deadbeat dads" of the United States.

Within neighborhoods like La Matera, perceptions of state welfare are different, although not a few neighbors reproduce the surrounding stigma. There, "welfare" is closely linked to subsistence. State assistance is an essential part of the monthly budgets of the vast majority of families we spoke with (and became even more vital during the pandemic). Although not always articulated discursively as a "right," access to aid is seen as something that the state should provide to help those who have less. At the same time, beneficiaries perceive welfare and workfare programs as intricately related to the pernicious functioning of grassroots politics in the neighborhood. For many neighbors, Pancho and other brokers represent those "sly ones" that he himself criticizes, because they either mishandle state aid and distribute it in an arbitrary fashion (demanding "things" in exchange) or because they personally and cunningly profit from it.

It is an open secret in poor neighborhoods that many local brokers keep a percentage of the workfare plans they help acquire for their constituents. At least 10 percent of what the beneficiary receives usually returns to the broker: "If you don't give the money to him, he will cross you off the list." It is important here to quote Ana, a long-time resident, at length:

> When the first workfare programs came out, they would be something like 140 pesos. Pancho registered me. I had nothing, I lived in a wooden house. Thanks to him I got the money. I got paid for two months and I had to give half to him. As soon as I got paid the first time, I went to the store and spent everything on bricks and bags of cement. I told him I spent the money. The second month, I did the same, I spent everything. The third month I wasn't paid. And he told me that he was not going to register me for any other state program. "You will never be paid again," he told me, because I did not give him the money he asked for. I reckon he did something to kick me out. I signed up for every possible program, and I never got paid again. Because I didn't give him a cent. He took from everyone he registered; he made a lot of money . . . He would pass by me and would be dog-faced. Can you believe that I never got paid again?

"Pancho had six houses in La Matera. Six houses and six women," recalls Alma, referring to Pancho's reputation. "He said that he helped the neighbors.

After the first flooding, we got slippers, mattresses, beds, and food. He kept a lot of things for himself, he didn't give them away to us." The same suspicion circulates around the public works and housing plans that Pancho obtained for the neighborhood: according to many, he pockets a percentage of their cost. Although they do not normalize this situation, and vent a resigned criticism, neighbors do not have many alternatives in the face of such abuse verging on extortion.

The predatory behavior of many neighborhood political brokers is not limited to profiting from state aid. "Pancho gave us drugs," Juan told Sofía. "I would go to the bar. He would come and throw two *tizas* [cocaine] on the pool table. He would say, 'Guys, we have to go and put up the posters' . . . Pancho is a son of a bitch."

"Let's go, let's go, I'll bring the dessert," Miguel heard Pancho telling all the youth congregated around the bus. The drums and the banners were ready. Miguel knew what kind of "dessert" Pancho was talking about: a good *rodaja de merca* (cocaine), three or four bottles of red wine, and one hundred pesos for each participant. It was 2008, and Miguel was Pancho's right-hand man. "Fetch me three or four *tizas* . . . you can keep half. Now, let's go." The pills they would get before each political rally, remembered Miguel, "were the most delicious thing."

Not everyone in La Matera is critical of Pancho. There are also several neutral opinions about him ("The times I spoke with him, he treated me well. He had a lot of people working with him; they told me he was kind of a badass, but whenever he saw me, he greeted me well") and a variety of laudatory views ("Pancho gave a lot of welfare subsidies . . . He gave subsidies to people, and they dug the ditches, they cleaned the streets. Pancho was in charge of the neighborhood; thanks to him, we have an elementary school, a kindergarten, the community center, the plaza . . . the neighborhood has advanced a lot").

We spent several afternoons with Teresa before she told us about the heated argument that she and Pancho had had a few days before he was arrested, an altercation that escalated into physical aggression. "He left a purple mark on my neck," she told Sofía, "the first time in eighteen years that he got mad at me. I told him the truth: 'You have your own wife and I want to meet other people.'"

One morning, while Sofía shared maté with Teresa and her friend Alejandra, one of Pancho's daughters, they both agreed that Pancho and his wife were extremely jealous people: "Now we can't call him [in jail] because he's with her. She doesn't like him saying 'my love' to me. She says that I am a 'fat and old woman,' but Pancho never left '*this* fat and old lady.' He is in prison, and he is going crazy because I am not visiting him." Alejandra laughed when she listed the various women in her dad's life and then added: "I have many half-sisters."

Alejandra doesn't seem to have a moral objection to her father's lush sex life. Teresa does not talk much about the aggressive macho behavior of Gordo Amor. They are, however, adamant about the unfairness of the accusations of drug dealing that weigh on him: "Do you think that I," queried Alejandra, "would be starving or trying to make ends meet with my little store if my old man was a drug dealer? I would have bought a nice new truck!"

Just as Pancho arouses the affections and jealousy of his various lovers, he generates disparate reactions among many residents of La Matera. There are those who, as we just saw, truly appreciate him and his work, despite his alleged crime. Others, although they criticize him harshly for "what he does to the kids" (i.e., feed them drugs), do not deny that his "tireless political work" has translated into infrastructural improvements—La Matera went from a vacant lot with tents in 2000 to a neighborhood with a plaza, a school, a health center, and several paved streets in 2021.

Whether they valorized or criticized him, our many interviewees agreed: without Pancho's intervention, resources (the welfare benefits, the public works) would not "have come down to the neighborhood." Pancho can keep food that is destined for soup kitchens, he can appropriate a percentage of the welfare subsidies, he can give *paco* or marijuana to his young followers, he can abuse his neighbors. But they all know that without him, their lives would be even more fragile and miserable. And after all, many of them think, a lot of local politicians and grassroots leaders do some version of what Pancho does, particularly when it comes to keeping a portion of the state aid they distribute.

This dialogue between Sofía's relatives, recorded just under a month after Pancho was released from prison, illustrates the diversity of opinions about him and the ambivalent moral and political assessment of his actions:

BLANCA: Pancho is a son of a bitch, true, but if Pancho hadn't lifted his ass off the chair and mobilized people, there would be no community center, no school, no kindergarten. There would be none of that, because he took the initiative. He mobilized a lot of people to do it.

DANIEL: So what? And the other stuff?

BLANCA: What other stuff? It does not matter.

OLGA: It doesn't matter.

DANIEL: How come it doesn't matter? So, I build a community center for you and I keep ten houses for myself?

OLGA: I don't care; others also steal, but they keep it all. He, at least, stole and half was for us and the other was for him.

DANIEL: You both shake hands, you are two morons.

BLANCA: But we have an elementary school, there is a kindergarten, there is a health center, there is a plaza. Did you see how nice the plaza looks?

The dialogue continued between jokes and laughter. Olga had just found out that Pancho was registering people to receive "some bags of food," and she commented that she was going to sign up. Her sister Susana added, "Everyone should just try to do what they can [to stay afloat] [*Cada uno se salva como puede*]." Not missing a beat, her brother-in-law Daniel, who had already criticized Pancho, ironically commented, "That's why we are the way we are." The conversation continued like this:

OLGA: It doesn't matter. If we don't steal, someone else will come and steal...[Many] say that those of us who receive welfare are lazy.

DANIEL: Why do they have to deduct so much money from my salary to give it to those scoundrels?

SOFIA: They are not scoundrels!

DANIEL: Yes they are. Your grandfather worked all his life and receives a $15,000 [US$215] check, and someone who never contributed to a pension fund received money without working. Is that right or wrong?

SOFIA: It's wrong.

DANIEL: Well, then...

ROXANA: No, but they are not all like that.

DANIEL: The state built their homes, the state built everything for them. What else do you want? That's it! How much more should the state keep giving? That's the way it is in La Matera and in many other places.

BLANCA: Do you think that people don't have needs?

DANIEL: In La Matera, more than a few don't need anything!

BLANCA: Many do! I invite you to count how many people are living in houses that are falling apart... Pancho signed me up for a housing program, and they built my house. I was one of the first who got a home. But there are many people out there who still need one.

The conversation then turned to some neighbors who, according to Daniel, did not "deserve" what they received from the state, and then to the case of other local brokers, who coordinate soup kitchens and, presumably, also benefit financially from them. While the exchange was friendly, the viewpoints were diverse—the state is seen as either giving "too much" or not giving enough.

The conversation highlighted an argument that we heard many times during our fieldwork. Nobody denies that politics serve to enrich local political brokers like Pancho. However, the brokers are not judged by what they appropriate but rather by what they distribute: "He steals but he gives away." Pancho is no exception.

Perhaps the term "soguero" is the one that best captures the ambivalence of neighborhood brokers' actions. One of us first heard the word "soguero" fifteen years ago when Estela, a resident of a poor neighborhood of La Matanza, used it to refer to a powerful local broker. With that word, Estela described a person who throws a rope to a neighbor, someone who gives you a hand when you need it, like the local broker who helps you and others. Susana illustrated this (helpful) dimension of the broker's actions when she told us that she and her husband, Chori, obtained their house in La Matera thanks to Pancho. "Chori was Pancho's close follower. We got the house because of Pancho. He was involved in politics and had a lot of leverage back then. With Pancho, you got things, medicines, things for your friends, you got things ... It was good to have him as a friend. Even though he had a bad reputation, he did things around the neighborhood."

"Let's tell the truth," Frasca said when Pancho was in prison. "He was the only one who mobilized residents in La Matera. If the power went out, he was the one who called the company or organized a protest until the problem was solved ... The guy did a lot here. And all the people who spoke badly of him are now feeling that because when he is not around, things go bad, we get flooded, and nobody pays attention to us. When the guy was around, bulldozers would come and clean the ditches, you would see bulldozers everywhere."

However, the same rope (or the same hand) that is extended to help can also be used to hang you—as Estela illustrated by wrapping the imaginary rope around her neck. The same relations that assist residents in day-to-day survival problems are also used by brokers to control them. Brokers may demand that their followers do things they otherwise would not, such as attending a rally, or they may extract resources from them, requesting, for example, a percentage of their state assistance subsidies.

Rosario and Mariana, two La Matera residents, illuminated this second meaning of the term "soguero" very clearly. Rosario told us that "when you receive foodstuffs from the broker, you have to go to the rallies because if you don't, you won't receive the food, they cut you off ... [Food] is helpful, but you have to march." Mariana remembered the long lines to collect a check from a state aid program: "The same day that we got paid, we spent everything ... We bought the things that we normally couldn't eat, yogurt, cereal." Fifty percent of the amount she received, however, had to be given back to "the guy who registered you in that program."

Some neighbors will attend a party organized by their broker because they understand that this is the expectation; others pay brokers a percentage of their subsidy because brokers explicitly demand it. Some do both. Not all brokers engage in predatory or extractive behavior, although all of them expect some kind of reciprocity for their services.

Beyond the two meanings of *soguero* that Estela conveyed, there is a third possible connotation. A rope is used to tie and climb. The aid that brokers like Pancho distribute among neighbors and the infrastructure they obtain for the neighborhood (often through a combination of interpersonal transactions and disruptive collective action, or "negotiations and pressure") allow him to enlarge his pool of followers. With a larger number of followers comes greater negotiating capacity and a stronger ability to exert collective pressure—in short, accumulated power. As such, the "rope"—the *soguero*—also serves to "do politics."

Brokers as Time Goes By

"I learned how to organize a roadblock [*piquete*] from my dad," Alejandra (one of Pancho's daughters) proudly stated. Another broker, Lili, described how, alongside her neighbors, they jointly fought for public lighting and water: "We were the best picketers." In straightforward terms, these two statements capture a key transformation in the brokers' way of doing politics. The brokers that were portrayed in *Poor People's Politics* (Auyero 2001), the book on clientelist practices in a Buenos Aires shantytown that one of us authored, were mediators between a *patrón* (a state actor or someone with close links to one) and the neighborhood residents. They were problem solvers—they would distribute medicine, speed up paperwork, or obtain food for their followers, the "clients." These were personalized, individual favors provided in exchange for political support—attendance at a rally, for example. That assistance, those favors, those always partial and precarious "solutions," were offered in a context where state services and programs were only starting to be rolled out. The actions of contemporary brokers like Pancho, on the other hand, take place in a context of dense state presence in the form of multiple welfare programs. But this is not the only difference between mid-1990s brokers and contemporary ones. Back then, it was rare for brokers and their clients to resort to contentious collective action—they were not "picketers."

In contemporary Buenos Aires, brokers have adopted many tactics from the existing repertoire of collective action. They assert their claims not only at party rallies, with flags and drums, but also in the streets, blocking traffic on a busy thoroughfare or organizing a protest with "their people" in front of city hall. Today, *piqueteros* and brokers—actors who at one point defined themselves in opposition to one another—share a similar logic of action in their attempts to capture state resources. The actions of Pancho and many other brokers show that clientelist politics and collective action are not opposite or contradictory political phenomena, but rather dynamic processes that maintain recursive relationships.

Pancho for the Time Being

While he awaited his trial, Pancho was required to stay home for all but five hours a day. One hot morning in January 2021, still in the midst of the pandemic, Sofía chatted with him in his "office"—the place where he was arrested. With bare white walls, cement floors, a few plastic chairs, a long table, and a pool table off to the side, Pancho's place (he calls it "el local") is modest. He was sitting at the head of the table while Toni, one of his loyal followers, prepared him some maté. Toni was nineteen, lived adjacent to the office, and acted as a janitor and night watchman of sorts. Neighbors stopped by, and Pancho asked them about their health, their latest jobs, their relatives. While chatting with residents, he kept an eye on two of his sons (nine and ten years old) who were mowing the lawn outside the office. Pancho liked to keep them busy—the next time we visited, the two boys were sweeping the sidewalks.

Holding his maté in one hand and his cell phone in the other, Pancho couldn't stop talking about his many "projects." In addition to a shopping center, he wanted to build a pay-by-the-hour hotel (*un hotel para parejas*—locally known as *telos*) in the center of La Matera. A few blocks away from where he and Sofía were talking, a bright street banner advertised a recently opened hotel with "new technology for more pleasure." He told Sofía that every neighborhood had a *telo*, and that La Matera deserved one, too.

"Wild dreams, I know," he said, "but I think beyond how things are now, always thinking about the future. Other people buy new cars, I buy cement bags, because it's all about the future." As noted earlier, many say that Pancho has as many lovers as he has homes in La Matera. We don't know the truth of those claims (though we suspect he obtained a couple of his homes through negotiations with the contractors building new units for a state housing program in La Matera). What we do know is that one of his sources of income is the rent he makes from his properties there. He told us so when describing the way he paid for his lawyer: he sold one of these homes.

But Pancho was not only thinking about money-generating "projects." Shortly after leaving prison, he was already setting up meetings to organize his neighbors to make claims for new infrastructure: drains, sewers, bridges to cross streams, pavement, bus lines, garbage. "That's why they say I'm the bad guy . . . because I complain." While he and Sofía were chatting, neighbors came by to greet him, and he invited them to one of several meetings he was planning. He also wrote their names down for a new workfare program. He would collect personal information from other applicants over the phone, telling Sofía that the mayor's private secretary was the one who asked him to make a list of potential beneficiaries. Even under the supervision of the prison system, Pancho's activity was unremitting.

As Pancho tells it, the infrastructure works he fought for are the reason he ended up in jail. "Politics imprisoned me [*a mí me mete preso la política*]." The government sent me to jail. They wanted to build an embankment to stop water from flooding the neighborhood. But they were doing it wrong. I stopped the job. And then I denounced the government in front of the TV cameras of Channel 13. I spoke about the open-air landfill that is right here, in the center of La Matera. I have been fighting for garbage collection . . . I always fight." Predictably, not all neighbors share his version of the events that ended with him in prison. For many, he is still a drug dealer. As soon as he got out of jail, on the wall of a house near his office, he painted "Pancho wishes you a Happy Holiday." Under his name an anonymous neighbor added "transa" (drug dealer). The accusation did not last more than a couple of hours. Pancho himself covered it up with a coat of fresh paint.

Notes

1. See chapter 9.
2. The details of his arrest can be found at https://www.infobae.com/sociedad/policiales/2018/03/16/detuvieron-a-un-ex-candidato-a-concejal-k-que-vendia-droga-en-quilmes.
3. On the stigma of the *villa* and how squatters distanced themselves from it, see Cravino and Vommaro (2018). This article provides a useful overview of land occupations in the metropolitan area of the province of Buenos Aires.

Suggested Reading

On Squatter Settlement Politics in Latin America

Álvarez-Rivadulla, María José. 2017. *Squatters and the Politics of Marginality in Uruguay*. New York: Palgrave Macmillan.

Cravino, Maria Cristina, and Pablo Ariel Vommaro. 2018. "Asentamientos en el sur de la periferia de Buenos Aires: Orígenes, entramados organizativos y políticas de hábitat." https://ri.conicet.gov.ar/handle/11336/85947.

Holland, Alisha C. 2017. *Forbearance as Redistribution: The Politics of Informal Welfare in Latin America*. New York: Cambridge University Press.

Holston, James. 2009. *Insurgent Citizenship: Disjunctions of Democracy and Modernity in Brazil*. Princeton, NJ: Princeton University Press.

On Clientelistic Politics in Latin America

Auyero, Javier. 2001. *Poor People's Politics: Peronist Survival Networks and the Legacy of Evita*. Durham, NC: Duke University Press.

Vommaro, Gabriel, and Hélène Combes. 2019. *El clientelismo político: Desde 1950 hasta nuestros días*. Buenos Aires: Siglo XXI Editores.

Zarazaga, Rodrigo. 2014. "Brokers beyond Clientelism: A New Perspective through the Argentine Case." *Latin American Politics and Society* 56 (3): 23–45.

On Piqueteros *in Argentina*

Pérez, Marcos E. 2022. *Proletarian Lives: Routines, Identity, and Culture in Contentious Politics*. New York: Cambridge University Press.

Rossi, Federico M. 2017. *The Poor's Struggle for Political Incorporation: The Piquetero Movement in Argentina*. Cambridge: Cambridge University Press.

CHAPTER 12

Alberto
SERVICE WORK AND SOCIAL CHANGE IN ARGENTINA

Katherine Sobering

In October 2020, Alberto faced a life-altering decision. For the past two decades, he had worked at the Hotel Bauen, a worker-run hotel in downtown Buenos Aires.[1] Different from most hospitality workers the world over, Alberto was a member of a worker cooperative, one of nearly a hundred waiters, housekeepers, and receptionists who democratically managed the hotel by voting on major decisions, electing their managers, rotating jobs, and even paying everyone equally. Alberto's participation not only provided him deep insight into service work but also ushered him into a fight for social change: through his career at the Hotel Bauen, he had joined a movement demanding better jobs and more equitable workplaces.

In 2020, however, everything he had worked for was under threat as the novel coronavirus spread across the globe. In response, the Argentine government mandated that most hotels close their doors, part of a sweeping lockdown that brought sectors of the economy to a halt. Of the over one thousand hotels that once operated in Argentina's capital city, less than 1 percent were open for business in September 2020, according to the Argentine Association of Tourism Hotels. After months of uncertainty, Alberto and his fellow coworkers, called *compañeros*, gathered to discuss their options. The twenty-story tower equipped with 180 guest rooms, seven ballrooms, a theater, and a café had always been costly to maintain. But without typical sources of revenue or sufficient state support, debts were piling up. After an extended debate, the group voted to abandon the iconic hotel.

The closure of the Hotel Bauen was not the first time that Alberto had seen the building vacated in a moment of turmoil. Almost two decades earlier, he had witnessed a massive economic crisis. As people took to the streets

Fig. 12.1. *Press office in the Hotel Bauen in 2011.*

in protest, the private owners of the Hotel Bauen quietly closed their doors. In the months that followed, the former workers of the Hotel Bauen appealed for months of unpaid wages they were owed. But after making little headway, they eventually decided to occupy the hotel and form a cooperative, joining a growing movement to recover jobs and democratize work.

I first visited the Hotel Bauen in 2008, about five years after workers reopened the hotel to the public. Alberto, then in his early thirties, was my initial contact. At the time, he worked in the press office, which was tucked away from the bustle of customers and eventgoers on the third floor of the hotel. In contrast to the hotel's public spaces, the office was adorned with political posters, including black-and-white photographs of Che Guevara and Fidel Castro, a flyer for a worker-run factory in Brazil, and a portrait of Eva Perón. Over the years, members continued to add images, plastering the walls with portraits of longtime members and supporters of the cooperative. While our initial meetings took place in this office, our conversations about the cooperative hotel, Alberto's experiences there, and his work history continued for nearly a decade. Over the years, I would come to learn about the deep connections between Alberto's experiences doing service work and his persistent fight for social change.

Precarity and the Expansion of the Service Sector

Alberto was a rebellious child. When I asked about his youth early on, he told me that he was disenchanted with school and eager to enter the workforce. He developed a love for punk and heavy metal music as a young adult, sporting long hair and a growing collection of facial piercings and tribal tattoos. In one of the many interviews we would have over the next decade, he described himself as "really punk, really anarchist." He clarified that he never affiliated with a political party: "I never carried any flag."

Alberto came of age in the 1990s, a time that was marked by relative stability and economic growth in Argentina. Like other Latin American countries, Argentina had experienced a debt crisis in the 1980s. To address the problem of hyperinflation, in 1993 the government implemented the Convertibility Plan, which pegged the Argentine peso to the US dollar in an attempt to stabilize the currency. Officials then set out to reform the financial system, privatizing public services, liberalizing trade, and opening the economy to globalization. In due course, the state removed export taxes, duties, and quotas that had long protected internal markets, while borrowing increasing amounts of cash from international lenders.

These policies had immediate effects on local businesses. In a country once known for its strong industrial sector, many factories struggled to keep up with the demands of foreign competition. By the turn of the twentieth century, the share of industrial production had shrunk and the service sector had expanded tremendously, making up 60 percent of the GDP by 2001.

A key part of these reforms included efforts to reshape labor markets following neoliberal policy prescriptions. State officials targeted labor regulations to create more "flexible" conditions that would supposedly allow wages to adjust to the market rate. Politicians modified labor laws to ease the costs of hiring and firing, facilitate the use of temporary and part-time employees, and reduce employers' contributions to social security. With increasing leeway, individual workplaces began to permit working conditions well below standards that had long been protected by collective bargaining agreements.

Amid these labor market changes, Alberto took his first job at a hotel in the gentrified neighborhood of Puerto Madero, the former port of Buenos Aires. Such jobs were not easy to come by. Alberto had relied on his father's connections to get the job as a bellhop. "The first thing I learned was how to work under pressure," he told me one day in 2012. "Most of the places [in the hotel] related to hospitality were really watched by the managers. So mostly they taught you how to walk where you should walk and do what you had to do. There was never a part of you that was thinking and developing something your way. You were following orders and trying to make sure that the person who was above you or who was controlling you didn't give you some sort of suspension or sanction for something you did wrong." In addition to learning how to labor under strict managerial control, Alberto felt a "double responsibility" to both his employer and his dad: "I had to be good because

I had been hired through a recommendation, so the person who recommended me weighed in on what I did at work."

Alberto remembered working a grueling schedule. "I worked on a rotating shift [*de turnante*], which means I covered other people's days off. So I was there two days in the morning, two days in the afternoon, two days at night." The constantly changing work hours upended his life outside the workplace. He explained that the rotating shift "really causes problems in everyday life because you have to sleep when everyone else is up, or arrive late, eat in your house alone, you don't see your family . . . At most in the morning, I'd have a couple of [yerba] matés with my mom or dad." On top of that, he was also finishing high school. "What most exhausted me," he remembered, "was that I also studied. So, imagine that! In my life, I didn't have time for anything."

After three years, Alberto was promoted to work the night shift in reception. He was ready for the change: "It was there that I started to work with better conditions because, well, the salary was different, the hours were regular. I worked at night, but for the most part, I started to see the possibilities I had outside the hotel." Having recently completed high school, he also had more time to enjoy the fruits of his labor. Aside from splurging on CDs and rock band T-shirts, he saved his money and eventually purchased a motorcycle. He loved riding through the congested highways of Buenos Aires, and his purchase freed up more time, since riding a motorcycle cut his commute by nearly half.

One day on his way home from work, Alberto was hit by a car and thrown from his bike, suffering a badly broken leg and severe road rash that would leave scars across his body. His bike was totaled in the wreck, and for weeks, he was unable to walk. Alberto recovered at home, supported by his parents and sisters. After months in a cast, he was able to return to work, but he remembered having trouble standing for any period of time. His return to work also coincided with a new manager, who took steps to push him out of the job.

Looking back on that time, Alberto reflected: "At some point, perhaps, I could have been a militant or joined some social group or got into politics. That seemed really far away from me. It didn't attract my attention at the time . . . All I was looking for was economic capital . . . I wanted the things that one believes the son of the family [should have]." As Alberto explained, he joined the labor force to make money. But the jobs he held were changing rapidly. Without strong labor regulations, Alberto's boss was able to push him out of the position due to his disability.

This experience was especially difficult for him, since he knew the kinds of protections and benefits that had once been afforded to hotel workers. He explained, "My father worked in hotels, and he lived that lifestyle, [in the] upper middle class, um . . . He lived well, and after leaving [my job] and seeing how they treated me after an injury . . . I was really angry."

Entering and Exiting the Middle Class

As the family's oldest son, Alberto followed in his father's footsteps. During his childhood, he remembered visiting his dad at what felt like an opulent lobby in the Hotel Bauen. His father, Tito, had a long career in hospitality. A tall and imposing man with a tidy appearance and authoritative speech, he started working at the Hotel Bauen in 1981. The facility had been open for just over two years when he was hired as a doorman.

For much of his career, Tito enjoyed a stability that his son would never experience. His job at the Hotel Bauen allowed him to enter the middle class over the next decade. At the time, he was also a member of the Gastronomy Union and enjoyed a predictable schedule, working from 6:00 p.m. to 6:00 a.m., with a competitive salary, paid sick leave, and generous vacation days. With that stability, he was able to build a comfortable home with a beautiful kitchen and ample patio that I had the pleasure of visiting once for a weekend lunch. He recalled, "Thanks to the extra income [from tips], I could build my house."

Eroding social stability hit home during the 1990s when Tito's employer at the Hotel Bauen sold the business to a Chilean company. When the new managers arrived, they set out to subcontract parts of the hotel to different firms to reduce labor costs. Tito remembered witnessing the transition, explaining, "Like the history of the country, everything became precarious. The role of concierge disappeared, and [the] receptionist started to also work at the register." In effect, when third parties took over, jobs were dissolved and combined, and longtime employees were rehired into these new roles without full benefits, seniority, or labor protections.

When Alberto started his career in hospitality nearly twenty years later, he entered a labor market very different from the one his father had initially navigated. As labor protections were rolled back or removed and trade unions lost bargaining power, Alberto weathered the instability of what Arne Kalleberg (2009) calls "precarious work"—formal and informal work that is characterized by low wages, the lack of benefits, unpredictable schedules, stressful conditions, and even physical hazards.

After he lost his job following the motorcycle accident, Alberto sued the

Fig. 12.2. *The Hotel Bauen after its inauguration in 1978. Source: Wikipedia.*

company for indemnity while going back to school to study gastronomy. He then set out to find work, eventually landing a job at a restaurant in the wealthy neighborhood of Recoleta, just blocks from the famous cemetery where Evita Perón is interred. Alberto shifted from working with customers to laboring behind the scenes. He liked his boss and thrived in a role coordinating operations, assessing the quality of products, managing payments, and coordinating delivery schedules.

It was during this time that his career path first crossed with his father's. He recalled that when the owner of the Hotel Bauen began subcontracting parts of the business, "my boss's company managed to get in." The subcontracting started in food service and the bar. As part of this process, Alberto explained, "I started to work here in the Bauen . . . I wasn't visible. I was in the basement where the storage is and the suppliers' trucks enter through the loading dock . . . I would more or less oversee the cuts of meat, make sure they were good." Despite working behind the scenes, he was eager to do the job. "The first day of work here, I came with lots of energy [*todas las pilas*] because, well, my dad was here," Alberto remembered. But he soon realized that things in the Hotel Bauen were much worse than he anticipated. In his role as a subcontractor, he remembered seeing a list of workers who were forced to resign, only to be rehired by a subcontracting firm to keep doing the same job. Even his boss, who stood to profit from the arrangement, thought that what was happening was wrong. "My boss wasn't Jesus," he noted, "but [he thought] this was bad." When I asked more about the things he witnessed, Alberto speculated that using subcontractors provided the company running the Hotel Bauen with a financial buffer. The business's checks could bounce, but the hotel would still stay open for business.

Early on, Alberto suspected fraudulent business practices were occurring, but he opted to turn a blind eye. He described his frame of mind at the time: "Sometimes you see things that the boss does or something and you don't really pay attention, you don't judge them. You don't draw conclusions."

He summarized his individualized mentality toward work: "If he [the boss] does something, well, fine. But just don't screw me over."

Out with Them All!

At the end of the twentieth century, Argentina's economy entered a depression. Small- and medium-size businesses closed. Unemployment rates rose. And the number of people living in poverty surged. In 2001, Argentina's president and economic advisers made a series of policy decisions that had reverberating effects. To avoid the rapid withdrawal of money from banks, the government froze all domestic bank accounts, effectively locking residents out of their hard-earned cash. In response, people took to the streets, looting supermarkets, blockading roads, and banging pots and pans. In what was called the *corralito*, people expressed their discontent by chanting "Que se vayan todos!" (Out with them all!), demanding the removal of the politicians responsible for the deepening economic woes.

The national crisis erupted on the heels of a series of internal upheavals that roiled workers in the Hotel Bauen. Earlier that year, the owners had filed for bankruptcy and started to cancel reservations and events. As a subcontractor, Alberto had already moved on from the Hotel Bauen. But the remaining employees knew these were ominous signs. In addition to shedding staff, the remaining Bauen workers were paid only a fraction of their salaries with the weak promise that they would be compensated later on. And at the peak of the popular protests in December 2001, the owners permanently shut down the hotel and fired the remaining employees.

Alberto remembered the aftermath: "The hotel closed on December 28. So, imagine that one day, I come home, and I see this: my old man devastated [*hecho mierda*], my mom crying. It was messed up. It was really intense because at that moment, it was like the man of the house was working and the woman stayed home as a housewife. It wasn't like it is now when . . . both have to work." For Tito as the family breadwinner, unemployment was devastating. But Alberto was also aware of his family's relative privilege. "Thank God that when my old man hit rock bottom, he already had his home and didn't have a lot of problems. Others had a lot of debt, and it was really tough." Reflecting on the Bauen closure, Alberto felt that the experience was a wakeup call. Not only was the experience "belittling" but it was also a call to action: "I think that is the biggest realization for a person who has lived in the middle class all their life—without activism, without anything—to see so much mistreatment around you."

Occupy, Resist, Produce

In the months following the hotel's closure, former Bauen workers met periodically to discuss their options and appeal for unpaid wages and benefits. Alberto attended some of the gatherings, remembering them as "very, very disorganized." He attributed this to the lack of professional support: "The truth was, there were no professionals who wanted to work for free, lawyers who would work for free. Forget it." Eventually, the group connected with organizers from the National Movement of Recuperated Businesses (MNER). Made up of lawyers and activists, the MNER had been integral to supporting the growing movement of *empresas recuperadas por sus trabajadores*, or worker-recuperated businesses: companies that were being converted from privately owned enterprises into worker-controlled cooperatives. In and around 2001, hundreds of groups of newly unemployed workers had occupied bankrupt, closing, or owner-abandoned firms with the goal of restarting them under worker control.

In March 2003, a small group of former employees entered the Hotel Bauen to stake a claim on the property. Occupation was the first step of the process, Alberto explained. "What we did at first was try to follow the slogan of the movement that was the one that got us in here." He was referring to a slogan that members of worker-recuperated businesses borrowed from the Landless Workers' Movement in Brazil: "Occupy, resist, produce." On its significance, he said, "It gave us the push we needed to go head-on." Despite the ideological support, however, the group soon confronted the challenges of collective decision-making. Alberto recalled, "We were seeing that... a lot of things could be done, but we always needed to get [one another's] support. You couldn't just raise your hand and say, 'Yes, go ahead. Let's do it,' and then just one of us shows up. Rather, to vote is to say 'Yes, let's do it and let's *all* do it.' And that was really what created our group; we were given the tools and the training of a cooperative that was purely our own."

When workers entered the Hotel Bauen, they were joined by activists, leftist politicians, and members of local neighborhood associations who supported their cause. Almost overnight, the vacant hotel was infused with energy and excitement for a hopeful but still undefined future. In these early days, occupying workers negotiated with both police and the bankruptcy judge charged with overseeing the property. But as weeks and months passed, they set their sights on an ambitious goal: to join the growing movement of worker-recuperated businesses.

Most workers who occupied businesses eventually organized as worker cooperatives, which offered an accessible organizational form to reorganize work democratically, as well as practical benefits like an exemption from tax on revenues. Worker cooperatives have long existed throughout Latin America. But worker-recuperated businesses are part of what Manuel Larrabure, Marcelo Vieta, and Daniel Schugurensky (2011) call a "new cooperativism." Different from the traditional cooperative movement, this new cooperativism centered on developing alternative economic organizations that utilized horizontal labor processes, enacted democratic values, and prioritized deep connections to local communities and other social movements.

Despite its promises, workplace recuperation required the contentious act of *breaking the law*—in this case, by illegally occupying private property. Once they organized as a cooperative, however, the workers started to appeal to legalize their use of the facility. To build their case, the newly formed BAUEN Cooperative referenced part of Argentina's constitution that allowed for the takeover of private property for the public good, especially in cases of fraud or abandonment. Expropriating private property for public use is not unique to Argentina. The practice of eminent domain is used by countries around the globe, including the United States. For some recuperated businesses, the state successfully expropriated private property on behalf of the worker cooperatives. But others, including the case of the Hotel Bauen, would prove far more contentious.

A Family Affair

By the age of twenty-five, Alberto had held a series of jobs in the service sector—working in hotels and restaurants across the city—but ultimately decided to join his father in the Hotel Bauen. Tito had played a critical role in the occupation. After being elected to serve as the first president of the cooperative, he would go on to hold several different leadership positions. In a show of solidarity, Alberto packed a bag of clothes and personal belongings and moved into the Hotel Bauen.

Initially, he kept another service job while spending his free time "doing security, painting, sweeping [in the hotel] . . . anything they needed." Alberto told me with pride, "I'm a founding member [of the cooperative]." He went on to explain that he was one of many young people who joined the cooperative around the same time: "Fundamentally, we started in solidarity as a group of kids of *compañeros* who had recuperated [the hotel]." He initially contributed his youthful energy not only to prepare to reopen for business but also to defend the hotel from the threat of eviction. He moved into a small single room to join other members with few personal constraints—in this case, young, energetic, and often single people with no children—who could provide twenty-four-hour security and keep watch over the occupied building.

Alberto and Tito were not the only family members I would come to know during my fieldwork in the BAUEN Cooperative. Parents and children, siblings, and relatives all came to work in the hotel. Some of this was made possible by the cooperative's early efforts to prioritize providing jobs to former Bauen employees, and then to offer them to family members. Years later, that policy had long been struck from the books. But members of the cooperative continued to rely on their personal networks to recruit new members.

Research on worker cooperatives around the globe documents similar practices. Since cooperatives operate democratically, hiring like-minded members can help make that process less difficult. In the BAUEN Cooperative, commitment to the broader purpose was encouraged; activist experience was not a prerequisite. I met many folks over the years who had joined the cooperative without knowing the hotel's history and struggle. But founding members like Alberto and Tito were quick to share their stories of occupation and resistance with new members, teaching them not only how to provide hospitality but how to self-manage their time and participate in the democratic governance of the cooperative.

Even with family ties and a shared commitment to cooperativism, practicing democracy at work was rarely an easy task. All members of the cooperative could participate in the Workers Assembly, where the group made important decisions ranging from voting on budgets to resolving disciplinary issues. These meetings were often contentious affairs, with members passionately sharing their views and dissents. In one of the many comparisons he would make to conventional firms, Alberto explained that a traditional boss would tell you to "leave your personal problems at the door." But this was never the case in the BAUEN Cooperative. For Alberto, "the hotel is like a big home, and we compound many of the messes [*amortizamos muchos de los quilombos*] that *compañeros* bring from home." In addition to the blurry boundaries between home and work, the challenges of practicing democracy at work were also exacerbated by the cooperative's size. After starting with about thirty members, by 2012, the cooperative had grown to over one hundred. Alberto explained, "With one hundred people, we already have a scammer, a thief, a liar . . . You have everything . . . It's not because one chooses them or because it is planned like this."

Securing Service Work

When Alberto moved into the Hotel Bauen in 2003, he undertook the enormous task of reopening a twenty-story conference hotel *without a boss*. As Alberto explained, "It's not like it was before [under private ownership] when everything was broken into sectors and you didn't know what anyone else was doing." He continued: "Usually here in the hotel, we worked twelve hours. That's when we said, 'Well, how many hours are we going to work? We said that we were going to do everything we could to maintain an eight-hour shift and benefits for the *compañeros*." As Alberto signaled, reopening the hotel involved reconsidering the workplace practices that they had long taken for granted with the goal of making hospitality work more humane and just.

In 2005, workers successfully reopened the Hotel Bauen as the country began to recover from the economic crisis. With the election of Néstor Kirchner, the government moved away from some of the austerity policies implemented in the 1990s. The next decade would be marked by relative stability and growth as unemployment rates improved and the economy entered a period of calm. But institutional arrangements allowing precarious work remained relatively unchanged. In the BAUEN Cooperative, however, workers set out to recover the job security that had once characterized service work, ensuring members could rely on stable jobs and a regular paycheck. But the cooperative took additional steps to encourage democratic participation in the workplace. Alberto referenced the importance of the cooperative's long-standing practice of job rotation. He explained, "Here, there is a possibility to rotate [jobs] so that you can train yourself, and the cooperative always supports that training."

"How do you organize the rotations?" I asked.

He replied, "Instead of going out into the normal market to ask for a sector change, a *compañero* is asked if they want to change places and there are others who [want to rotate] for their studies or other things like their schedules." He gave an example of housekeeping, which involves especially physically demanding jobs: "We try to find rotations for them every two or three years. Today, I can tell you that all the women in administration were housekeepers ... We try to ensure that the girls don't break their backs working." To Alberto, job rotation was both practical and developmental, offering members of the cooperative a possibility to learn new skills, change their schedules, and mitigate the physical toll of their labor.

Over years of visits to the hotel, I observed my contacts shift from one role to another. I personally experienced the practice of job rotation first-hand in

2015 when I worked in the Hotel Bauen for nearly a year. Every couple of weeks, I rotated positions, traversing the tower to understand everything from how elected officers managed the cooperative to how purchases were made, how reception and reservations were run, and how housekeeping and the laundry operated. During that time, I received on-the-job training as my coworkers introduced me to their daily tasks. I also observed workplace democracy in action by attending weekly meetings and assemblies in which groups large and small made decisions through majority vote.

In addition to job rotation, the BAUEN Cooperative also provided opportunities for job sharing and options to earn extra cash. "Here, you have eight hours of work," Alberto explained about their shifts. "For those who have more time . . . they can join a list for when there are events . . . dinners or whatever other events you can work overtime. So, after your shift, you change and put on your uniform to attend to the people. There's always a *compañero* who is going to teach you; we never leave you there so you can't do shit." Overtime work, too, provided a way for workers to develop a more holistic understanding of hospitality work by gaining hands-on experience across multiple roles.

In conversation with workers, I also discovered that the practices of job sharing and rotation were closely tied to the cooperative's policy of pay equity. Although rates hovered around the minimum wage, all members received the same base pay, whether they worked a desk job, in reception, or as a housekeeper. Members debated these pay policies vigorously and openly. But in maintaining a policy of equal pay, the cooperative not only incentivized job rotation, but also symbolically reinforced that all members were *valued* equally.

Legalizing the Occupation

In 2005, the BAUEN Cooperative reopened the hotel for business. But when they opened the doors to the public, they did so illegally. Over the next two decades, the workers fought for the legal right to use the facility. The solution, they argued, was for the state to expropriate the hotel and entrust it to the cooperative. Alberto played an important role in this effort. Through his job in the press office and as part of the informal guard living in the hotel, he helped coordinate protests to support the campaign for expropriation. Marches organized by the BAUEN Cooperative reflected Alberto's youthful resistance, featuring support not only from neighbors, social movement actors, and politicians but also from rock musicians. Younger members even formed a band called "Los Incorrectos," writing lyrics in support of the hotel. Through these events, the cooperative shared the sordid history of the Hotel Bauen with the public, framing it as a symbolic space to reclaim workers' rights. The hotel had been built in 1978 with generous public financing from the military dictatorship, but workers had discovered that the massive loan from the state had never been repaid.

Despite the persistence of workers like Alberto pushing for expropriation, the cooperative had conflicting and sometimes contradictory support from state actors like politicians, government bureaucrats, and the police. For example, while city officials conducted inspections and levied fines, federal agencies under the presidential administrations of first Néstor Kirchner (2003–2007) then Cristina Fernández de Kirchner (2007–2015) offered limited sources of material support. In the houses of Congress, a bill to expropriate the Hotel Bauen had been introduced multiple times with no progress.

When the bill was finally put up for a vote in 2015, I marched with Alberto, Tito, and many other members of the cooperative to show our strength in numbers. The bill passed that night, marking the first legislative victory. Yet the success was short-lived. Soon after, the new president, Mauricio Macri, and his conservative coalition swept major elections in the country. During his single term, one of the few bills that he vetoed was the expropriation of the Hotel Bauen. To add insult to injury, the administration implemented a series of policies that were even more detrimental to cooperatives and self-managed businesses like the BAUEN Cooperative. In particular, policies to deregulate utility costs resulted in skyrocketing rates for public services like electricity, water, and gas.

Despite these major challenges, the Hotel Bauen remained a hub of social activism. It provided a downtown venue for social movements and community-based organizations. The BAUEN Cooperative was also an important player in the creation of federations that coordinated mutual support among cooperatives. Alberto was proud of this advocacy work. As he explained, "For us, the federation is a huge win, but we can't take our eyes off the goal here, which is tourism."

Service Work *sin Patrón*

Time and again when describing the cooperative, Alberto referred to its organizational structure as an upside-down triangle. Instead of a boss at the top of the hierarchy, all the members of the cooperative shared authority as a collective. During one conversation in 2019, Alberto drew an upside-down triangle on a paper napkin to help me visualize the order of things. Although it was a cooperative, he assured me, this didn't mean that the hotel had no coordination. "The structure is actually a really good thing." Alberto circled the area in the middle of the pyramid that housed different collections of jobs—the work sectors, shift managers, and elected officers who created the "rigid part" of the organization.

As Alberto made clear, the BAUEN Cooperative was not a flat organization with no internal structure but a democratic organization where workers had an equal voice and equal pay. While this sounds good in theory, running the hotel as a cooperative was never an easy venture. In a press interview when he served as president of the cooperative, Tito reflected on the challenges of working in cooperation: "There are people who have the idea that a cooperative is like a pseudo-business." He cautioned the reporter against this perspective. "If you don't address this [assumption]," he warned, "you are just going to become another rat exploiting your *compañeros*, enriching yourself with two cars or with whatever you withhold." For Tito, reverting to exploitative ways of doing business was an issue that, in his words, "could be woken up" at any moment. Reorganizing service work without a boss would require more than just the creation of a worker cooperative. It would demand a full-on organizational transformation. Early on, Tito expressed his concerns about overcoming these challenges: "I know that it is going to be difficult. This is one of the things that keeps me up at night."

Like his father, Alberto was also attentive to the expanded social purpose of the hotel and regularly contrasted his work in the cooperative with a private company. "In a private business, maybe you would be able to comment on something because it was related to your work sector, you know? You didn't know when the boss was going to invest . . . or where the money went. This was something you'd never know." He went on to compare this to work in the cooperative: "But [here], it's different. Here, the cooperative is open about all of this . . . Here inside we have an understanding that we can all have an opinion, all of us, with equal points of view." Alberto spent nearly ten years rotating through various positions. By 2011, he had moved from his job in the press office to working in purchasing. In his new role, he coordinated the inflow of supplies that kept the hotel open for business. In addition to his day job, he continued to oversee the cooperative's social media accounts and advocate for the group.

Over the years, Alberto and his coworkers not only learned to provide hospitality through cooperation but also confronted the challenges of operating in a capitalist market. As a co-op, the organization struggled to get access to financing that they needed to repair the aging facilities. Drawing on his years of experience, Alberto knew this was critical to staying open for business. He explained, "To be able to continue working, to be able to be inspected today and not be fined, we have to be able to comply with codes because here, what we are fighting for is to be at the level of any other company . . . We have to be even better in that respect because we are receiving clients." In the absence of conventional support like access to businesses loans, the cooperative relied on a handful of small and infrequent government subsidies and grants, but mostly on their hard-earned profits to make repairs, updates, and improvements. Alberto was often on the scene to lend a hand. During each period of research, I documented different internal crises that required immediate attention, from investments in the boiler room to repairs to the elevators, exterior cladding, and façade.

Hospitality and Democracy

A hotel is not a place where you might expect people to experiment with democracy at work. Providing hospitality is usually predicated on subservience, in which the worker uses body, mind, and emotions to make customers feel cared for and considered. Decades of research on service work have detailed how service workers interact with managers and customers to "produce" a service. In her study of flight attendants in the 1970s, Arlie Hochschild (2012) drew attention to the particular nature of service work. Paid work takes on an even more sinister dimension, she argued. Service workers have to use not only their physical and mental capacities to labor but also their emotions and their bodies in ways that can disconnect them from their *selves*.

In 2019, I undertook a different role when I stayed in the Hotel Bauen as a guest for the very first time. The intent of my visit was to share my book manuscript with the many people in the hotel who had contributed to the research. There were some new faces, and others had moved on to different jobs or retired. For example, Tito had retired after nearly a decade of working in the cooperative. But the majority of people I had worked closely with in 2015 were still active in the downtown hotel. As I settled into my modest room on the sixteenth floor, I marveled at the sweeping views of the densely populated city. I spent the next couple of weeks eating meals in the café, taking long walks, and reconnecting with members of the cooperative, going sector by sector to share my findings and publication plans with the folks who had so generously received me.

On a chilly night in July of that year, Alberto and I met after his shift at a nearby bar to catch up. I proposed writing his story for this volume, and Alberto agreed. He filled me in on his election as the trustee of the cooperative the year before, a job that entailed overseeing democratic processes and ensuring transparency in the workplace. With this newfound responsibility, he turned his focus to maintaining the cooperative's viability in the face of mounting political and infrastructural challenges. While he lamented that he couldn't put his hospitality skills to use in his current position, he wanted to talk about tourism.

He told me that one of the most important things the cooperative was doing was training people in hospitality. He envisioned the cooperative as a training ground, a place where young people with scant labor market experience could learn how to provide customer service. In the bar where we sat, the floor was littered with peanut shells. Alberto dropped a napkin on the floor and then picked it up to prove his point. He explained that when people learn to pick up after themselves, it has a ripple effect. A person who learns about cleanliness at work will pick up after themselves at home and also in public. This simple training compounds into a much bigger change. More than teaching young service workers to become "useful," however, Alberto thought they were also learning how to maintain a certain "quality of life." Unlike factory work, where many sought stable jobs, Alberto thought that hospitality work had the potential to transform society. "It adds to things socially," and so hospitality workers learn to take "social responsibility."

After returning to my room in the hotel, I reflected on our conversation. For many, recuperated businesses injected democracy into the workplace. Scholars have even argued that economic democracy has a "spillover effect" that cultivates greater democratic engagement in other spheres of life. But that night, Alberto emphasized the importance of building cultural capital through customer service. He was explicit: learning how to "provide services" was a way to address what he referred to generically as "social problems" and prepare people for their future.

The End of an Era

With the outbreak of the global pandemic in 2020, Argentina implemented a stringent lockdown that had rippling effects. Alberto described the situation to me on the phone: "The truth is that [President] Macri couldn't throw us out, but the virus could. Because if we don't have work, the wheels don't turn. So, we started to accumulate debt in the millions [of pesos] and we had to fix it."

Many of the challenges that worker-recuperated businesses like the Hotel Bauen have confronted intensified during the pandemic. Soon after the lockdown, the national government implemented a series of measures to reduce the costs to workers and subsidize wages. A report from the Open University Program directed by Andrés Ruggeri (2020) documented the profound effects of the pandemic on worker-recuperated businesses. Because of their particular legal configuration, worker cooperatives operate in a gray zone that complicates their access to state financial support and subsidies directed at small businesses. In practice, this means that recuperated businesses have difficulties accessing any sort of meaningful financial support.

When I asked Alberto how the final worker's assembly went, he emphasized that the decision was genuinely collective, made by the group as a whole. In October 2021, the remaining members decided to vacate the hotel, liquidate the items they could, and distribute as much of the money they had saved to the members. They chose not to wait any longer, as jobs were hard to come by and members needed to be freed from their responsibilities in the cooperative to look for work. Alberto explained, "We made the decision to do the auction where we sold off the things we could. That also was sad . . . but we made good money, thankfully, and this is something we could also distribute to members. They also bought some of the things at low prices for their homes."

Alberto was one of a handful of members who texted me the news after the decision was official. His message, which he sent with a picture of city police, rang with distress: "Yesterday at 11 in the morning, Judge Hualde [the bankruptcy judge] appeared with her lackeys . . . to receive something bigger than the key to the city: the key to the BAUEN, one of the most emblematic towers in the power struggle against the Argentine proletariat, full of stories, laughter, and death . . . Closed like it was in 2001, the great iron mass will once again rest with the ghosts who will be able to walk and dance in the great halls."

To announce the news publicly, members of the BAUEN Cooperative released a heartfelt press release explaining their collective decision: "Over these seventeen years, we have overcome all sorts of adversities. We won many battles, resisted the attacks of the neoliberal project headed by Macri, all without having the property ownership resolved by the state. We have been joined by everyone who feels that the BAUEN was a collective construction, committed to gender inclusion and diversity, a space that mirrors social struggles. We have not been able to do any of this during the pandemic. That invisible fury that has affected millions of people around the world has also affected us in the hotel by totally paralyzing our services." The letter went on: "We are putting our operations on pause, but it will be short. We leave the hotel and take the BAUEN Cooperative Space with us. Nothing ends here. Everything begins here."

Months after the press release was disseminated, I asked Alberto if the cooperative might find another location. He was skeptical. For Alberto, the closure of the hotel marked the end of an important chapter in his life. When we spoke again on the phone, he described the significance: "It was hard, hard. So much effort, and to lose it because [of] something that we didn't do ... But you have to accept it. Because if someone keeps denying it, it'll make you sick. It'll stress you out. These are problems that don't have a solution."

"If You Don't Keeping Moving, You Freeze"

With decades of experience in hospitality, Alberto witnessed the industry collapse in the wake of the global pandemic. "Hotels are doing really badly," he told me as he contemplated the wide-ranging effects of state-mandated shutdowns on the service sector. "The hotels that could open are ones that are part of international chains that can follow the new regulations and compete with everything at the height of the situation. The small hotels ... there just aren't any open." After the Hotel Bauen had closed for good, Alberto cobbled together a handful of jobs. He told me, "I do all sorts of work. Maintenance, those types of things." During one of our conversations, he was at his day job working as a doorman in a small hotel near his house. He also worked online selling goods on commission from a Facebook page while also starting an online program in auto mechanics. "Right now, I work for two hours in the morning and two hours in the afternoon. And after that, I work online more than anything." Although the official unemployment rate at the end of 2020 was 11.7 percent, this number did not capture people like Alberto who hold jobs but are underemployed.

Despite the circumstances, Alberto counts himself lucky given the circumstances. His partner was able to continue work from home, which allowed them to keep food on the table and pay rent. Reflecting on the situation, he reminded me, "If you don't keep moving, you freeze." He went on: "I'm always looking for something else. I'm looking for something permanent, and also, I'm starting to think about something that will support me beyond just what I can earn." Despite the uncertainty that characterized his career, Alberto clearly saw his work as more than a paycheck.

Finding New Hope

Since the hotel closed, Alberto seems to have found some peace with the turn of events. "In reality, it's an unexpected ending for the struggle [*lucha*]," he admitted. "You know that, in this respect, I am really participatory and, well, I believe that's why I left the Bauen feeling okay. I left content because beyond the things that I lived and that I learned, I can share it with a lot of people. Beyond providing material things, it's about the possibility that people can open a little to think that it's not all about the money and ambition and consumerism." For Alberto, the years of work and energy that he poured into the BAUEN Cooperative had not been wasted effort. Those experiences had meaningfully changed the way he interacted with and understood his work.

As he grieved the loss of the cooperative, he also welcomed a new baby into the world. After the birth, he shared numerous photos of his happy family with pride. On having a child during the pandemic, he told me, "I was just telling [my partner] that amid all the people who have died, to bring a person into the world, it's something important." For Alberto, the birth of his child brought new hope to his life. "I have someone to fight for. Before, I fought for the Bauen . . . And now, I'm fighting for my children." His close connection with his family has been a major source of comfort throughout this time. His parents were thrilled to have another grandchild, and he felt like his partnership had really deepened after "so much time locked up."

Alberto thinks that cooperatives are going to be key to recovery from the coronavirus pandemic. "After these events, the forms that are going to emerge again will be cooperatives . . . You have to find a way out for people who can at least get together to work as a team." When I didn't offer any insightful analysis about the future of work post-pandemic, he chided me for not doing my job as a sociologist. We laughed, and he concluded, "It's all really strange. Better times will come."

Note

1. In this chapter, I use pseudonyms and change small details about the people involved. Hotel Bauen, however, is the real name of the hotel that was managed by the BAUEN Cooperative. For more details on this decision, see Sobering (2022).

References

Hochschild, Arlie Russell. 2012. *The Managed Heart: Commercialization of Human Feeling*. Berkeley: University of California Press.

Kalleberg, Arne L. 2009. "Precarious Work, Insecure Workers: Employment Relations in Transition." *American Sociological Review* 74 (1): 1–22.

Larrabure, Manuel, Marcelo Vieta, and Daniel Schugurensky. 2011. "The 'New Cooperativism' in Latin America: Worker-Recuperated Enterprises and Socialist Production Units." *Studies in the Education of Adults* 43 (2): 181–196.

Ruggeri, Andrés. 2020. *Cooperativas de trabajo y empresas recuperadas durante la pandemia: Impacto sanitario y productivo y alcances de las medidas de asistencia del Estado*. Buenos Aires: Ministerio de Desarrollo Productivo, INAES, and Universidad Nacional Arturo Jauretche.

Sobering, Katherine. 2022. *The People's Hotel: Working for Justice in Argentina*. Durham, NC: Duke University Press.

Suggested Reading

On Inequality and Service Work

Sherman, Rachel. 2007. *Class Acts: Service and Inequality in Luxury Hotels*. Berkeley: University of California Press.

On the Organizational Possibilities of Worker Cooperatives

Chen, Katherine K., and Victor Tan Chen, eds. 2021. *Organizational Imaginaries: Tempering Capitalism and Tending to Communities through Cooperatives and Collectivist Democracy*. Vol. 72. Bingley, UK: Emerald.

On Worker-Recuperated Businesses in Argentina

Vieta, Marcelo. 2019. *Workers' Self-Management in Argentina: Contesting Neoliberalism by Occupying Companies, Creating Cooperatives, and Recuperating Autogestión*. London: Brill.

AFTERWORD

Javier Auyero

To "write the truest and most authentic stories for our readers," states Isabel Wilkerson (2007, 176), we need "to gain time and insight into their worlds." We have visited the homes of the protagonists of this book; hung out with them and their families; shadowed them during their shifts at work; joined them as they cooked, folded laundry, talked to neighbors, friends, clients, or public officers; and accompanied them to community meetings, rallies, and other social gatherings. We have, in other words, spent time with each of the individuals featured in this book so that we could meaningfully write about their lives, about what they do, what they think about what they do, and how they make sense of their plight and their hopes for the future.

This time spent is what defines good ethnographic fieldwork (Wolcott 2008; Desmond 2009; Hoang 2015; Lareau 2021). In this sense, the research on which these essays are based (long-term engagement and a combination of participant observation and formal and informal in-depth interviews) emulates what other ethnographers have done before us. We paid attention to specific stories, local circumstances, and concrete explanations that actors on the ground gave for their particular actions. We then translated, clarified, and amplified this specificity, rootedness, and concreteness into narratives readers could understand and engage with, narratives about violence, patriarchy, environmental suffering, patronage politics, collective contentious action, labor precarity, and other processes that are crucial for understanding the Latin American region today.

This work of translation, clarification, and amplification is unthinkable—not truly feasible—without theory. Readers might wonder where the theories are that make this work possible. And they are right to speculate, because we intentionally submerged extant scholarly work on vigilance, violence, collective action, gangs, politics, state bureaucracy, and other topics so as to facilitate reading by different, wider audiences. But although not foregrounded in the chapters, theories are everywhere as principles of pertinence and protomodels of the phenomena at hand (Wacquant 2002). Hinted at in passing reference, mentioned at the end of each chapter as suggested readings, theory indicated to us which material should be examined in detail and which should not, which observations should be carefully reconstructed in a story and which could be left aside.

Where this book departs from most ethnographic work is in the way authors impart what they have learned. Here, knowing people's lives well goes hand in hand with an attempt at writing them well. We strived to convey the results of our "deep hanging out" in narrative form so that, as Katherine Boo puts it (2007, 14), readers "finish the stories and maybe give half a damn." We certainly do not claim to be the first to conduct social science research (being rigorous, systematic, and careful in the production of data) while also narrating what we learned in nonfiction form. Although scattered, we are now seeing more and more of this type of writing in sociology and anthropology. *Portraits of Persistence* thus joins, and celebrates, this slowly emerging narrative trend.

Neither knowing people well nor writing them well is an individual endeavor. This is another way in which the project on which this book is based distinguishes itself from most academic work: it was, from its very inception, a collective effort. Early on, and modeled on what many of us had done previously in *Invisible in Austin*, we met to discuss content and form. Together, we thought about potential topics, protagonists, and narrative strategies; together—over Zoom during the long pandemic and then face-to-face in Austin—we workshopped each chapter and discussed ideas for the introduction and even different titles. In this way, we enacted what I, borrowing and adapting from Norbert Elias (1984), would call an "ethnographer *aperti*"—not the singular, closed individual Elias calls *homo clausus*, that is, the type of scholar highly praised and rewarded these days in academia, but the open scholar who works in connection with multiple others.

A sense of a collective "we" and the intellectual promise of cooperative endeavors are difficult to create—let alone maintain—in the highly individualized world of contemporary academia. This is because collective intellectual projects such as this require and rely on notions of ongoing reciprocity, which starkly combat dominant notions of the optimization of time, clearly measurable outcomes, and individual success that students and scholars confront. We hope readers are able to read and enjoy this book as a counterexample to this prevailing (and to many of us, pernicious) academic trend. Resulting from a long, difficult, and, at the same time, fun and stimulating process, one that cultivated an approach to scholarly work based on collaboration and interdependency, *Portraits of Persistence* is a joint product—one to be digested, discussed, and hopefully emulated in the years to come.

References

Boo, Katherine. 2007. "Difficult Journalism That's Slap-Up Fun." In *Telling True Stories: A Nonfiction Writers' Guide*, ed. Mark Kramer and Wendy Call, 14–18. New York: Plume.

Desmond, Matthew. 2009. *On the Fireline: Living and Dying with Wildland Firefighters*. Chicago, IL: University of Chicago Press.

Elias, Norbert. 1984. *What Is Sociology?* New York: Columbia University Press.

Hoang, Kimberly Kay. 2015. *Dealing in Desire: Asian Ascendancy, Western Decline, and the Hidden Currencies of Global Sex Work*. Berkeley: University of California Press.

Lareau, Annette. 2021. *Listening to People: A Practical Guide to Interviewing, Participant Observation, Data Analysis, and Writing It All Up*. Chicago, IL: University of Chicago Press.

Wacquant, Loïc. 2002. "Scrutinizing the Street: Poverty, Morality, and the Pitfalls of Urban Ethnography." *American Journal of Sociology* 107 (6): 1468–1532.

Wilkerson, Isabel. 2007. "Playing Fair with Subjects." In *Telling True Stories*, ed. Mark Kramer and Wendy Call, 172–175. New York: Plume.

Wolcott, Harry F. 2008. *Ethnography: A Way of Seeing*. New York: AltaMira Press.

ACKNOWLEDGMENTS

This book would not have been possible without the generous participation of the people whose lives we portray in the chapters included herein. They opened their homes and their hearts to us; they allowed us to shadow them, to ask them all sorts of (sometimes even silly) questions. We are immensely grateful for the opportunity they gave us to learn from them. We hope we have done justice to their stories.

The Urban Ethnography Lab was the intellectual home for this project. We were blessed by the unwavering support of Daniel Fridman, the lab's director, as well as that of the chair of the Sociology Department at the University of Texas at Austin, Pam Paxton. We are also extremely grateful for the financial support of the Lozano Long Institute for Latin American Studies (LLILAS). LLILAS funded the workshop where, after many months of Zoom meetings, we were finally able to meet face-to-face and discuss the almost final version of each chapter. *Gracias*, Adela Pineda, LLILAS director, and Paloma Díaz, assistant director of programs, for your encouragement and support. We are also extremely grateful for the hard work of the marvelous staff at the UT Austin Sociology Department. To Anne Bormann, Valerie Goldstein, Kevin Hsu, Julie Kniseley, and Benjamin Romero: *Gracias totales*.

For the past ten years, the Urban Ethnography Lab has been a place of fruitful intellectual exchange and scholarly production. It was also a space where we were able to share and debate the emotional ups and downs involved in ethnographic fieldwork. At the lab, various events such as brown bags, updates from the field, lectures, and workshops fed and nurtured our sociological imaginations. From its inception, this book has been a collective endeavor made possible, to a great extent, by this wonderful intellectual and affective atmosphere.

As with our previous collective project, Kerry Webb trusted us and guided us throughout with her expert hand. Thank you for being such a stellar editor!

Proceeds from this book will go to the Urban Ethnography Lab, from which they will be distributed among some of the organizations featured throughout this book.

CONTRIBUTORS ⎯⎯⎯⎯⎯⎯⎯⎯⎯⎯⎯⎯⎯⎯⎯⎯⎯⎯⎯⎯⎯⎯⎯⎯⎯⎯⎯⎯⎯

Cinthya E. Ammerman is an assistant professor in the Department of Native American Studies at California State Polytechnic University, Humboldt, where she enjoys working alongside many first-generation, Indigenous, Latinx, and Chicanx students. Her research is focused on hemispheric relationality, land defense movements, and Indigenous knowledges. She participates in various initiatives that support Indigenous sovereignty and autonomy throughout Turtle Island and Abya Yala.

Javier Auyero is Lozano Long Professor in Latin American Sociology at the University of Texas at Austin and Ikerbasque Research Professor at the University of the Basque Country UPV-EHU, Bilbao. His latest book (coauthored with Sofía Servián), published in 2023, is *¿Cómo hacen los pobres para sobrevivir?* (Buenos Aires: Siglo XXI).

Alison Coffey is a PhD candidate in sociology at the University of Texas at Austin. Her main areas of research include the politics of climate change and urban development, conflicts over land and property, housing, and social movements.

Jorge Derpic is an assistant professor in sociology and Latin American and Caribbean studies at the University of Georgia. He works on collective responses to violent crime in urban Bolivia. He has published his work in *Population Research and Policy Review* and the *Wiley-Blackwell Encyclopedia of Urban and Regional Studies*, among others.

Alex Diamond is an assistant professor of sociology at Oklahoma State University. His ethnographic research explains the relationship between peacebuilding, rural development, and the formation of state power from the perspective of a rural Colombian village that is critical to a landmark peace process. His writing has been published in *Social Problems, Qualitative Sociology,* and *Revista Maguaré,* among others, and he is codirector of the in-production feature-length documentary *An Uncomfortable Peace.*

Maricarmen Hernández is an assistant professor of sociology and urban studies at Barnard College, Columbia University. Her research focuses on environmental sociology, Latin American studies, informal communities, ethnographic methods, and the study of urban marginality.

Katherine Jensen is an assistant professor of sociology and international studies at the University of Wisconsin–Madison. As an ethnographer, she studies race/racism, the state, and immigration in Latin America. She is the author of *The Color of Asylum: The Racial Politics of Safe Haven in Brazil*, published by the University of Chicago Press.

Eldad J. Levy is the Alfred J. Hanna Distinguished Postdoctoral Fellow at Rollins College. He studies a variety of sociological themes in Latin America, including crime, violence, urban insecurity, and political and economic sociology. His doctoral dissertation investigates the emergence of private security in Mexico City. His work has been published in the *American Journal of Cultural Sociology* and the *Annual Review of Criminology*.

Marcos Emilio Pérez is an assistant professor of sociology at Washington and Lee University. He is the author of *Proletarian Lives: Routines, Identity, and Culture in Contentious Politics*. His research has appeared in the *Latin American Research Review*, *Mobilization*, *Qualitative Sociology*, *Conflicto Social*, *Sociedad*, *Argumentos*, *Latin American Perspectives*, and the *Bulletin of Latin American Research*.

Dennis Rodgers is a research professor in the Centre on Conflict, Development, and Peacebuilding (CCDP) at the Geneva Graduate Institute of International and Development Studies, and principal investigator of the European Research Council (ERC)–funded project "Gangs, Gangsters, and Ganglands: Towards a Comparative Global Ethnography" (GANGS).

Jennifer (Jen) Scott is an associate professor in the School of Social Work at Louisiana State University in Baton Rouge. Her research focuses on the social determinants of health and well-being, in particular economic access (e.g., work, informal supports) and migration (e.g., legal status, identity, discrimination). She was awarded an Early Career Research Fellowship from the National Academies of Sciences, Engineering, and Medicine's Gulf Research Program for her current project on H2 workers in Louisiana.

Sofía Servián is an anthropology student at the University of Buenos Aires. She is the coauthor (with Javier Auyero) of *¿Cómo siguen sobreviviendo los marginados?* (Buenos Aires: Siglo XXI, forthcoming in 2023).

Katherine Sobering is an assistant professor of sociology at the University of North Texas. She is the author of *The People's Hotel: Working for Justice in Argentina* and, with Javier Auyero, *The Ambivalent State: Police-Criminal Collusion at the Urban Margins*. Her research has also been published in the *British Journal of Sociology, Qualitative Sociology, Social Problems, Socio-Economic Review,* and *Work and Occupations,* among others. She is a Fulbright Scholar, and her work has been supported by the National Science Foundation.

INDEX

Abrego, Leisy, 180
activism. *See* social movements
Afro-descendants: in Brazil, 41–44, 47–48, 52, 56; in Ecuador, 124, 129–130; and extractivism, 5
agroecology, 83, 84–85, 95, 99–103
Almeida, Paul, 6
Alvarez, Sonia, 54
Añez, Jeanine, 205
Arendt, Hannah, 160
Argentina, 185–204, 225–242, 243–262
asylum policies: in Brazil, 146–151; in United States, 148–149. *See also* refugees
Auyero, Javier, 36, 48, 126, 240
Aylwin, Patricio, 110
Aymara, 208, 211–212. *See also* Indigenous communities

barrios. *See* informal settlements
Bauen Hotel, 243–261
Berti, María Fernanda, 36
Beyond Smoke and Mirrors (Massey), 169
Biden administration, 179
biodiversity, 5, 115–116
Bolivia, 205–224
Boo, Katherine, 264
Bracero Program, 169
Brazil, 39–58, 145–162
brokers: neighborhood political (Argentina), 225–242; private security (Mexico), 62
bureaucracy, 50, 60, 80, 147, 150

Cajun Creole culture, 166–167
campesinos, 5, 82–83, 89–93, 95–98, 100–103
Cancer Alley, 164
capitalism, 95, 114
carceral system, Brazilian, 39–58
Chile (Wallmapu), 104–123
Christin, Rosine, 14
citizenship, 147, 152–153, 159, 179
climate change, 105–106, 117–122
coca, 87–90, 97
cocaine, 26, 28, 42, 83–84, 88–89, 235
Cold War, post-, 24
Colombia, 82–103
colonialism, 5, 105–120, 165
Comfort, Megan, 47
conditional cash transfer programs, 207
Corazón de Dixie (Weise), 169
corruption: of Brazilian police, 42, 154; in Mexican justice system, 60–61, 66–68, 70–75, 79; and narco-states, 22
COVID-19 pandemic, 15n2, 205, 206–208, 223, 243, 258–261
crime: organized, 42, 61–64, 66, 70–77; and stigma, 43, 54–55; and urban life, 7, 59. *See also* drug trade; violence
Cuvi, Jacinto, 152

Davis, Diane, 61
debt: business, 243, 258; national, 185, 245; personal, 213–214, 217–223, 249

INDEX

deindustrialization, 8, 191–192
delinquency, youth, 27
democracy: returns to, 110, 188, 191, 203, 211; in the workplace, 243–244, 251–258
dictatorship: in Argentina, 54, 188, 190, 255; in Brazil, 148; in Chile, 110, 115
displacement: due to climate change, 105, 117–120; due to conflict, 83, 89, 92, 145–148; due to development, 5, 93–95, 98; due to disaster, 100, 119, 137–143
Drug Enforcement Agency, 63
drug trade: in Argentina, 225–226, 228–230; in Brazil, 42–44; in Latin American cities, 7; in Mexico, 60–63, 176; in Nicaragua, 21–58; across US-Mexico border, 176. *See also specific drugs*
Durán-Martínez, Angélica, 63

Ecuador, 124–144
Elias, Norbert, 264
elites: in Colombia, 103; in Ecuador, 130; in Mexico, 63–66, 80; and urban space, 7
empowerment, 23–24, 34, 36–37
environmental injustice, 116–118, 124, 129–130, 141–142
extractivism: and colonialism, 5, 105–106, 113–117; and development, 5, 103; *See also* hydroelectric dams; oil industry

FARC. *See* Revolutionary Armed Forces of Colombia
Farias, Juliana, 44
Favela: Four Decades of Living on the Edge in Rio de Janeiro (Perlman), 51
favelas. *See* informal settlements
FBI (Federal Bureau of Investigation), 63

Fernández, Alberto, 191
Fischer, Brodwyn, 126
Free Trade Agreement (Colombia), 99

Geertz, Clifford, 14
gender: inequality, 2, 23, 34; and machismo, 9, 24, 29, 34, 36; and masculinity, 24, 190, 201; roles, 40, 48, 54–55, 189. *See also* patriarchy
Gender and Society (journal), 29
Genova, Nicholas de, 180
Gibson, Julia, 121
Gleissman, Steve, 83
González de la Rosa, Mercedes, 223

Haraway, Donna, 120
Hatton, Erin, 180
HB-2 nonimmigrant visa program, 169, 179
healthcare systems, Bolivian, 205–224
Hochschild, Arlie, 220, 257
Hoffman, Kelly, 6
Hundred Years' War, 113
hydroelectric dams, 82, 84, 89–95, 97, 99. *See also* extractivism

IMF. *See* International Monetary Fund
immigration. *See* migration
imperialism, American, 63
import substitution industrialization, 190–191
Indigenous communities: and agroecology, 83, 103; and extractivism, 5; and resistance to colonialism, 104–122. *See also* Aymara; Mapuche
industrialization, of agriculture, 98–99
inequality: environmental, 129–130; in Latin America, 2–9; and neoliberal reforms, 186, 190–191, 223; reductions in, 207; and refugee integration, 146–147, 151. *See also* gender: inequality; labor
informal settlements: Argentine villas,

225–228, 232; in Bolivia, 211; Brazilian favelas, 40–43, 51; in Ecuador, 126, 130–141; Nicaraguan barrios, 24–25; and urban inequality, 7
In Harm's Way (Auyero and Berti), 36
Institute for Counterterrorism (Israel), 62
International Monetary Fund, 6, 207
Invisible in Austin (Auyero), 15n1, 264
Israel, 62, 64, 158

judicial system, Mexican, 60–61, 63, 66–69, 72–75, 80

Kalleberg, Arne, 247
Kandiyoti, Deniz, 29
Kessler, Gabriel, 26
Kilanski, Kristine, 48
Kirschner administrations, 191, 231, 253, 255

labor: blue-collar, 187, 201–202; emotional, 54–55; exploitative, 110, 178, 202; informal, 43, 135, 151–154, 156, 170, 192, 208, 212–221; precarious, 177–178, 180, 191–192, 247, 253; seasonal, 168–170, 178–180; service industry, 109, 135, 244–249, 253–258
Lamont, Michèle, 200
Lancaster, Roger, 24
Larrabure, Manuel, 251
Leeds, Elizabeth, 42
Leite, Márcia, 54
Ley, Sandra, 61
Life Is Hard (Lancaster), 24
Lomnitz, Larissa, 208

Macri, Mauricio, 191, 255, 258, 259
Manchung, Anne, 220
Mapuche: homelands, 104, 112–113, 120–122; Lafkenche people, 104–105, 112, 120; language and culture, 106–108, 111–113. *See also* Indigenous communities

marijuana, 28, 236
MAS. *See* Movement toward Socialism
Massey, Douglas, 169
McCann, Bryan, 126
Mérida Initiative, 62–63, 65
Mexico, 59–81, 163–184
middle class: in Argentina, 247–249; in Bolivia, 210; in Ecuador, 130; shrinking, 15n2
migration: rural-to-urban, 87, 133–134, 211; seasonal, 168–170, 179; undocumented, 179–181; to United States, 158–159, 168–170, 172. *See also* displacement
military: Brazilian, 49; Chilean, 116; Colombian, 89, 91, 96. *See also* dictatorship
Mills, C. Wright, 13
mining, 5, 94, 211
Morales, Evo, 205, 207, 213, 220
Mothers of the Plaza de Mayo, 54
Movement toward Socialism (Movimiento al Socialismo; MAS), 207–208

National Movement of Recuperated Businesses (MNER), 250
neoliberalism: and agriculture in Colombia, 98; and extractivism in Chile/Wallmapu, 115–116; impacts and dismantling of, in Bolivia, 207–208; and inequality in Argentina, 186, 190–19, 245, 259; across Latin America, 6, 8; and state repression in Brazil, 52
Nicaragua, 21–38

oil industry: in Ecuador, 124–127, 131–134, 142; in Louisiana, 164–165. *See also* extractivism
Ortner, Sherry, 14

pacification, 48–49, 83, 97, 114
Palestinians, 158

INDEX

paramilitaries, 83–84, 88–89
Partido Revolucionario Institucional (PRI), 61, 77
patriarchy: in Nicaraguan drug trade, 24, 29, 36–37, 40; in rural Brazil, 40. *See also* gender
patronage, 61, 208, 240
peace process, Colombian, 83–84, 96, 97–99
Pearce, Jenny, 80
Peréz Martín, Amalia, 6
Perlman, Janice, 51
Peronism, 225, 231
persistence, 13–15
"Perverse State Formation" (Pearce), 80
Pink Tide, 5, 6, 207
Pinochet, Augusto, 110, 115
piqueteros, 186–187, 190, 192–198, 203–204, 225, 240
police: Argentine, 230; Brazilian federal, 149–150; Brazilian military, 42–44, 48–49, 51–52, 56, 151–152, 154; Colombian, 93; in Latin American cities, 7; Mexican, 27–28, 31, 35, 61, 65–66
Politics of Drug Violence, The (Durán-Martínez), 63
Poor People's Politics (Auyero), 240
Portes, Alejandro, 6
poverty: in Argentina, 186, 190, 249; in Brazil, 146, 151–152, 156; across Latin America, 4–7, 15n2; and poor people's politics, 225–227, 233, 240; and race in Ecuador, 127–130, 143; in rural Colombia, 97–100, 103; and socialism, 5, 207, 212, 223
PRI. *See* Partido Revolucionario Institucional
private security: in Mexico, 59–80; and urban space, 7
Public Enterprises of Medellín (EPM), 90–95

Race and the Chilean Miracle (Richards), 116
racial democracy, 41
racial segregation: in Brazil, 52; in United States, 165
racism: in Brazil, 41–48, 52, 56, 147; in Bolivia, 217; in Chile, 114–116; in Ecuador, 129–130
Ramsay, Georgina, 160
Refugee Act, Brazilian, 148
refugees, 145–161. *See also* asylum policies; displacement
Reina del Sur, la, 21, 23, 36, 37
Revolutionary Armed Forces of Colombia (FARC), 83–84, 87–90, 94, 97–98
Richards, Patricia, 116
Rugerri, Andrés, 259

Schugurensky, Daniel, 251
seafood processing industry, 165–168, 177–178
Second Shift, The (Hochschild and Machung), 220
"Silent Witness, A" (Christin), 14
slavery, 52, 165
socialism, 8, 207
social movements: of campesinos, 83, 92–97; and collective action, 4–5, 13–14, 186, 190, 194, 239–240; led by mothers, 49–50, 53–57; and road blockades, 92–93, 95, 96, 230, 240; of workers, 250, 254–255. See also *piqueteros*
Sociological Imagination, The (Mills), 13
structural adjustment, 8, 223
survival strategies, 15n3
Syrian conflict, 145–146

Talley, Jared, 121
testimonio literature, 3
toxicity, 126–143
transportation system, Bolivian, 213, 216

Unemployed Worker's Movement. See *piqueteros*
United States: and intervention in Latin America, 63–64; Louisiana, 163–184. *See also* migration
urban development, 7, 61

Vianna, Adriana, 44
Vieta, Marcelo, 251
villas. *See* informal settlements
violence: against activists, 95; in the Colombian conflict, 83–92, 97–103; gender-based, 23–25; against Indigenous communities, 106, 114–117; state, 42–44, 48–52, 54–57, 116; urban, 6–7, 36, 190, 192, 203. *See also* crime; drug trade; police
Viterna, Jocelyn, 94
Vizenor, Gerald, 106

Wacquant, Loïc, 15n3
Wallmapu (Chile), 104–123
Washington Consensus, 6
Weise, Julie, 169
welfare, 190, 229–231, 233–234, 237–238, 240. *See also* workfare
Whyte, Kyle, 121
Wilkerson, Isabel, 263
Wilkis, Ariel, 223
Women in War (Viterna), 94
worker-recuperated business, 243–261
workfare, 193, 200, 229–232, 234, 241. *See also* welfare
working class, 191, 209, 211
World Bank, 6, 207

The Zone: Making Do in the Hyperghetto (Wacquant), 15n3

Printed in the USA
CPSIA information can be obtained
at www.ICGtesting.com
CBHW020857260824
13331CB00005B/3

9 781477 328989